..., Inc.

g Center
Rd.
905

**PRICE LIST - MAY 1988**

Tom Crutchfield

HOURS 9:00 A.M. – 5:00 P.M. — E.S.T.
MONDAY - SATURDAY

FAX (813) 694-0097        (81...        21        Chris McQuade

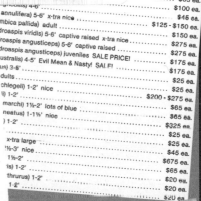

# EXTREMELY RARE NEW FROG!

## » THEOLDERMA CORTICALE «

WE ARE PLEASED TO BE ABLE TO OFFER A LIMITED NUMBER
AN EXCITING AND *EXCEPTIONALLY BEAUTIFUL* NEW SPECIES
TREE FROG FROM A SMALL AREA OF THE REMOTE JUNGLES
NORTH VIETNAM. THIS MAGNIFCENT CREATURE HAS THE LAT...
NAME OF *Theolderma corticale* AND WAS ONLY RECENT...
DISCOVERED BY SCIENCE. IT IS A *LARGE* SPECIES WITH A...
ADULT SIZE SIMILAR TO A WHITE'S TREE FROG !!! THEY HAVE A...
*INCREDIBLE BODY MORPHOLOGY* > THE ENTIRE FROG (HEA...
ARMS, BACK - EVERYTHING) IS COVERED IN *SPINES!!* TH...
SPECTACULAR BLACK & GREEN COLORATION HIGHLIGHTED WIT...
RED AND GOLD IS SUCH THAT THEY LOOK WE...
THEY ARE SLOW, DELIBERATE CLIMBERS. IMPO...
ARE **NOT** "DESTRUCTIVE JUMPERS & NOSE BAN...
SPECIMENS FROM THREE BLOODLINES FR...
CAPTIVE BREEDING IN RUSSIA. THEY AR...
FEEDERS ON CRICKETS AND SUPERWORMS A...
FAST. IF YOU ARE REALLY SERIOUS ABOUT FRO...
CONSIDER THIS MAGNIFCENT SPECIES. *PRICE*...

# Stolen
# World

# Stolen World

A Tale of
Reptiles,
Smugglers, *and*
Skulduggery

**Jennie Erin Smith**

Crown Publishers
*New York*

*Photograph Credits*
Endpapers and page 1: Roy B. Ripley;
page 83: Bill Love/Blue Chameleon Ventures

Library of Congress Cataloging-in-Publication Data

Smith, Jennie Erin, 1973–
Stolen world : a tale of reptiles, smugglers, and skulduggery /
Jennie Erin Smith.
p. cm.
1. Reptile trade—United States—Anecdotes.   2. Wildlife
smuggling—United States—Anecdotes.   3. Animal dealers—
United States—Anecdotes.   4. Snakes—United States—
Anecdotes.   I. Title.
SK593.R47S65 2011
364.1'33670973—dc22          2010009548

ISBN 978-0-307-38147-7

PRINTED IN THE UNITED STATES OF AMERICA

*Book design by Donna Sinisgalli*
*Illustrations by John Burgoyne*
*Jacket design by Oliver Munday*

1  3  5  7  9  10  8  6  4  2

First Edition

For my late grandfather Joseph McGrath, the most devout reader I have ever known and whose *Times* clippings we still miss. And for my late grandmother Frances Smith, who liked her stories a little on the rough side.

# Contents

**Part III**

## Dr. Wong

**Part IV**

## Old Age and Treachery

# Author's Note

This book is derived from interviews, court records, and published and unpublished documents. Nearly all quotations derive from interviews; a very small number are derived from sworn testimony. All names are real save for three: Benjamin Bucks, Stefan Schwarz, and Karl Sorensen, which are pseudonyms.

# Stolen World

# Part I

## The Kraftsman

**The reptile** vendors stood at their convention tables and kept watch over their stacks of deli cups—the same clear, covered plastic containers used at grocery stores to dole out olives or cream cheese. The cups were punched neatly through with air holes, and each contained a baby snake or lizard.

It was August 1996, and the National Reptile Breeders' Expo had just opened. Spread out through several ballrooms of an Orlando hotel, vendors displayed their deli cups under canvas signs bearing curious, vaguely propagandistic slogans: "Conservation thru Commercialization," "Assured Survival Through Applied Scientific Economics." Almost all were men; at least half of them wore a tattoo, a ponytail, or a T-shirt bearing a reptile design, and some had all of the above.

The hobby of keeping reptiles, once obscure, was growing very fast, and it had a new name: "herpetoculture." It sounded like "herpetology," but you needed a Ph.D. to be a herpetologist. If you woke up to find your pet snake had laid eggs, you were a herpetoculturist. The vendors were breeding reptiles for unusual colors, or mutations like albinism, and such manipulations only increased the animals' value. Years before, the vendors said, they had relied on importers and smugglers to bring them rare and wonderful reptiles from abroad. Now, thanks to herpetoculture, they simply created their rarities at home, reptiles that were just as valuable, yet perfectly legal. Better still, they said, they'd by now bred so many species that they were saving endangered reptiles from extinction.

It was all very noble sounding, except that only a few weeks before, the *New York Times* had run a front-page story about plowshare tortoises, a species said to be on the very precipice of extinction, stolen from a special breeding facility in Madagascar that had been set up to save them. The story implied that some of the missing tortoises could turn up at this expo in Orlando. And three days before the expo, federal wildlife agents had arrested a German for possessing sixty-one smuggled snakes and four tortoises, not plowshares but Madagascar species nonetheless, at a diner in Bushnell, Florida, an hour away.

Who was the German supposed to meet in Bushnell? The agents wouldn't say, but the reptile vendors all knew.

Only one reptile dealer lived in Bushnell, Florida. His name was Tom Crutchfield. At the expo, Crutchfield had the showiest booth and the slickest signs and some of the best animals. Next to his table were two albino iguanas—handsome, motionless ghosts—priced at $75,000 for the pair. Crutchfield was short, thickly built, and mustachioed, and looked extraordinarily testy.

The U.S. Fish and Wildlife agents were closing in on something larger than a single German, and everyone seemed to know it.

The owner of the expo, a Florida native named Wayne Hill, was in good spirits despite the fuss, and invited me up to his penthouse suite to talk. Flanked by half a dozen of his associates, Hill reclined on the couch and pontificated about the reptile business, and how it had gotten so big.

Wayne Hill was a retired petroleum engineer, and had spent some years in Saudi Arabia. He was an oil man, but above all a reptile man, and there in the desert, he said, he'd had a vision—like Jesus and Moses before him.

This speech had the marks of one delivered many, many times, but Hill's friends leaned in anyway. In the desert, Hill said, he envisioned a forum where reptile breeders could freely trade their live animals. Before the first of his reptile expos, he explained, the reptile dealers had been confined to selling their animals at zoo and science symposiums, until a backlash against the animal trade caused them to feel unwelcome. Hill encouraged the animal dealers to abandon these conventions, and he started one just for them, in 1990, at a Howard Johnson's in Orlando. And now, six years later, here we were. At a much bigger hotel. Why did the *New York Times* think the plowshare tortoises would show up here? I asked Hill. Now Hill sounded mad. Someone hostile to the trade must have planted the idea, he said, a zoo person or an "animal-rights Nazi." After that, I didn't bother asking Hill about the German or Tom Crutchfield, or why this brave new reptile-breeding industry, where snakes emerged from sterile containers like Aldous Huxley's fetuses, would have any more use for smugglers.

But then, weirdly, Hill pointed me to a smuggler he said he was very fond of, a smuggler without whom, he said, a great many of these species wouldn't be in Orlando at all.

I found Hank Molt a day later, just where Wayne Hill said he'd be, alone at a table by the pool. It was late afternoon. I can't remember if Molt had a Heineken in his hand, but in the years that followed I would seldom see him in such settings without one.

He was in his mid-fifties then, tall and lean. He seemed delighted by what was happening to Tom Crutchfield. Like Crutchfield, Molt eschewed the whole tattoo-and-ponytail aesthetic for a clean, almost soldierly look—brush cut, cargo pants. He had the quick, bulging eyes of someone very smart and easily unhinged. Molt said he was annoyed that someone beat him to the plowshare tortoises, a heist he'd been pondering for years, though he would have taken only a few animals, he said, not the seventy-five that were stolen.

Molt had no sign at the reptile expo, no slogan, no table of his own, no animals.

To him this thing called herpetoculture, with its genetic mutations and deli cups and pretensions to science, held limited appeal. He lived for the natural animals, he said, for their rarity and beauty and where you had to go to get them. Now, he complained, the animals have lost their stories.

In the years when Molt styled himself not as a shameless veteran smuggler but as a "specialist dealer in rare fauna," he would arrive at the zoos, fresh from the world, with snakes and lizards in his knotted cloth sacks.

He would open the bags one at a time and let the animal crawl out as he told its story. This was not the most efficient way to sell animals. It was theater, and it took hours.

"It was the romance of the snake," Molt said. And what a terrible, twisted romance it would turn out to be.

# 1

## I Fly Around the World

In 1965, Henry A. Molt, Jr., took a sales job at Kraft Foods, where he was given the use of a company station wagon and an exurb of Philadelphia as his territory. Molt hated everything about the job except the station wagon, which he would commandeer on weekends to visit zoos. Molt had been collecting reptiles since the age of six, when he carried a sickly king snake around school in a knotted sack; as he grew older, he sought reptiles more far-flung and dangerous. Now, at twenty-five, he kept cobras, rattlesnakes, Gila monsters, and pythons in the basement of his parents' home.

Kraft Foods was proud of its eccentric young salesman, and mere months after hiring Molt it put a drawing of a cobra—erect, hooded, and ready for action—on the cover of its employee magazine, *The Kraftsman*. Tucked next to a recipe for salmon loaf with cheddar sauce was an article about Molt. Kraft Foods had dispatched a reporter to learn all he could about Molt and his unusual hobby, which, Molt was happy to imply, involved the occasional illegality:

> Molt next showed me what he considered to be his most valuable specimen. It was a beautiful Diamond python which had come from Australia and for which he had paid $90. Molt says the Diamond python is found only in Australia and New Guinea and is fast becoming extinct. For this reason Australian authorities have forbidden its exportation.

"How did you get yours smuggled out?" I asked. Molt gave me a sly glance but said nothing.

When Molt's workdays of counting mayonnaise jars and issuing credits for moldy cheese ended, he would retreat to his bedroom at his parents' house and write letters to foreign animal dealers, whose addresses he'd found in "The Animal People's Directory," a booklet that circulated in those days to zoos and film studios. Molt wanted only the rare animals, reptiles even the zoos couldn't get, so he sought out dealers in countries that restricted, or banned, the export of wildlife to the United States: Australia, Mexico, Communist states. "I would follow the most obscure lead," Molt said. "If I saw a picture in *National Geographic* of a missionary holding a snake, I would try to write him, too. Most of the letters probably never reached their destinations."

BEFORE RESIGNING himself to a career at Kraft, Molt had presented Roger Conant, the Philadelphia Zoo's curator of reptiles, with a gift of some Mexican pit vipers. Molt hoped to curry favor with Conant and land a job at the zoo, but Conant only thanked Molt for the snakes. Molt had majored in English in college, not any sort of science, had spent most of his time in a fraternity house, and, anticipating his graduation draft notice, had enlisted in the marines, calculating correctly that they would be less likely than the army to send him to Vietnam. He still owed the marine reserves a weekend a month, and would for quite some time.

Molt's tedium was broken by the monthly lectures of the Philadelphia Herpetological Society, at the Academy of Natural Sciences. The academy was one of Molt's favorite places; by twenty-five he had already spent hundreds of hours in its library, reading snake articles amid its ancient leathery smells and glass cabinets. There Molt met Joe Laszlo, a Hungarian who had escaped the Soviet invasion in a hay wagon bound for Austria, then emigrated to Philadelphia, where he maintained multitudes of lab rodents for the Albert Einstein Hospital. Laszlo was tired of mice; all he'd ever wanted was to work in a zoo, with snakes.

After his experience with Roger Conant, Molt doubted his chances with the zoos, but even a bad zoo job would trump Kraft, so Molt and Laszlo synchronized their meager vacation time and drove the Kraft station wagon to zoos in Columbus, Ohio; Atlanta; and Fort Worth, Texas, all of which were building new reptile houses.

The moneyed old northern zoos, like those in Philadelphia and the Bronx, had long maintained reptile houses with interesting foreign species, but at most zoos, "reptile house" traditionally meant a cement floor scattered with half-starved local rattlesnakes that died every winter and were replaced in the spring. By the mid-1960s, though, the smaller zoos in the South and the West were talking about hundreds of species, climate control, skylights, indoor jungles, and curving cages with nonreflective glass. The new reptile buildings housed the aspirations of a crop of freshly minted reptile curators, men weaned on the snake books of the 1930s, '40s, and '50s, books by writers like Frank "Bring 'Em Back Alive" Buck; Raymond L. Ditmars, the Bronx Zoo's first reptile curator; Carl Kauffeld of the Staten Island Zoo, a rattlesnake hunter; Clifford Pope of the American Museum of Natural History, with his fondness for giant pythons and boas and anacondas; and poor Karl Schmidt of Chicago's Field Museum, who loved African snakes and then died from one's bite. The reptile curators at the emerging zoos were only a generation removed from these snake writers, and they scrambled for rarities, competing fiercely with one another. "Everybody wanted to get something somebody else didn't have," said Wayne King, the Bronx Zoo's curator of reptiles at the time.

MOLT AND LASZLO had no luck finding jobs in the new, high-tech zoos. They returned to Philadelphia.

If they couldn't work for zoos, they could buy and sell reptiles, they decided. Together, they shipped a box of rattlesnakes to a laboratory in

Hungary, a deal for which they created a business name and an onionskin letterhead. They called their fake firm the Philadelphia Reptile Exchange, just to call it something. When Laszlo was eventually hired by a zoo, Molt hung on to the stationery, on which he sent out more letters seeking reptiles. Every so often, someone responded.

A man wrote from Holland, offering to sell Molt some Australian reptiles. He was acting as an intermediary for his son, he said, who lived in Australia.

Splendid, unique reptiles—straw-colored pythons with ebony heads, bright green snakes that coiled elegantly over branches, river turtles with piglike snouts—were tantalizingly abundant in Australia and New Guinea, but very hard to get. Australia had some of the strictest wildlife laws in the world, a result of its bad experiences with alien species. Rabbits, introduced by hunters in the nineteenth century, had made a crumbled moonscape out of its vast grasslands. Cane toads, native to South America, had been introduced to eat beetles that plagued the continent's sugarcane fields, but they didn't jump high enough to do even that; instead, they swelled to the size of Chihuahuas, and their poison skin killed native predators. Foreign species had done so much damage in such a short time that Australia responded in the 1960s with a blanket ban: no foreign animals or plants in, no native ones out, and the same went for its protectorates, like Papua New Guinea. Only government zoos could send their representatives to Australia or New Guinea and expect to return with animals, and even they had a tough time of it.

Australian zoos were equally frustrated in obtaining foreign species, which meant that any Australian zookeeper had the potential to become a smuggling partner, and this Dutchman's son turned out, to Molt's surprise, to be head keeper of the Melbourne Zoo. In 1965 he began shipping Molt diamond pythons and carpet pythons in crates marked "china" and "glassware."

Just as this connection started to bear fruit, Molt received a letter from Megot Schetty, the owner of Schlangenpark Maggia, a private snake zoo on the Swiss-Italian border. Schetty was a widow of indeterminate age, small and gray. Her scientist husband had been killed by a swarm of bees in Africa. In her lush greenhouses, Schetty kept species Molt coveted: giant hog-nosed snakes from Madagascar, vipers from Israel and Jordan. Schetty sent Molt whatever animals he asked for. In return Schetty wanted what every European snake fancier wanted: rare dwarf rattlesnakes from Arizona and Mexico, maroon-and-orange-patterned corn snakes from the Carolinas, the black, lustrous indigo snakes of Florida.

All this exchange was leaving Molt with a reptile collection of impressive variety and value. In May 1966, Molt married and moved into an apartment, but returned daily to his parents' basement to feed his bushmasters and fix the heat lamps on his Palestine vipers. His Kraft job became harder to bear. "We'd have these regional sales meetings where the managers would say, 'Okay, tigers, go out and get 'em!'" he said, "and they'd make us growl like tigers as we went down the stairs—*grrrrr!*" At the company's annual convention in Chicago that year, the vice presidents dressed as cowboys, exhorting the team to "shoot for higher sales." Molt had just about had it. He spent the Sunday of the convention alone at the zoo, where he saw alive, for the first time, a Dumeril's boa from Madagascar. There is nothing particularly spectacular about a Dumeril's boa—it is brown, it is not too big, it hides in the leaf litter. But the sight of one ignited something in Molt, who was by then fairly combustible.

On the plane back to Philadelphia, Molt sat next to an executive from IBM, fresh out of a similar convention. The man asked Molt what kind of business he was in.

"I fly all around the world collecting animals for zoos," Molt answered. Somehow, it sounded more natural than the truth.

MOLT'S IDEAL was not without precedent. Natural history had always been an outsourced business. Someone had to fill the cabinets of curiosity, to steal the world from the world and bring it back, or no one would believe it.

Even Carolus Linnaeus had his students do the collecting for him. Of the seventeen young men who scoured the earth for the Swede, whose own farthest journey was to Lapland, just over half survived their travels, and one went mad. The students died of malaria in Java, North Africa, and Guyana; of fever in the East Indies, tuberculosis in Turkey; gastroenteritis in Guinea; suicide on a Russian steppe. None of this discouraged their successors as the centuries wore on, as the royal cabinets grew into royal museums and as wars and revolutions opened those museums to the public, which only wanted to see more specimens. The trouble was, collecting them required a tougher constitution than most of the leaf-sketching aristocrats who walked those museum halls possessed. In 1819 France's Muséum national d'Histoire naturelle, insatiable in its appetite for life pickled, pressed, mounted, and dried, began training young men from working-class families as traveling naturalists, who would shoot, label, and preserve on behalf of those who preferred not to. It sent these mercenaries of natural history to Madagascar, India, and Australia, where they, too, often met splendid misfortunes. Many of the young travelers hoped that this route would provide them a back door into science, but generally, if they were lucky, they found work as taxidermists. There simply weren't enough museum jobs to go around, and the well-born occupied the best posts.

Natural history's class divide deepened as the traveling field men, the shooters and baggers, came to view themselves as the true naturalists. They saw life in the field, with its complex interactions, whereas all that happened in museums, sneered the English collector Philip Gosse, was that "distorted things are described, their scales, plates, feathers counted; their forms copied, all shriveled and stiffened as they are; their colours, changed and modified by death or partial decay, carefully set down; their limbs, members, and organs measured and the results recorded in thousandths of an inch; two names are given to every one; the whole is enveloped in a mystic cloud of Graeco-Latino-English phraseology . . . and this is Natural History!"

But the museum men kept wanting, so the collectors kept collecting. Natural history became a veritable industry as the Victorian age advanced, with elite taxidermy firms holding their own stables of collectors, steering them toward the profitable species, those the museums most desired.

Were it not for such firms, a young Alfred Russel Wallace might well have remained a frustrated lecturer at the Victorian equivalent of a community college, pinning the beetles of Leicester and reading Charles Darwin's *Voyage of the Beagle* as he drifted off to sleep. It was Samuel Stevens, a specimen dealer, whom the twenty-four-year-old Wallace approached in 1847 about an expedition to Brazil to collect insects that Stevens would sell to the British Museum.

Seven years had passed since Charles Darwin, born into the Wedgwood pottery fortune, had secured his fame and a permanent seat among the science Brahmins of London with an account of his *Beagle* journey, nearly a year of which was spent in Brazil. Wallace, a middle-class amateur, could hope to make a similar trip only by collecting for money. His three-year turn in Brazil was marred by heartbreaking setbacks—shipments held up at ports for his failure to bribe, and a cargo fire that destroyed all his specimens and his notes. In 1855, Wallace was back in the field, collecting for Stevens in the Malay Archipelago, when he mailed to Stevens a rather ambitious-sounding monograph, "On the Law Which Has Regulated the Introduction of New Species." The obscure specimen collector, on the fringes of science, had touched upon the mechanism by which species changed or died off, edging close to Darwin's still-unpublished theory of natural selection.

In February 1858, while shooting birds of paradise in eastern Indonesia, Wallace contracted malaria. In the ensuing fevers, he seized on what he needed to round out his theory, which he drafted in two days and mailed to Charles Darwin, whom he greatly admired, for an opinion. It had been a century since Linnaeus's *Systema Naturae* had attempted to put Creation in order; here, Wallace laid bare its secret law. The life of wild animals, wrote Wallace, is a "'struggle for existence,' in which the weakest and least perfectly organized must always succumb."

What happened next is well-known: The similarities caused Darwin and his colleagues to panic. The result was a hasty joint reading of both men's works at the Linnaean Society in London, an arrangement that protected the "priority" of Darwin's theory while acknowledging Wallace's independent formulation of a like one.

When Darwin's *On the Origin of Species by Means of Natural Selection, or the Preservation of Favoured Races in the Struggle for Life* was published in 1859, Wallace was back in the jungle, skinning his primates, pinning and labeling his insects. He had a living to make. Six years later, he was still in Borneo, shooting orangutans for Stevens. In May 1865, he wrote: "I found another, which behaved in a similar manner, howling and hooting with rage, and throwing down branches. I shot it five times, and it remained dead on the tree ... I preserved the skin of this specimen in a cask of arrack, and prepared a perfect skeleton, which afterwards was purchased for the Derby Museum."

By his final return, Wallace had amassed some 125,000 specimens, 1,000 of them new to science.

At the dawn of the twentieth century, Darwin was dead, Wallace surveyed his gardens from a wheelchair, and the specimen collectors continued in the perilous ministry of science, skinning and preserving for their distant patrons. England's Walter Rothschild, the most prodigious, generous, and voracious museum man who ever lived, employed no fewer than four hundred—this not counting the insect men—to fill his personal zoo and museum in Hertfordshire. Most of Rothschild's field men were also adventurers of limited means, who died now and then of typhoid, cholera, dysentery, and yellow fever; one had his arm bitten off by a leopard. Rothschild's niece and biographer, Miriam Rothschild, worried for them. "[If] they survived the occupational health hazards of their trade, they seemed to lose much of their *joie de vivre* as time went by," she wrote. "Bouts of fever and other tropical diseases undermined their constitution, and they lost their sense of well being. Furthermore they were rarely able to save any money for an honourable retirement, and the life they led did not fit them for so-called civilization."

When specimen mania leaped, like a long-reaching brush fire, to the New World, the same roughed-up collectors came to work for American institutions. America's natural history craze had been delayed by the Civil War, and in the years after it ended, new museums and zoos went up fast. The scramble for specimens was every bit as intense as it had been in Europe. But at least there was a place for the field men in America. With no scientific aristocracy firmly established, anyone was free to take part. P. T.

Barnum, a museum man before he was ever a circus man, promoted natural history like some sort of patent medicine, a cure for the discontents of an industrial age, and though Barnum's version of natural history included taxidermic hoaxes like his "Feejee mermaid," a fish sewn to a monkey, he forged lifelong ties with the curators at the Smithsonian, Harvard, and the American Museum of Natural History, donating dead animals to them and underwriting their expeditions. When William Temple Hornaday, a specimen collector, buffalo hunter, and the Smithsonian's chief taxidermist for a time, started the National Zoo, he brought Barnum on as a consultant. The zoo's head keeper was hired away from Barnum's circus.

In 1906, Hornaday left Washington to build the Bronx Zoo, where he added to its exhibits a vast number of horns and mounted heads. The horn craze had started in England, with trophies from African safaris, but it suited America, where natural history was fast becoming a more macho affair. The eighteenth-century naturalist wandering the Jardin des Plantes, filling notebooks with musings on lichens—this would not do. The new naturalist was rugged to the extreme. The Nile and the Amazon were no objects to him, and he emphasized, over all else, the dangers of his journeys: glaring lions, flesh-munching piranhas. The new naturalist was meaty, bass-voiced, the fictional Professor Challenger of A. Conan Doyle; or he was like the real-life Theodore Roosevelt, a hybrid of naturalist and sportsman: fearless, yet virtuous. Not content with merely shooting and stuffing, he brought the best of his animals back alive.

The next crop of field men embraced the new ideal, and then some. In the 1920s and '30s Frank Buck, of Gainesville, Texas, wore a mustache and pith helmet and collected for American zoos their tigers, snow leopards, pygmy water buffaloes, and crocodiles. This involved substantial risks in the days before tranquilizer darts, and Buck's adventures building traps and bossing around natives became fodder for his wildly popular, if ghostwritten, books. Buck's formal education had ended in middle school, a fact he was always touchy about, but he called himself a scientist when it suited him. In *Bring 'Em Back Alive,* Buck explained why he deserved the title, disparaging the museum men like his forebears a century earlier:

I know a man on the staff of a great museum who by the hour can trace back for centuries the feathered ancestors of birds that I have collected by the thousand . . . This man is an authority even though he has never left the United States. He is primarily a student. I am a student, too, but in a different way. I have had to make a study of such hard-boiled details of the collecting business as the best way to get a snarling tiger out of a pit cage without getting messed up in the process, how to transfer a murderous king cobra from a crude native container to a modern snake box.

Rather than shirk from the field men's affronts, the museum men just borrowed their testosterone.

As a very young man, Raymond L. Ditmars had toiled unhappily in the entomology department of the American Museum of Natural History, starved for adventure, labeling insects and keeping a live rattlesnake on his desk, waiting for the day the museum opened a reptile department. But the museum was slow to do that, and Ditmars quit in frustration. Ditmars's friends feared that he'd thumbed his nose at the scientific establishment a tad rashly for a young man with only a high school degree, at a time when college was starting to mean something at zoos and museums. In 1899 Ditmars was relieved to be hired by W. T. Hornaday as the Bronx Zoo's first curator of reptiles.

Within a decade Ditmars had penned two books: *Snakes of the World* and *Reptiles of the World*. Theodore Roosevelt, president at the time, liked them enough to send Ditmars a letter, but they were dry, survey-like volumes, nothing to read with a flashlight under the covers. Then, in the early 1930s, Ditmars retooled the same books into wild collecting yarns that proved far more popular.

Stretched in undulating fashion in the trunk of a fallen tree, lay the big "cotton-mouth." Huge he looked in the light of our lamp, his sides showing olive green, while the rough scales of the back seemed as black as velvet. Slowly turning toward the boat he gave us a glassy stare and a flash of forked tongue. It was easy work slip-

ping a noose over that wicked head, when we swung him, writhing furiously, into the boat.

A strong odor of Frank Buck now permeated Ditmars's prose. Indeed
Ditmars and Buck knew each other well. Buck collected for the Bronx
Zoo and boasted in his books of his services to "Dr. Ditmars, America's
greatest reptile authority." And Buck had taught Ditmars that in the public
imagination, the quest for the specimens mattered more than the specimens themselves.

By the time Ditmars died, in 1942, the great museum and zoo expeditions had ended. Museums found themselves bloated with specimens,
some of which were burned deliberately in bonfires. Specimen collecting,
one of the few reliable business opportunities natural history had ever
provided, had become unprofitable and in certain cases illegal. Few of
America's once-copious taxidermy firms survived the Second World War.

But Ditmars's fraying, yellowing volumes long outlived their author.
The reptile curators at the new zoos had devoured them in their youth; a
young Hank Molt all but memorized them.

In the long-reaching light of the Bala Cynwyd, Pennsylvania, middle
school library, Molt had read his favorite part of Ditmars's autobiography,
*Thrills of a Naturalist's Quest,* over and over. In it, a teenage Ditmars, alone
in his parents' attic, opens his first crate of serpents, fresh off a ship from
Trinidad: a rat snake, a tree snake, a coral snake, a fer-de-lance, and finally
a very large and deadly bushmaster, which Ditmars pauses, appropriately
enough, before unveiling: "It made considerable displacement in the bag,
and where its sides pressed outwardly upon the cloth, rough scales showed
through like the surface of a pine cone . . ."

"When he opened that box I was right there beside him," Molt said.
"Each snake was a ceremony, a transformation." He stole the book.

In his high school years, Molt made contact with the surviving con-
temporaries of Ditmars and Buck, adopting, gradually, the posture of a sophisticated herpetologist. He wrote Roger Conant, the Philadelphia Zoo's
curator of reptiles, to request information about rat snakes—specifically,
how he could get some. Conant advised that the fifteen-year-old Molt try

to "get into the country, far away from Philadelphia, and take a look." But at fifteen one cannot get far away from anything, and all Molt had were his books.

"Ditmars working in the museum for ten cents a day, with all these stern people," Molt said. "Frank Buck going to get rhinos or elephants ninety fucking years ago, when there was no treatment for malaria, just some gin and tonics when you got a chance. Overcoming these odds like they were nothing." They were inspiration enough.

MOLT QUIT Kraft Foods. With his mother-in-law's money, he bought a pet store in the northern suburbs of Philadelphia. He sold puppies and kittens and continued to receive his special packages from Melbourne and from Maggia, Switzerland. In September 1966, he mailed to zoos a mimeographed sheet introducing himself as Henry A. Molt, Jr., proprietor of the Pet Emporium: "We specialize in rare and unusual reptiles and are currently importing many species seldom seen in captivity! Are you interested in specimens from Madagascar, Australia, New Guinea, Israel, North Africa, Ghana, Thailand, Argentina, and Peru to mention several?" On the back he listed the thirty-five species he had.

"Within days the phone started ringing off the hook at my parents' house," Molt said. He made up his prices on the spot, and they were outrageous. The zoos were not deterred. They could spend months negotiating, with meager success, for Australian export permits, or they could pay through the nose. Molt, who had earned $400 a month at Kraft, made $5,000 that week. He never sent out another mailing as the Pet Emporium. From now on he was the Philadelphia Reptile Exchange.

Molt quickly gained repute as a boutique dealer, someone with excellent taste, if such a thing can be said, in reptiles. In list after list, Molt increasingly made mention of his animals' aesthetic "perfection." "To all Zoological Parks & Museums," he began his mailings. "Enclosed you will find our latest listing of reptiles. Unless noted otherwise all specimens are perfect display quality." He joined the American Association of Zoological Parks and Aquariums and learned to play the curators well, seeking animals that would foster competition and garner high prices. The Carnegie Museum bought any of his reptiles that died.

With each list, Molt's descriptions grew longer and more emphatic: "Calabar's ground python *(Calabaria reinhardti)* VERY RARE!! Burrowing python from limited range in West Africa. Gun metal blue and brick red, $200. Australian water python *(Liasis f. fuscus)* rich glossy brown with bright apricot belly, rare in U.S. Zoological collections, collected in N. Queensland, Aust. $325." Some of his animals were so seldom seen that he had to describe what they ate, the natural landscape they inhabited, or the dead museum specimen from which they were known. He did nothing to hide the fact that his best specimens were taken in violation of foreign laws.

Which wasn't, at the time, much of an issue. In the mid-1960s, little thought was given to regulating the animal trade, a business that was "totally devoid of conscience in those days," Molt said. A gorilla was about the only animal that required a special permit to import. Medical research labs, carnivals, game farms, and pet stores relied on cheap and copious imports of wild animals. The animals were transshipped through import firms in Florida, giant wholesale warehouses where nursing baby monkeys were crated without their mothers, parrots came in with half the box dead, and profits were made by drastically marking up what survived. Some two million reptiles were imported every year through these channels, and though the vast majority were farmed baby turtles meant for dime stores, the rest were wild. Stressed, dehydrated, and full of parasites, few survived far past the point of sale. That the animal trade could be cruel and wasteful was not news to members of conservation groups like the Audubon Society and the newly formed World Wildlife Fund, which were pressuring governments to curtail it. But a middle-class family could still return from Florida in those years with a baby alligator, and once in a while a forklift driver at an airport would drop a whole crate of monkeys, sending blood and entrails all over the place.

Only smuggling animals from one of the few "closed" countries, like

Australia or Mexico, violated federal law, and that law was the Lacey Act, a largely forgotten turn-of-the-century hunting statute that made it illegal to import game, live or dead, in contravention of a foreign law.

So Molt saw little cause for restraint. His zookeeper in Melbourne scheduled the big shipments of snakes, lizards, and turtles for around Christmas, when postal and cargo workers were overwhelmed. If a shipment contained venomous snakes, the package was mislabeled on the outside. Inside was a warning sticker, "in case the guy got bit," Molt said. "If they opened it that much we were fucked anyway."

Every year Molt's ledgers grew longer. With the exception of a woman wrestler who slept with snakes in her bed, his big customers were all zoos. The Houston Zoo bought four thousand dollars' worth of animals from Molt in 1968, when a Triumph Roadster cost three thousand. Roger Conant, whom Molt had only a few years before pressed for a job, wrote Molt that the Philadelphia Zoo's old reptile house was being torn down to make room for a bigger one with a crocodile-filled "jungle river," among other marvels. "We will be in the market for many things," Conant told Molt, "and perhaps you might be able to help us obtain them."

Molt's timing couldn't have been better. Zoos were suddenly interested in reptiles, but weren't particularly good at breeding or caring for them. Mortality was always high, and in a period when exhibits were expanding, a good dealer relationship helped. What if you walked into your jungle river one morning and found the crocodiles belly-up?

THANKS TO Megot Schetty in Switzerland, Molt now had the Dumeril's boas that had enraptured him in his final days at Kraft. Jonathan Leakey, son of the famous paleoanthropologists in Kenya, was sending him African dwarf adders. But the Australian animals were by far the most profitable, and Molt suddenly found himself with a serious supply glitch there.

After a long silence from Melbourne, the zookeeper's father sent

Molt an obituary: His son had died, at only thirty-seven, of a heart attack brought on by obesity.

Molt needed another Australian smuggler. The Australian animals had become Molt's specialty, and if he didn't keep them coming in, the zoos would find them elsewhere. He turned to the widow Schetty, who was always good for a contact.

Schetty gave him a woman's name: Gisela Szoke, of Perth. She didn't know much about the woman, she confessed. Molt tapped out a letter.

A man responded. His name was Henry, too—Henry Szoke, the brother of Gisela. Gisela didn't deal in reptiles, it turned out; Henry did.

Henry Molt and Henry Szoke corresponded for a year. They experimented with boxes of different materials and dimensions. Now and then they failed. A box of baby crocodiles was intercepted in Australia when an inspector felt air holes. A taipan mailed to Philadelphia in a cookie tin came in dead and rotten. Air holes had to be concealed, and cookie tins were out. When shipments were large, Szoke sent them in red shipping crates labeled "art."

Henry Szoke shared Molt's interest in rare and obscure species, and had good smuggling techniques. Molt paid him cash, which he mailed in Hallmark cards. Almost everything Szoke sent arrived healthy. Molt barely missed the ill-fated zookeeper he had earlier depended on. Between price lists, Molt sent out bulletins of "specials," whatever was fresh from Szoke. The Bronx Zoo emerged as a major buyer of Szoke's New Guinea crocodiles. The Dallas Zoo had a thing for his Australian lizards.

Without Henry Szoke, Henry Molt was nobody. "He was the steak," Molt said. "Everyone else was pickles."

THANKFULLY, MOLT'S institutional clients seldom visited his retail shop, whose giant sign still said "Pet Emporium," and whose shady frat-house atmosphere contrasted sharply with the scholarly tone of his mailings.

Fellow reptile dealers, carny snake handlers, kids from the suburbs, small-time poachers with something to unload—all found a hangout there. In place of the kittens and puppies, which he'd expunged, Molt kept a hatchling snapping turtle in a glass jar by the register, feeding it and changing the water until, like a living ship in a bottle, the thing had grown so big it could not escape. At which point the "snappy in a jar" would be liberated with a hammer, and a new one would take its place.

The apartment upstairs was occupied by an ex-convict named Bob Udell, a bearish young man in and out of mental institutions and jail, who would set police cars on fire, or shoplift large quantities of meat. Udell decorated his apartment with bead curtains and a naked mannequin lying in a coffin. He darkened his windows because it reminded him, in a comforting way, of jail. Udell was nonetheless very good with rare snakes, and became a constant presence in Molt's shop, a quasi employee. "Udell had a talent with the animals. He could walk by a cage and see a snake not lying right, and sure enough the animal was dehydrated," Molt said. "Plus you couldn't make him go away—he would burn your house to the ground." Udell minded the store and packed up the reptiles for deliveries. Molt, the only one around with any college, drove the boxes to zoos in a Volkswagen minibus, and did all the talking.

A PECULIAR man phoned the Philadelphia Reptile Exchange one day. He sounded like a hillbilly, almost cartoonishly so, and yet he was on his way to Madagascar, he told Molt, "to get some lemurs." He was thinking of picking up some snakes while he was there. "The problem is," the man said, "I can't tell one from the other." He was on his way to Philadelphia, he said, right now.

The hillbilly turned out to be a towering, freckled, elfin-eared man named Leon Leopard. He lived in Waco, Texas, on a street called Parrot Street. Leopard was new to the animal business. He owned a string of gas stations, and, like many station owners in an era of cheap gas, had resorted to gimmicks to boost sales. Leopard's gimmick was live monkeys. So for a certain number of fill-ups you could have a free squirrel monkey.

Leopard bought his monkeys from Miami's biggest animal importer in those days, a man named Bill Chase, whose compound housed ostriches, tigers, all manner of parrots, venomous snakes, ponds filled with alligators and marine toads and tortoises soaking in the sun. Chase's monkeys arrived on night flights from Peru, a thousand at a time. It occurred to Leopard, the first time he drove to Miami and saw Chase's incredible, teeming place, that there might be money to be made in the animal business. What was the most valuable monkey of all? he asked Chase. Lemurs, Chase told him, which are not actually monkeys, he explained, but another sort of primate, found only in Madagascar. Leopard left Miami thinking about lemurs, and Madagascar. He checked in at the zoos, where the curators told Leopard that there were Madagascar snakes worth money, too. They handed him Molt's price list.

Leopard was impressed with Molt's business, and Molt was impressed with Leopard. For a yokelish Texan who owned gas stations and spoke no French, Madagascar was not an easy trip. Besides being isolated, poor, and barely navigable, it was in the middle of a Marxist insurgency that would soon sever it from France. The country was literally burning—political points were made by torching thousands of hectares.

Leopard left for Madagascar wearing a gas station uniform that he had converted into a zoo uniform with the addition of a few patches. He carried doctored stationery, too, with his own name printed under the Central Texas Zoo's logo with the title "Director of Zoo Biology." Leopard returned from Madagascar with the rarest of the rare—lemurs, boas, plow-share tortoises—all with stamped permits from the Ministère des Eaux et Forêts. Molt could barely contain his awe or his envy.

Now Leopard wanted to fly to Papua New Guinea, where it had been only a decade since the Australians outlawed cannibalism. The populace was so notoriously hot-tempered that the American embassy advised visitors to keep driving if they hit someone's dog on the road. Leopard urged

Molt to come along. But Molt still owed the marines one weekend a month. If Molt couldn't come and lend his knowledge, Leopard suggested, perhaps he could supply some cash.

They agreed that Molt would put up $2,000, and that Leopard would go collect the elusive Boelen's python, an iridescent black-and-white snake from the highlands. No one had ever returned from New Guinea with a live Boelen's python, but the snakes had been studied sporadically since the 1930s, and a few sat pickled in museums. Molt scrutinized the jarred Boelen's pythons at the Academy of Natural Sciences and studied a map of New Guinea, pinning it with locales from the museum labels. At least Leopard would know where to look. Molt and Leopard agreed to sell the animals together, and split any profits.

Leopard readied his fake zoo stationery and his fake zoo uniforms. He carried Molt's map.

Leopard fared even better in New Guinea than he had in Madagascar. Wildlife officers found him a coffee farmer in the highlands who was also a government-licensed animal collector. The coffee farmer provided Leopard with not only Boelen's pythons but also birds of paradise and oddball indigenous mammals. It took Molt and Leopard a whole year to sell everything; Molt had to run a two-for-one special on tree kangaroos, which he kept in dog kennels and tried to feed figs. "I was freaking out. I didn't know how to take care of them," he said, and he hated mammals, anyway. Molt and Leopard drove to the zoos in Leopard's Cadillac, entertaining zoo directors at restaurants, where Leopard enraptured them like a country preacher. "He had really good stories— probably many of them bullshit but they sounded good," Molt said. "All we'd seen was *Wild Kingdom* and *National Geographic*. Here was a guy who'd been there." Molt was increasingly enamored of the Texan, as were the zoos. "Leon made a very, very rapid rise," said Robert Wagner, a longtime president of the American Association of Zoological Parks and Aquariums. "He knew frightfully little about animals—he was for most of his life the equivalent of a used car salesman. But he just became fascinated with it."

THE MARINES cut Molt loose in the summer of 1970. In anticipation of this day, Molt solicited requests from the zoos, just the way Leopard had done. He purchased himself an around-the-world ticket: Philadelphia–London–Lagos–Accra–Johannesburg–Maputo–Antananarivo–Nairobi–Cairo–Istanbul–Frankfurt–Philadelphia. He carried new business cards stamped with the logo of the American Association of Zoological Parks and Aquariums:

HENRY A. MOLT, JR.

---

ZOOLOGICAL EXPEDITION

---

*Authorized Agent for:*
LINCOLN PARK ZOO
100 W. WEBSTER AVE
CHICAGO, ILL. U.S.A.

The Lincoln Park Zoo, in its lust for lemurs, had furnished Molt with these nominal credentials. Its assistant director sent him a wish list: "At present we need a female White-fronted, female Red-fronted and male Fat-tailed Dwarf Lemur . . . we also want ruffed, either color phase, Black Lemurs and Crowned Lemurs . . . if you can come up with Gray Gentle Lemurs (Hapalemur) we'd be interested in those too."

Molt had no idea what he was doing. He had a map of Africa, a handful of contacts, and the vicarious experience of Leon Leopard to go on. If he could get lemurs, he would, but lemurs didn't keep him up at night. What did was the Angolan python, deemed by the *Guinness Book of World Records* to be "the world's rarest snake." None of the zoo people had seen one alive, or even a decent photo of one; all Molt could find was a photo with a grainy image of a dead specimen in liquid, from an old German article in the Academy of Natural Sciences. He could barely make out its pattern.

When he got to Accra, Molt headed for the university in search of snake people. He found some American graduate students and installed himself in their rental house. The authorized zoological expedition of the Lincoln Park Zoo then blasted through the cacao plantations of Ghana in a Land Rover, finding Gaboon vipers, Cameroon toads, and ropelike aggregations of army ants that could be lifted with a stick. Here and there they stopped to pull stunts on local people. They picked up a hitchhiker, but only after measuring his arms and legs; they explained that they were selling him to a shaman, laughing mercilessly as he fled the Land Rover into the darkening forest.

The students shipped Molt's snakes and toads back to Philadelphia. Molt flew to South Africa. To actually try to collect an Angolan python in its native range would be suicidal. The snakes occurred on the Namibian-Angolan border, a mined war zone patrolled by South African and Cuban troops and an independent faction of guerrillas. But an Afrikaner naturalist promised to find Molt four—his contacts were brave or desperate enough to cross minefields for snakes—and send them cash on delivery. Molt continued with confidence to Madagascar, where he stormed about the offices of the Ministère des Eaux et Forêts, acting the veteran zoo collector, seeking lemurs for his sponsors in Chicago. The officers were not budging: Duke University's lemur experts had by then effected a ban on the collection of lemurs by anyone but themselves.

Molt loudly invoked the name of Leon Leopard, director of zoo biology at the Central Texas Zoo. He worked very closely with Leopard, he told the bureaucrats, and Leopard would not be pleased to hear about his ill treatment.

While Molt was trying to look indignant, a wiry man gestured to him from the hallway. It was Leon Leopard's guide, Folo Emmanuel. Within days Emmanuel and Molt were in the Perinet national forest, stuffing reptiles into bags. They slept in Emmanuel's smoke-filled hut, eating fish tails with Emmanuel's children, an arrangement Molt could tolerate only briefly. He tried to sleep on the floor at a nearby train station, because that was more comfortable, until after a few days he gave up on the lemurs, and on Madagascar. He departed for Kenya with a single sack of Madagascar ground boas in his luggage. At the Nairobi Intercontinental he ordered room service.

At noon the next day Molt gathered his snakes and his suitcase and rented a tiny Fiat. The man at the rental firm asked him if he had any plans to leave the city with it. This was not, he emphasized, a car that could be driven into the bush. "Hell, I know that," Molt said, and started immediately toward the estate of Jonathan Leakey, two hundred miles to the north. As Molt drove, the pavement became dirt, the dirt became stones, and the stones grew grapefruit-sized, then pumpkin-sized, until finally one broke the Fiat's manifold and killed it. In the early evening, somewhere on the high plain spanning Kenya and Ethiopia, Molt found himself alone with his snakes. A group of Masai shepherds passed. They regarded Molt with what may or may not have been pity, then moved on. Roger Conant had advised the teenage Molt to get far away from Philadelphia. This he had accomplished. "I figured I would be eaten by lions or hyenas or something," Molt said.

A few hours later, at dusk, Molt was rescued by some passing Kenyan soldiers. He jumped onto their Land Rover and waded with them through a chest-deep river, carrying his snakes and his bags above his head. The soldiers dropped him off at Leakey's house. By then it was night, and Leakey was not home. A servant allowed Molt to rest on the couch and brought him tea, while Molt took in his elegant surroundings—terraces and gardens, oriental rugs and carvings, the frog calls from the lake's edge, and the smell of teak furniture. The generator shut off, and it was dark. Molt tried to sleep, only to be roused by a growling in his face. A caracal, with tall, tufted ears, was investigating him.

Jonathan Leakey ran a snake farm and a melon farm on this sprawling lakefront homestead, and unlike his famous parents and brother, he was more interested in money than in digging up fossil hominids. At twenty-nine, Molt's age exactly, Leakey had a reputation already compromised by the frequent deaths of his employees, who got killed packing his poisonous snakes. Leakey was surprised to find Molt on his couch, but obligingly shuttled him around the lake, with its wading hippos and flocks of flamingos. He radioed to have Molt's wreck of a Fiat repaired well enough for a return trip to Nairobi, where Molt left it parked in the rental lot, with a polite note and nonworking credit card number. He had a plane to catch. With him was his bag of Madagascar ground boas and some little horned vipers from Kenya, which he bagged and stuffed into a sneaker. He left for home, where a customs officer picked up Molt's sneaker, and seemed poised to insert a probing hand into its toe, when he changed his mind and returned the sneaker to Molt's suitcase, sparing himself an excruciating and noteworthy death.

NOT MUCH could keep Molt at home after that. As a husband, he was indifferent on a good day. The Angolan pythons arrived from South Africa and turned out to be stunning after all, a beautiful caramel brown with rounded scales like beads and white, lightning-shaped markings on their sides. Yet the high Molt felt on opening a crate of the world's rarest snakes quickly gave way to boredom and wanderlust. He let Bob Udell take over the pet shop while he retooled himself into the itinerant reptile collector he longed to be. Molt changed his business ads. Instead of classifieds for forty-dollar pythons in the *Philadelphia Daily News,* it was full columns in the American Association of Zoological Parks and Aquariums directories. "SPECIAL COLLECTING TRIPS ANYWHERE IN THE WORLD AT NO RISK TO YOU," Molt now promised. "YOU PAY ONLY FOR RESULTS!!"

In 1971, Molt and Leon Leopard fell out over shipments Leopard continued to receive from New Guinea. Molt had a feeling Leopard was getting more animals than he claimed, and not paying Molt his half. Molt phoned around to the zoos to see who had what animals, then billed them, ostensibly on the partnership's behalf, pocketing $6,000. Just in case Leopard thought of trying the same, Molt sent the zoos an emergency bulletin:

"Until further written notice, no person(s) or business other than myself, Henry A. Molt, is authorized to represent PHILADELPHIA REPTILE EXCHANGE in any respect whatsoever." Incidentally, he added on the bottom of the page, "I am planning to leave shortly on an extensive collecting trip to South East Asia and the Pacific."

After Africa, the world seemed smaller to Molt, and Leon Leopard's achievements less extraordinary. New Guinea no longer sounded far or foreboding. Molt would fly there and seek Leopard's coffee farmer in the highlands, undercutting Leopard. On the way he would stop over in Sydney to see Henry Szoke, purveyor of marvelous illegal Australian animals, whom Molt knew nothing about and was very curious to meet. Szoke told Molt he was welcome to visit, but he had something to confess, he said: He was not Henry Szoke.

Henry Szoke did not exist. Henry Szoke was Stefan Schwarz, a German from Stuttgart. He would explain the rest when they met.

STEFAN SCHWARZ was not tall, and he walked with a slight limp, but he was tan and handsome, a few years older than Molt. His German accent was barely detectable under his Australian one. Together Schwarz and Molt made an abbreviated tour of Sydney—the still-uncompleted Opera House, the harbor, and the botanical gardens.

"Within hours he had told me his whole life story," Molt said.

Schwarz had been born in Stuttgart to a family of academics. Most of them still lived there, except his sister Gisela, who had also emigrated to Australia, and was married to a Hungarian named Szoke.

Before leaving for Australia, Schwarz had been a keeper at the Stuttgart Zoo. The Germans, along with the Belgians and the Dutch, possessed some of the finest and oldest zoos in the world, and skilled keepers like Schwarz fanned out to guide new zoos as they sprung up on other continents. In Sydney, Schwarz became general curator of the Australian Reptile Park, which had emerged in the 1950s from a venom-extracting operation just like those common then in the American South—except that instead of rattlesnakes, the Australians milked the insanely deadly and fast-moving taipans. Schwarz continued to maintain his ties to zoos in Europe, and in 1964 he finessed for the reptile park Australia's last big legal importation of foreign reptiles, a huge sampling from dealers and zoos in Germany, the Netherlands, and Belgium, which arrived in Australia on a Dutch freighter. Schwarz accompanied the reptiles for the ten-thousand-mile journey, changing dirty snake bags and administering live rodents. When an Amazon tree boa died toward the end, only a few miles offshore of Melbourne, Schwarz blithely tossed it overboard. A young man found it on the beach and toted it to the National Museum, whose head herpetologist embarrassed himself with wild hypotheses of how the snake had crossed the Pacific.

Years later, when he was settled in Sydney, Schwarz took it upon himself to return the European zoos' generosity. He boarded a plane to Stuttgart with a Tasmanian devil in his hand luggage. He collected monitors and snakes in Australia and New Zealand, sending them to Europe in his red boxes labeled "art."

When Molt came to visit, Schwarz was in the process of divorcing his German-born wife. He was leaving Sydney and the zoo, moving north to a property in Cairns. There he would build a private collection of reptiles in pits and wooden cages, and expand his side business in cane toads. Schwarz collected the monstrous invasive toads and sold them, dead and preserved, for dissection and novelty wallets. He was finished with zoos; now, for the foreseeable future, it would be cane toads and smuggling.

Schwarz and Molt got on like brothers. They visited the zoos and forests of New South Wales and slept under the stars. They sensed, even then, that they would be working together a long time.

IN PORT Moresby, Papua New Guinea, Molt boarded at the Civic Guest House, a hostel run by an Australian widow who fed her guests in a common mess. The Civic Guest House was Molt's type of place—a frat house. He drank away the thick humid nights with American service-men and a guy hunting for downed Japanese warplanes. Already, he liked New Guinea. It was, in its way, crazier than Africa. The roads around Port Moresby teemed at night with snakes, and Molt would enlist the Ameri-cans to pile into his rental car and go hunting. They drove in heavy rains along the Brown River, packing a rifle and machetes and a case of South Pacific lager, taking pains not to hit any dogs.

Unfortunately no Boelen's pythons lived along the Brown River. These Molt would have to get from the highlands. Leon Leopard had been the first to bring them back alive, which annoyed Molt. He would just have to bring back more.

All Molt knew of Leopard's coffee farmer was that he lived in a place called Wau. Two flights a week left Port Moresby for the Wau airstrip, and Molt boarded a plane so small that passengers had to be weighed before boarding. Its wing had been bandaged with what appeared to be duct tape.

Pilots in Papua New Guinea were mostly Australians who shuttled mail into the mines and plantations of the highlands. They knew where everyone lived. And so Molt found himself, without extraordinary effort, a guest of Peter Shanahan, Leon Leopard's supplier and the biggest cof-fee farmer in Wau. Shanahan lived with his American wife in a plantation home on a grassy hill, where thick fogs blocked the sun for days at a time. They were attended to by tenant farmers and servants who called Shana-han "master," which simultaneously creeped Molt out and thrilled him.

Shanahan was a third-generation New Guinean, thirty-one years old. His maternal grandfather, a German, had planted the country's first coffee farm with seeds smuggled from Jamaica. Shanahan's parents had sent him to boarding school in Sydney, but he was called back before college—fam-ily fortunes, once huge from gold mining, were flagging, reduced to the coffee plots. Shanahan's dreams of becoming a biologist were shelved to save them. Yet Shanahan ended up a skilled and sought-after animal collec-tor even as he farmed coffee. He netted butterflies for the Bishop Museum in Honolulu, and birds of paradise for the Rotterdam Zoo.

Shanahan had seen his first Boelen's python only a few years before, in the mountains above Wau. It was sunning itself in a tree, its skin shimmering like taffeta. Finding a python at that altitude, Shanahan said, "was like, 'What the heck?' It was a snake I hadn't seen before, very pretty. I made a big pole and hooked it. When I looked around they were quite common." Shanahan collected several. He did not know what to call them.

When Leon Leopard arrived in Wau one day, wearing his ersatz zoo uniform, he showed Shanahan photos of the very same snake. "Leon Leopard. Central Texas Zoo," the Texan announced, extending his hand.

"That shook me up," Shanahan said. "I had never heard an accent like that before."

Shanahan didn't know what to make of Leopard, except that "he had a big opinion of himself and was full of stories. And he lived on Parrot Street, which was weird." Leopard didn't seem to know much about wildlife, which was odd for a zoo man—"but back then there weren't the books," Shanahan said. "Even the common species, we didn't know what they were. Libraries didn't exist in Wau."

Up in the Wau hills, any white visitor was accommodated—people were bored, and reflexively gracious in the colonial fashion. Leopard also came equipped with the approval of the wildlife department in Port Moresby, and as a licensed collector it was Shanahan's job to provide. Shanahan's wife, though, quietly made copies of Leopard's documents. The Texan was, in her estimation, "a spiv, a cheat," and maybe not a zoo man at all.

Now, only a year or so since Leopard's visit, here was Hank Molt: younger, far more knowledgeable, and every bit as suspect. "Hank worked on impressing," Shanahan said. "He was Mr. Sophisticated. He knew his stuff, that was pretty obvious—not birds and mammals, but reptiles." He wondered whether Molt had really fallen out with Leopard, as Molt had claimed, or whether the two were setting him up. "I was just a hick," said Shanahan. "We could handle crocodiles and cyclones but these boys from the city were something else."

Shanahan was sitting on tens of thousands of dollars' worth of animals Leopard had ordered, "a spectacular collection," Shanahan said, but Leopard had delayed so long in arriving that Shanahan had become panicked. He would dump it for a pittance if he had to, just to cover his costs. And now here was Molt. It certainly seemed like a setup.

Molt offered to buy all the animals, to get Shanahan out of a bind. "Hank actually took out his checkbook," Shanahan said. "Right then and there." But Shanahan said he would have to wait for Leopard. And then Leopard called.

Molt said he'd like to stick around awhile longer.

MOLT SAT on Shanahan's porch, staring at the hills, drinking a South Pacific lager. He had come to New Guinea hoping to make $250,000. He would be lucky, now, if he broke even. It was a failure, but failure can be mitigated by small reprisals, and Molt had one in mind.

A nervous Shanahan had driven off in his old Land Rover that morning to collect Leon Leopard at the airport in Port Moresby. This would have been a relief to Shanahan, but then, there was Molt still drinking beer on his porch, for reasons that were not clear to him, and Molt had insisted that Shanahan say nothing to Leopard about him. "That whole situation caused me so much angst and trouble," Shanahan said. "I never knew how to handle these guys. I just figured I had to bring them together."

It was evening when the Land Rover returned. Shanahan's servants were relaxing on the grass, chatting and picking lice from one another's hair. Molt waved from the porch. Leopard had to squint, shut the car door, then amble closer on his long, slender legs.

The entire reason Molt had remained in Wau was to savor Leon Leopard's expression. It was a stricken one, just as he'd hoped: wide-eyed, pale, a hint of bile rising to the throat.

"Mercy, mercy," said Leopard. That was enough for Molt.

AN INVIGORATED Molt flew on to Fiji. He introduced himself to museum officials as a zoologist.

The museum men, expatriate Britons, directed Molt to the island of Ovalau, where children followed him wherever he wandered. He drank kava in a thatched hut with two kindly brothers, who taught him the words for the two species he sought—the Fiji banded iguana was *voiki,* and the Fiji boa *nanka*. Both were seriously coveted by zoos. In the United States, only the San Diego Zoo had ever exhibited Fiji iguanas—demure, emerald-colored creatures, the males bearing stripes of robin's-egg blue, that are by some unexplained phenomenon related to the iguanas of Central America and the Caribbean, seven thousand miles away. Leon Leopard and Molt, in happier days, had made a pilgrimage to San Diego to view a pair of Fijis. They were taken aback by the iguanas' diminutive size, their alert red eyes, and their jewel colors.

On Ovalau, the brothers assembled some kids to catch Molt's nankas and voikis. To Molt's dismay, the kids set the trees on fire, raining reptiles to the ground and charring them in the process. Giant tree-dwelling crabs had nipped off the boas' tails, so they were stubby as well as charred. Molt climbed a tree after a Fiji iguana, to demonstrate its proper capture. He fell from the treetop into a brook, then rose from the water with one lizard triumphantly in hand. Molt returned to Philadelphia with a crate of them.

When Molt delivered his iguanas to the zoos, he made sure to tell a story, like Leon Leopard before him.

There were four or five women on the base of this tree all pointing up and yelling "voiki! voiki!" Finally I saw it—it was a solid green female. I started climbing the tree, pursuing this thing from branch to branch. Higher and higher it went onto smaller and smaller branches, eluding me at a deliberate pace. All of a sudden it's about to hop over to the next tree! I lunge my body forward so I go crashing out of the tree right into a stream of water six feet deep. But the iguana is in my hand and I rise slowly from the water, wielding it above my head, like the Statue of fucking Liberty.

He sold them all.

## 2

### Willow Grove

Molt's new retail store, a brick storefront in Willow Grove, Pennsylvania, did much to discourage casual shoppers. His old store, the Pet Emporium, had been cursed with a metal sign the size of a truck—there was no way to remove it, and therefore no way to curtail the incessant foot traffic. Police were constantly coming around, too, looking for Bob Udell. So Molt decided to move. He discouraged Udell from following.

In Willow Grove, Molt covered the windows in bamboo mats and marked the shop with a small, simple sign:

The Exotarium

IMPORTERS

EXPORTERS

Artifacts, Natural History Specimens

The effect was perfectly forbidding.

MOLT HAD just about recovered from his South Pacific trip the year before. He'd lost $20,000, and though he'd enjoyed spooking Leon Leopard in the Wau hills, the reality was that Leopard wrote thousand-dollar checks to the American Association of Zoological Parks and Aquariums and lived in a lush Texas compound with apes and gazelles, while Molt's own membership to the AAZPA had been canceled for his failure to pay a hundred dollars in dues, and the association wrote him a cease-and-desist letter for using its logo on his stationery. More than once, his electricity was shut off.

All Molt had, really, were his connections overseas. After their meeting in Sydney, Molt and Stefan Schwarz took boyish glee in encrypting their correspondence. They established a numerical code for dozens of species and memorized it, never committing the key to paper. If Molt wanted a shingleback skink, he'd send a yellow carbon paper requesting a "no. 17." Molt signed off as "Junior," Schwarz as "Vegemite." Molt took charge of the bookkeeping, as Schwarz burned anything that could incriminate him. Australian penalties for wildlife crimes were stiff and getting stiffer, so even on the phone, Schwarz spoke to Molt in code. "The photos looked good, but one of the children's pictures was blurry" might mean a Children's python came in dead; "It's sunny out, I think I'll have a schnapps" meant Molt's cash had arrived.

Molt and the Swiss widow Schetty, after eight years' correspondence, dropped all pretenses that their dealings were legal, and Schetty's aid was invaluable to Molt, for Switzerland had no statute like the Lacey Act, and no endangered species list. Any foreign animal that reached Switzerland was home free, and could be reexported to the United States. Molt advised Schetty not to label her boxes in too much detail, and, in a pinch, to call everything a venomous snake, discouraging close inspection. Molt asked Schetty for Komodo dragons, gavials, whatever she could get, and had no qualms about peddling to her marked-up Australian reptiles from Stefan Schwarz, the contact she had provided Molt years before.

Molt had upset Schetty by returning from the South Pacific with nothing left for her, particularly the Fiji iguanas she so badly wanted. He'd shipped the bulk of his Fiji animals to the Dallas Zoo, and the rest to Atlanta.

He promised to go back. "This fall I return to Fiji, Solomon Islands and New Guinea and Philippines," Molt wrote Schetty in the Tarzan-speak he deemed suited to her English. "This time I send you stuff direct from there. Last time was first trip to area. I have learned a lot, have good contacts."

IN THE spring of 1972, a teenager wandered into the Exotarium, dressed in military surplus and a belt hung with survival tools. Karl Sorensen found Molt the way all the snake fanatics seemed to—"like flies attracted to dead fish," Molt said. Sorensen was a rugged type, an outdoorsman, and into psychedelic drugs. Already he'd traveled to Mexico and back, shrooming and snake-hunting. Sorensen was the son of schoolteachers, and had a scrubbed, Scandinavian look, but there was something unstable about him. He barely spoke, and when he did it was in sort of a whisper. He enjoyed knives.

Sorensen didn't like to work, but he liked to be out in the woods, and Molt was starting to see potential in this young adventurer, who hankered to return to Mexico and catch more snakes. "Think bigger," Molt told him—think, say, Southeast Asia.

Molt had begun to see the young Karl Sorensen the way, he guessed, Leon Leopard had seen him just a few years before. Sorensen was no innocent—he dug up graves for fun, and had burglarized Princeton University's natural history museum. That the kid was a druggie Molt regarded as an advantage, something to use against him as needed.

MOLT HAD to delay his return to Asia by a year. His wife had become pregnant.

Nine months later, Megot Schetty wrote Molt excitedly to congratulate him. "My wife had a nice little baby girl born on 22 January thank you for your kind wishes," he replied, then got on to some business about dead Mauritanian vipers.

Molt retreated to the Exotarium for much of the winter. He composed price lists, which, though not issued with much regularity, were painstakingly designed in whatever fonts and inks caught his eye. His envelopes got tattooed all over with "Urgent" and "First Class" stamps. Every transaction resulted in a paper trail; if someone wrote Molt just to call him a cheat, he copied the letter and filed it in three places. Frequent infusions of drama relieved a landlocked Molt's boredom. "There was always some crisis or confrontation, crazy people coming around," he said. Bob Udell was a free agent now, roaming back and forth to Florida, returning with trash cans full of indigo snakes that he kept in his apartment. He hired kids to break into Molt's shop for animals, certain he'd been cheated by Molt. Molt hired Sorensen to break into Udell's place.

At thirty-three, Molt could not call himself rich or even solvent. He nonetheless had the pleasure of being treated as a colleague by his childhood idols. Roger Conant summoned Molt to the Philadelphia Zoo to help unload mambas into the new reptile house. The National Zoo's reptile curator popped by the Exotarium to talk shop, braving the rogues' gallery of regulars. Molt made frequent deliveries to the Bronx Zoo, where the curator Wayne King added to his collection of New Guinea crocodiles.

When King's underling, a young reptile keeper named John Behler, refused to provide Molt some Gaboon viper babies from a pair Molt had sold the zoo—such kickbacks were expected in those days—Molt went straight to its famous director, William Conway, and made a stink.

"I was used to being treated like a king," he said.

MOLT ALWAYS made the zoo rounds before a big trip. He enjoyed the whole tap dance, meeting and tantalizing the curators. Fiji iguanas were an easy sell, as they made for beautiful displays. Molt sent around notices that promised not just pairs but "true sexual pairs in perfect condition with a 30 day live guarantee," collected with great difficulty from "the remote outer islands in the Fiji group." Washington, Memphis, Dallas, Sacramento, and St. Louis all placed orders. The Philadelphia Zoo authorized Molt to act as its agent in New Guinea, supplying him with a letter of introduction and a litany of its turtle and python needs.

Molt's plan was to send Sorensen as an advance man to Fiji, where he would collect the iguanas and boas. Molt would follow to Fiji and pick the best among them, then send shipments from the airport. The two would repeat this pattern of parting and reuniting through Fiji, the Solomon Islands, New Guinea, Thailand, the Philippines, Singapore, and India. Sorensen would have to invest $3,000 and pay his own airfare, but any profits would be split, and there would certainly, Molt assured him, be profits.

On June 7, 1973, Sorensen landed in Fiji with a piece of paper bearing the names of two brothers and one island—no phone numbers, no addresses. Two weeks later, Molt arrived at the Nadi, Fiji, airport in the middle of the night, to find Sorensen waiting with thirty iguanas and boas tied up neatly in muslin bags. The iguanas were unscathed and well colored; the boas' tails were intact, not crab-chewed. Except there were too many, and Molt and Sorensen were forced to release some in the dark field behind the airport.

They continued to New Guinea. In Port Moresby, Molt didn't bother to check in with the wildlife department. Three months before, it had rejected the Philadelphia Zoo's bid to use Molt as its agent. Molt and Leon Leopard were now recognized for what they were—commercial wildlife dealers, *personae non gratae* in Papua New Guinea.

Molt offered the Philadelphia Zoo a handy solution—to authorize Peter Shanahan as its agent. Molt would go pick up the animals, and hopefully persuade Shanahan to throw in a few extra for him. Philadelphia wrote New Guinea, which agreed to the arrangement.

Molt and Sorensen stayed a few nights at the rough-and-tumble Civic Guest House before heading to Wau, where Peter Shanahan had the zoo's nine reptiles packed and ready, with nothing extra for Molt. While Molt lolled around Shanahan's, enjoying a colonial society soon to be purged from its tranquil mountain homesteads, the mail plane came. The wildlife department demanded that Molt report to Port Moresby for a chat. Shanahan, weary of slick American animal dealers, had phoned them.

Molt returned with Sorensen to the capital, but before checking in at the wildlife office, he sent the kid out to find snakes. Sorensen found eighteen, including a rare Papuan olive python—a thick, blunt-headed constrictor, slate-colored on top, brown on its belly, that was hotly desired by zoos. There was no question whose baggage the snakes would travel in. Sorensen "did not balk at it a bit," Molt said. "He did not hesitate a second."

In the wildlife department, Molt noticed a map of New Guinea on the wall behind the officer's desk. It was stuck with pushpins, and each pushpin pierced a name impressed on rigid label tape: Henry Molt. Leon Leopard. Molt recognized the name of a third collector, a German. Leon Leopard's pin was in the distant ocean. Hank Molt's was in Wau.

The officer sent Molt away, and told him to return after lunch. When he did, he saw his pin had been moved to Port Moresby.

Papua New Guinea and Henry Molt smoothed things over. Molt was a good talker. Good enough that the wildlife department not only shipped Molt's nine animals to Philadelphia for him, they threw in three rare Fly River turtles as a gift to the zoo. That Karl Sorensen was by then on a plane to Hong Kong with eighteen New Guinea snakes, one lizard, and four crocodiles in his luggage, Molt did not bring to their attention.

AGAIN THEY separated. Molt chose to skip Australia, not wanting Sorensen to get too close to Stefan Schwarz. The kid was too crafty, and Schwarz was too important.

Mme Schetty was expecting the pair, and her Fiji iguanas, to show up any day in Switzerland. Molt had written her from New Guinea, boasting of their successes and their imminent arrival. Mysteriously, though, he failed to appear in Maggia. "Up to this day I have waited and waited for your visit . . . please be so kind and answer earliest and write what you have for me," she pleaded. Her letter lay unopened in Philadelphia.

Sorensen flew to Singapore and Molt to Manila. They reconvened in Singapore, whose wildlife traders operated on a scale unlike anything in the West. The Singapore traders were ethnic Chinese, some of them third-

or fourth-generation animal dealers, and their reach extended far—into Cambodia and Irian Jaya and even Bangladesh, where the rural poor carried animals to collection points. The Singapore traders sold slow lorises for twelve dollars and wild leopards for thirty-five, and listed 150 species of snake on a single onionskin price list. In one of their hangarlike warehouses might be ten thousand parrots, crated and labeled for a KLM flight to Amsterdam. So lucrative were the Asians' shipping contracts that the airlines entertained them at Raffles and the Shangri-La. They maintained memberships at colonial-era social clubs, where their mistresses were always welcome.

Molt was friendly with an animal dealer named Y. L. Koh, and a second Singapore dealer, Christopher Wee. The two were avowed enemies—Koh older and soft-spoken, Wee younger and brasher. Both packed animals in frequently lethal ways. Wee had already been convicted for wildlife offenses in Australia, and employed the Indonesian army to net black palm cockatoos in their roosts. He had once, notoriously, dyed a young orangutan black with Miss Clairol, so that American customs officers would mistake it for a monkey.

Neither Wee nor Koh thought anything of laundering a shipment for a customer—it was common courtesy. Wee treated Molt and Sorensen to a sumptuous dinner, sold them four crates of reptiles, and mixed their New Guinea hoard into the boxes, which they forwarded to Philadelphia.

This collecting trip was coming together smoothly. Specimens were in the air, and some already had arrived at the Philadelphia Zoo. Molt and Sorensen's frequent personality clashes were the only real problem. The kid was taciturn and always buying stuff. Molt was chiding and controlling. At a bird farm in Thailand, Sorensen decided he fancied some hornbills. He ordered them killed and mounted, annoying Molt to no end, and stuffed them in his luggage along with his newest hatchets and daggers. To make room for these treasures, he threw out all his clothes.

Sorensen was quick to find drugs in Thailand, and Molt could do nothing about it. While Molt kicked back with soldiers and mercenaries and the pretty prostitutes at Lucy's Tiger Den, Sorensen scrounged for opium. After a tense few days in Bangkok, Sorensen surprised Molt with a knife to the throat. "I was lying in bed in our hotel room, about to fall asleep," Molt said. "I couldn't tell if he was fucking with me or not." To be on the safe side, Molt assumed he was not.

They continued, unhappily, toward India. "He had a suitcase filled with knives and dead birds and LSD," Molt said of Sorensen. "I wouldn't go through the airport with him." In Calcutta, Molt ventured out to buy gavials, returning to his hotel room to find Sorensen "with guys in turbans cutting hashish the size of a placemat. He was always a pain in the ass," Molt said. "I put up with him because I was using him."

"DEAR MME Schetty," wrote Molt. "Thank you for your 2 letters and I apologize for not stopping by in Switzerland on my way home but we ran out of time and by the time I reached Europe I received word of an illness in my family and proceeded direct home."

There was no illness in Molt's family, but Molt was quite sick of Sorensen, and their tensions did not subside in Philadelphia. After their August 1973 return, they faced the daunting task of selling their cache of 150 rare reptiles equitably. Molt did nothing equitably, but it took Sorensen months to realize it.

Udell had done a fine job maintaining the animals he'd received, as had the Sacramento Zoo. Philadelphia's order arrived in good shape, and Molt charged them a thousand dollars apiece for the Fly River turtles meant as a gift from New Guinea. Dallas, Sacramento, and Rochester all got their Fiji iguanas. The National Zoo took four. Molt wrote to offer some iguanas to Mme Schetty, who confirmed that she would buy them—but then Molt did not respond. He had sold out. It sickened him to remember the night he and Sorensen had let loose eight iguanas behind the airport in Fiji, where they were certain not to survive.

Sorensen had yet to see profits from this immensely profitable trip. Fall became winter, and Molt hoarded in the Exotarium all the reptiles they had left. Sorensen demanded the remainder to sell on his own. Molt refused him. "I was gonna rip him off," Molt said. "Absolutely."

MOLT WAS still packing iguanas for the St. Louis and Memphis zoos when President Nixon signed the Endangered Species Act of 1973.

"At a time when Americans are more concerned than ever with conserving our natural resources," Nixon declared, "this legislation provides the Federal Government with the needed authority to protect an irreplaceable part of our national heritage: threatened wildlife."

The new Endangered Species Act also aimed to curb what the public was starting to view as a distasteful commerce in exotic animals, a trade that, it was said, was contributing to extinction. It came with a list of species, including foreign ones, barred from commercial trade. A few years before, the Lacey Act had been resurrected and reinvigorated, also in the hope of slowing trade. The Lacey Act now prohibited illegal imports not just of game animals, but of nearly every form of animal in an effort to stem, its sponsors in Congress said, "an accelerating rate of extermination of many of our planet's unique forms of life." The Lacey Act's penalties, formerly misdemeanors, became felonies.

Earlier in 1973, the United States had signed on to the Convention on International Trade in Endangered Species. CITES, as the treaty was known, would create a global list of species whose trade was banned or restricted, and this list, like the domestic one, was certain to grow. CITES aimed to curb the huge, often terrifically damaging commerce in timber and animal products—ivory, sea turtle shells, rhinoceros horns, bear bile, crocodile skins—but it made no exceptions for live plants or animals. By the end of that year, eighty nations had joined CITES, and Geneva was chosen as its administrative headquarters. The handy loophole Molt used to launder animals through Switzerland would close when the treaty took effect, in 1975.

Faced with this imposing new trinity of laws—the Lacey Act, the Endangered Species Act, and CITES—many wildlife dealers chose to get out of the business entirely. Molt saw only opportunity.

# 3

## Pine Barrens

The New Year began auspiciously.

A fresh batch of Fiji iguanas refreshed Molt's reputation in the zoo world. In January 1974, the American Association of Zoological Parks and Aquariums forgave him for stealing its logo and not paying dues, and sent him an invitation to its annual conference, to which Molt showed up in a safari suit.

Wish lists arrived in the mail. The director of the Knoxville Zoo, which was opening its own new "reptile complex" in the fall, demanded from Molt forty-three species, including half a dozen already on the U.S. endangered species list, the usual smattering of Australian animals, and sixteen reptiles newly proposed for CITES listing. There was no mention of permits.

Molt had big ambitions for his next trip.

Karl Sorensen was out, obviously. His new kid would be Steven Levy, a doctor's son from Pittsburgh. Levy was a serious, personable eighteen-year-old, neither a druggie nor the type to put a knife to your throat. Weeks after Molt and Sorensen returned from their trip, Levy had arrived at the Exotarium with a baby alligator and a ragtag bunch of snakes to sell. He was moving out of his parents' house and into a dormitory, he explained.

Levy, like Molt and the rest, possessed the gene that had caused him to chase after reptiles since he could walk, and the memory of the Fiji iguanas, olive pythons, and New Guinea crocodiles he'd seen at Molt's shop haunted Levy his whole first semester at Allegheny College. He wrote Molt a letter, asking if there was some way he could help.

Sure there was, Molt wrote back. It would require a passport, a round-the-world plane ticket, and $3,000.

"He said we'd be leaving around Christmas," Levy said. "Then Christmas became spring." Levy took a semester off from Allegheny College, only to be told the trip was delayed until summer. "My parents thought Molt was nuts," Levy said, until Molt took Levy's father to dinner. "I dressed really well and was driving a brand-new Oldsmobile station wagon," Molt said. "I believe I impressed him as upstanding."

Some Karl Sorensen drama was responsible for Molt's delays. By now Sorensen had figured out he'd been stiffed, that Molt had no intention of cutting him his share of earnings from their trip, nor so much as returning his original $3,000 investment, though Molt's check from the Philadelphia Zoo alone would have covered it twice over.

And suddenly the Exotarium was burglarized. All the leftover snakes from New Guinea were stolen, along with some baby crocodiles from Thailand and a couple of cobras from Singapore. The burglary "had all the earmarks" of Sorensen, Molt said. "He was able to lift these storm doors over the sidewalk and descend into the basement and enter the shop." Yet Molt could not resist sending hundreds of his customers, zoos included, a juicy bulletin: "During the night of April 8, 1974, thieves broke into our shop and stole the following live reptiles." He described each stolen specimen down to its "nice wavy dorsal pattern" or "few faint old scars." He offered a thousand-dollar reward.

Barely had Molt's bulletins gone out when Bob Udell arrived at the Exotarium with a bulletin of his own: The party responsible—not that there was ever much doubt who it was—demanded a ransom. Sorensen would return all the animals for his $3,000 back, and be done with it. For his negotiating services, Udell demanded a fee of $300.

Molt drove to Udell's place, where the kid was waiting. Molt flashed the money, and a silent Sorensen loaded the animals into Molt's car. Sorensen's own was parked several blocks away.

"I gave him the cash and I asked him if he wanted a ride over," Molt said. "He was stupid enough to get in my car. In my left hand I grabbed the gear shift and put it from drive into park. In my right I grabbed his ponytail and pulled his head back. I started choking him as hard as I could. It was broad daylight but no one was noticing.

"He was clenching the money. The door was open and his leg was pushing against the pavement. He had a huge Adam's apple and I squeezed and squeezed it until he released the money. He got out and slammed the door hard. There was the money laying on the floor of my car. He had clenched it so hard some of the bills were stuck together."

Molt never saw Sorensen again. Udell kept his fee.

A FEW factors distinguished Molt's 1974 trip from his previous three. It would be an intentionally criminal venture. The quantities of reptiles would be much larger. More money and people would be needed to carry it off.

Steven Levy would do fine as a bag boy, but Molt needed substantial financing and a second body. On one of his frequent trips to the bank, wearing his favorite olive twill safari jacket—an understated number without too many pockets—he met someone who fulfilled both requirements.

Edward Allen was the only other customer at the Bala Cynwyd branch of the Central Pennsylvania Bank who bought travelers' checks in $500 denominations. Allen, too, was an adventurer, a big-game hunter who had been to the North Pole and the Congo. Not too many of those lived in Montgomery County, Pennsylvania. Allen stood in line behind Molt. The teller introduced them with satisfaction. Molt, she informed Allen, travels all around the world collecting animals for zoos.

Molt and Allen retreated to a lunch counter in the bank building, where Allen also worked. A generation older than Molt, Allen was an investment banker, half of a firm called Allen & Rogers. His résumé was lustrous, all-American fare: a hot-air balloonist, U. Penn grad, and Chicago Bears fullback for half a season in 1947, until a Steeler ripped up his knee. He was a nondrinker and nonsmoker, with a loyal wife and four strapping sons. He zipped about town in a Mercedes convertible. Yet for all his trappings, Allen was restless. He hated his job; he was trying to sell the firm to his partner.

Over lunch, Allen learned about Stefan Schwarz's jungle compound, the copious profits from Molt's New Guinea trip, and the cute whores and the guns on the wall at Lucy's Tiger Den.

It helped that Molt, for all his jungle talk, hailed from reassuringly familiar circles. Molt's sister, it turned out, was friendly with Allen's sister. Molt drove a new Oldsmobile and maintained a healthy line of credit at the bank. The tailoring on his safari jacket was fine. Allen invited Molt to his home in the wealthy suburb of Newtown Square. In a barn behind his house, Allen had built an enormous den for his custom rifles and hunting trophies—a polar bear, kudus, impalas. "It was all very impressive," Molt said. "He was a man's man. A he-man."

Allen hadn't hunted Africa in years, and he'd never been to Southeast Asia. He had little pressing business while the firm's sale was pending; he was all but retired. Reptiles held no interest for Allen at all, but what he could really use about now, he told Molt, was a good, old-fashioned jungle quest.

"I said, 'Well, we're doing a trip in a couple months,' but then I said 'I don't know, this is a pretty rough trip. We're going into Fiji . . . ' It's the negative takeaway. You dangle something and then take it away."

Allen insisted he was more than up to it.

STEVEN LEVY landed in Fiji on September 1, 1974. He'd taken another semester's leave from Allegheny College and was quite unaware of how his predecessor had ended up.

Levy's job was identical to Karl Sorensen's—go to Fiji, get iguanas and boas, wait for Molt, move on. He'd spent the summer waiting for Molt to give him the word while he studied maps and got coached in the selection of Fiji iguanas—no missing toes, no missing tails, collect male and female specimens equally.

The only difference was that Levy was to collect five times as many animals. And they were going through Schetty in Switzerland this time, which was easier and safer than shipping them straight home.

"Best greetings to you after a long, long time!!!!!!" Molt wrote Schetty that July. "This year I am finally coming to Switzerland on my way home for a visit. The purpose of my letter is to find out whether you would be willing to accept some shipments from Fiji, New Guinea and Philippines during my trip . . . of course I would be willing to make available a good portion of the specimens to you." Schetty forgave Molt his lengthy and mysterious silences. For Fiji iguanas, much could be excused.

Now Levy, nineteen years old, stood in the Nadi, Fiji, airport, with a hard-sided Samsonite suitcase and a slip of paper. Molt had assured Levy that you can find anyone in the third world with just one name, and one name was all he had: Niumich. Molt told him to take a ferry to the island of Ovalau and ask for Niumich; Levy instead took a plane and landed on a gravel strip next to what appeared to be a wooden lean-to. This was the Ovalau airport. The Fijians awaited the plane in ripped shirts and sarongs.

"I'm looking for Niumich," Levy told the first person he saw, a young man about his own age.

"That's my brother," the young man said. He introduced himself as Epineri. He called himself Epi. Together he and Levy walked the mile and a half home, to a village called Navuloa.

Epi lived with his parents in a wooden house without electricity or plumbing, but by the standards of Navuloa, it was exceptionally well appointed. Within minutes after Levy arrived, he saw his first wild Fiji iguana, eating flowers in a tall tree. Epi scrambled up the tree and caught it.

It did not take long for the youth of Navuloa to mobilize for Levy, and they climbed every tree for miles while Levy adjusted to the quiet rituals of the village, sleeping on a hard bed in the family house, watching Epi's mother bake bread and weave palm-leaf mats to the sound of her transistor radio. He wore a sarong.

Molt had provided Levy with muslin bags for the snakes and iguanas, and with the kids returning sometimes twice a day, he was accumulating more animals than he knew what to do with. Five dollars was a lot for anything in Fiji, and Levy had to refuse the kids arriving with more. He was running out of money. Every day he rinsed the bags of snake and lizard feces, dried them, repacked the animals, and waited for Molt, who was two weeks late and counting.

Levy was unnerved by Molt's absence, but also found himself dreading his arrival. He'd become attached to this family, helping them carry huge sacks of flour from the market and following them daily to the ocean, where the women netted shrimp. In the warm afternoons, he showered, surrounded by giggling children, under an outdoor spout.

Another languid, idyllic week passed before Molt arrived, and by then, the sarong-wearing Levy was sad to see him. Molt was accompanied by an older man—Levy had not been briefed about Ed Allen, and this just made it worse.

Molt, all business, was thrilled with Levy's haul: forty-two iguanas, forty-six boas. They sought a carpenter and commissioned from him wooden boxes painted with the words "Natural History Specimens."

Epi, who was studying to be a policeman, secured the local police's stamp for the boxes, making them look official enough to pass muster. Straight to Switzerland went the iguanas and boas, and Levy left Fiji heartsick. He promised to return, knowing that he never would.

MOLT HAD departed Philadelphia with sixty-five dollars in his pocket, and some credit cards. A customer owed him thousands of dollars that he promised to wire Molt in Singapore, a few countries hence. Leaving home with sixty-five dollars was not a gamble Molt would likely have taken without Ed Allen by his side. Already, only one country into the trip, it was Allen who paid for the crates and shipping out of Fiji. Levy had already run through all his money, and his parents were wiring him more.

The group took a plane from Fiji to Australia, where Molt and Allen met Stefan Schwarz, and Levy proceeded alone to New Guinea.

Schwarz was still building his Cairns reptile compound, which amounted as yet to a patch of land with some bare wooden sheds and a tent where Schwarz slept. Molt and Allen slept in a tool-filled storage shed too low to stand in, and showered using a punctured bucket. For toilets, they dug holes in the ground. Allen didn't mind at all. "He was fifty-seven but fit and tough as a thirty-five-year-old," Molt said. "He loved that kind of shit." Schwarz organized a hunt for amethystine pythons, and the three descended in a cold rain into a volcanic gorge, where they were plagued by leeches and mud wasps and had to boil tea in tin cans for warmth. Allen filmed them with his Super-8 camera. On Schwarz's bare land they drafted a list of the specimens that Schwarz would hurry to collect, driving all over the country with his hooks and bags, before Molt and Allen's return the next month. Allen fronted Schwarz $5,000. Molt gave him nothing.

In Port Moresby, Papua New Guinea, Levy checked in at the Civic Guest House. Molt loved the place, as had Karl Sorensen, but it terrified Levy. New Guinea was nothing like the gentle Fiji. Everything about it was mean, drunk, raucous.

Levy's mission was to collect anything he could in New Guinea, then sit around and wait for Molt and Allen again. Levy was on his own: there was no use appealing to Peter Shanahan in the Wau hills, and the New Guinea wildlife office would be more likely to arrest anyone connected to Hank Molt at this point than to help. Levy's collecting efforts were hindered by weather: rain attracted the snakes to the roads, and this was the dry season. He scrounged up just a handful of frogs and snakes, and bought some baby crocodiles at a farm.

Before departing on this trip, Levy had some understanding of the new wildlife laws, but it was only when Ed Allen arrived in Port Moresby and began packing Levy's animals into a suitcase, Levy said, that he "sort of got the idea" that the venture was illegal. Allen and Levy would travel to Hong Kong next. Molt was already there.

The trip was going just as Molt had envisioned it—the three weaving around one another, meeting and taking stock, working multiple countries simultaneously. Except Molt was supplying none of the money, and this was not endearing him to his companions. Molt possessed only his credit card, with which he picked up the rare hotel room or meal. He clung to the hope of a wire transfer in Singapore.

Levy and the older man got on well, to their mutual surprise. At airport souvenir shops they chatted about cameras, bought suitcase stickers, and voiced their misgivings about Hank Molt.

The unlikely allies left for Hong Kong.

*4 October 1974*

*Dear Mme Schetty:*

*I have obtained a very good collection of Australian specimens, actually the best single collection of my lifetime and this will come to Switzerland by special courier Oct 15. My other 2 traveling companions are due to meet me in Hong Kong tonight and I am hopeful of good results from their efforts in New Guinea.*

*I am eagerly looking forward to my visit in Maggia and my opportunity to meet you after these many years.*

*Very Best Regards,*

*Henry A. Molt, Jr.*

FROM HONG KONG the three hopped over to Singapore, where Molt checked in frantically at the American Express office. Twice a day, for three days in a row, he was told no funds had been wired. His customer had stiffed him.

Allen had by then sized up this collecting trip for what it was—ill-planned at best, an elaborate con at worst. Yet Allen believed, or chose to believe, that there were profits to be had if they journeyed on.

They traveled to Bangkok, which was home to bustling wildlife markets and the biggest crocodile farm in the world, but Molt marshaled them straight to Lucy's Tiger Den. He could show them a good time, even if he couldn't pay for it.

"We entertained prostitutes. That was one of the highlights of the trip as far as I was concerned," Levy said. Molt was partially redeemed, even to Allen. "This was before AIDS, thank God," said Molt.

The fun finally wore off in Calcutta, where Allen, Molt, and Levy bunked in an elegant Victorian hotel, one of Molt's favorites, with cool marble passages and vaulted ceilings. Surrounding the hotel day and night were hundreds of beggars, who pressed their wretched faces to the windows throughout the afternoon tea service. "Hank and I were up-stairs in the room and Ed had gone outside with his eight-millimeter camera," said Levy. "Hank grabbed a handful of change and threw it out at them. People clambered all over each other," escalating into a near-riot around Allen. "Hank did it to create a scene, something pathetic for Ed to film." The police arrived later at the hotel, looking for Allen. Levy remembered the episode as shameful. Molt recounted it merrily for years.

MOLT DEPARTED for Karachi and Levy for Sri Lanka. Ed Allen flew to Sydney, bought three new blue hard-sided suitcases, and drove his rental car some 1,200 miles to northern Queensland, where Stefan Schwarz had the reptiles ready and organized in tree-shaded pits and cages. To anyone with the remotest appreciation for reptiles, this was, as Molt had boasted to Schetty, a collection of a lifetime: blue-tongued skinks, ridge-tailed moni-tors, black-headed pythons, frilled lizards, diamond pythons, and rare goan-nas whose range was restricted to a few square miles of the western desert or a patch of trees on the northern coast. One hundred and fifty specimens in total.

Schwarz measured Allen's suitcases and built thin fiberboard boxes to fit the reptiles inside them. His methods were time-consuming and painstaking, but worthwhile. He separated all the animals, and never pushed a snake into its compartment, but allowed it to slide in and form its own coil before he sealed it. This reduced the stress on the snake, and it was thus more likely to arrive intact. People like Christopher Wee and Y. L. Koh took no such precautions, and a terrible number of their animals got crushed, cannibalized, or maimed en route.

Schwarz's box building and reptile packing took days, and Allen helped while Schwarz, always certain government goons were lurking around the corner, interrupted himself to peer anxiously into the trees with binoculars. Allen fiddled with his clothes so that they popped out ever so slightly from the closed cases. He made the grueling return drive to Sydney and flew, with the reptiles in his bags, to Zurich. Levy, returning from Sri Lanka, joined Allen at the Zurich Airport Holiday Inn. He had no money left.

Molt was supposed to have greeted them both at the Holiday Inn and accompanied them to Schetty's. But Molt had already come and gone.

MOLT'S LAST collecting stop was so fruitless and miserable that he'd just given up. With Allen in Australia and Levy in Sri Lanka, Molt had flown to Karachi in search of a man named Arif, whose address label he had surreptitiously scraped off a crate at another animal dealer's house nearly ten years earlier. India had recently passed a law banning all exports of its wildlife, like Australia—now the only way to get an Indian python was by laundering it through Pakistan. But Ramadan had emptied Karachi, and Arif would not be found. Molt possessed a credit card, but only six dollars in his pocket, and there was no possibility, given the holiday, of getting to any bank. Molt's wife by then had no idea where he was. She called Ed Allen's wife in tears, hoping for news, but even Ed Allen had no idea that Molt was walking around Karachi, hungry, with six dollars in his pocket. Nor, by that point, did Ed Allen care.

Molt arrived at the Karachi airport with the handful of plane tickets he had left, pleading to be put on any plane flying west. On a twelve-hour flight to Paris, he ate everything on his tray, and begged other passengers for the uneaten food on their trays. From Paris, he flew to Zurich, got an advance on his credit card, and checked in at the airport Holiday Inn. The next day he left Zurich for Schetty's.

Molt's train lurched into the Alps, where snow was already falling. In Maggia, the widow Schetty awaited her American friend, and received him warmly. Schetty was stooped at the shoulders and wore thick black shoes, but her eyes sparkled when she smiled. She spoke poor English, so her assistant Hermann Hücker interpreted for her, guiding Molt through the immaculate greenhouses that held her ever-changing collection.

Schetty's home was lovely: nearly four hundred years old, with walls of zoological books and bound articles, her voluminous stamp collection, ladders and lofts, and a waterfall propelling an ancient mill wheel outside. The Fiji iguanas chewed fruit in their ample cages, perched on twigs, content.

Molt returned to Philadelphia, leaving Allen and Levy to deal with the rest.

MOMENTS AFTER Allen and Levy were reunited at the Zurich Airport Holiday Inn, Levy opened one of his boxes from Sri Lanka, and a cobra popped out. This was not good. "We didn't have anything to pin the snake's head with," Levy said. Allen pried a board from a neighboring box and after a tense, prolonged standoff with the snake, Levy managed to immobilize its head and force it back in as its body whipped about furiously. He then smoked a chain of cigarettes.

Molt called from Philadelphia with instructions. Allen and Levy were to proceed to Maggia, Molt said. There they would repackage all the animals except the Australian reptiles, which, thanks to Schwarz's box-building skills, could hold up in their suitcases for the flight home. The declared country of origin was to be Singapore. The suitcases would move as unaccompanied baggage into Kennedy Airport, and they would sign for the cargo boxes after five p.m., when the customs inspectors—the few who knew anything about wildlife, anyway—had gone home. They would deliver them straight to the Exotarium.

Allen and Levy had an even better idea. They would do as Molt instructed, a full day earlier, and not bother with the Exotarium.

By then they'd had it with Molt, and their mistrust ran so deep that as guests of Schetty's Schlangenpark, they insulted their hosts by demanding a full accounting of every animal, living and dead. There were copious dead. The Manila shipment had come in mangled, and the big animals in Y. L. Koh's boxes from Singapore seemed to have crushed the smaller ones.

The counting process took forever and infuriated the Swiss, who may have been smugglers but certainly weren't cheats. Allen and Levy apologized. It wasn't them, they explained, it was Molt. For all they knew, he'd already sold some animals in Europe, or put the best of them in his own luggage and would claim that they died.

Now, Allen and Levy planned to take every last reptile hostage until Molt paid them back.

They arrived in New York in the early afternoon, and rested outside on the curb, waiting for five o'clock to roll around. Levy chain-smoked, and Allen called his wife. Finally, that evening, they walked to the customs building to claim their shipment. The large crates from Switzerland were cargo, and would have to be inspected, but the retrofitted suitcases had made it through as baggage. Just as Molt predicted, the night officers "opened the crates but didn't have us open any bags. They didn't examine a single specimen," Levy said.

All that was left was to value the cargo, nine boxes of it, and pay the taxes. The animals inside were worth $50,000, but Allen declared them for $1,000. Molt had forgotten to coach Allen on matters of import tariffs. Allen happened to have $40 in his pocket, just enough to cover the 3.5 percent duties on a $1,000 shipment, with five dollars left for coffee and doughnuts. A nine-box shipment of wildlife valued at only $1,000 was almost certain to arouse suspicion, but Allen was damned if he would spend another cent on Hank Molt's reptiles.

Allen's wife collected her husband and Levy in a station wagon and drove them, reptiles and all, back to Newtown Square, Pennsylvania.

ALLEN AND LEVY found they had no idea what to do with fifty thousand dollars' worth of reptiles, most of them illegal, not to mention hungry, stressed, and in many cases dying. Allen knew nothing about keeping snakes and lizards. Levy knew a little bit, and owned some heat lamps and cages. They made for Levy's parents' house in Pittsburgh, and when they unpacked the animals they found that quite a few had died, including the New Guinea crocodiles and a fourteen-foot python. "We put all the dead stuff in a plastic garbage bag and my dad drove it to an incinerator," Levy said.

Molt owed Allen and Levy thousands of dollars, but the task of keeping three hundred rare reptiles alive, much less selling them off surreptitiously, forced the two to reconsider their hard stance. Here was Allen, a fifty-seven-year-old pillar of the community, stuck in a Pittsburgh basement with a college kid, the kid's pissed-off parents, and nine crates and three suitcases full of snakes, lizards, and turtles.

He drove home to Newtown Square and called his lawyer. Then he called Molt.

It was not until Molt walked out of the elevator in a downtown Philadelphia building that he realized Allen's "friend," in whose office they would "meet for coffee," was really Allen's attorney. Waiting for Molt was Ed Allen, one Jack Briscoe, Esq., and no coffee. Allen had spent the morning with Steven Levy on the phone, working out the precise amounts all three were owed from the proceeds of the reptiles. They agreed that Molt would have to retrieve the animals, as Allen and Levy had neither the skills to keep them alive nor the contacts to sell them. Molt, according to Allen's calculations, would garner 21.14 percent from all sales of the reptiles; Levy, 22.89 percent; and Allen, 55.97 percent.

Clearly, Jack Briscoe, Esq., didn't realize he had drafted a contract to divide contraband. Molt cheerfully accepted the terms.

"You can't enforce an illegal contract," Molt said. "You can't sue me if I don't deliver you your cocaine."

It was a Friday afternoon. Everyone shook hands. Molt would pick up Allen Sunday morning, and the two would drive to Pittsburgh to get their animals.

But late Saturday night, Allen phoned Molt again. He and Levy had changed their minds, he said. They'd made a deal with another animal dealer, a marginal fellow who lived in a Philadelphia row house and sometimes imported monkeys. This dealer promised to come to Pittsburgh and buy their reptiles in one lump sum. Molt would still get his 21.14 percent, Allen promised—if he and Levy felt like giving it to him. They hadn't quite decided.

"Everybody was trying to fuck everybody else over by that point," Molt said. "It was kind of fun."

Molt demanded that Allen accompany him to Pittsburgh, so that they could talk things through in the car. Allen agreed to ride along, and by the time they got to Levy's parents' house, "I was acting very threatening," Molt said, "trying to tell them I was their only hope." Reluctantly, Levy and Allen re-agreed to the original profit-sharing pact. Levy's father typed it up and copied it.

Molt slept that night on the Levys' living room floor. "My parents were really mad at Hank," Levy said.

THE SAME month, a man named Frederik Zeehandelaar was convicted of violating the freshly passed Endangered Species Act. He had backdated some import papers pertaining to a tiger.

At the time of his conviction, the Dutch-born Zeehandelaar was America's largest broker of zoo animals, and a valued adviser to the American Association of Zoological Parks and Aquariums. Zeehandelaar's reputation was solid—not just as a businessman, but as one with real respect for wildlife. He had imported some fantastic creatures: pandas, penguins,

Grévy's zebras, a Central Asian goat that had cost the Bronx Zoo as much as a Rolls-Royce. The zoos considered him a hero for having marched, once, into the Australian Embassy in Washington and emerging with permits for kangaroos. Australian farmers were shooting them by the thousand then, yet zoos couldn't legally obtain one. If he were a kangaroo, Zeehandelaar famously told the diplomats, he'd prefer life in a zoo to a bullet in the chest.

Naturally, the zoo people stuck up for Zeehandelaar. "I am totally dismayed," the association's director, Robert Wagner, wrote in a memo to members. "It is my opinion that Fred is being prosecuted to the fullest extent by our government and that they will hound him with indictment after indictment until he loses an appeal, gets out of the animal business, or they break him financially."

But the government's zeal had the zoo people confused. Why go after Fred Zeehandelaar? What was the aim of this sudden crusade—the animal trade, or them?

Molt was dimly aware of Zeehandelaar's case, and though it registered as a semi-significant development, "we were running more on testosterone than common sense at the time," he said.

MOLT'S JANUARY 1975 price list included none of his usual hyperbole. Just naming the animals was titillation enough. Indonesian frill-neck dragons! Green tree monitors! Thirteen species of crocodile! Fiji boas in small, medium, and large! Six hundred copies of the list were printed, on cheerful pink paper, but none of them got mailed. This New Year had not begun auspiciously.

Levy was back in school, and Allen and Molt weren't speaking. The week before Christmas, customs officers had contacted Ed Allen about his nine-crate, thousand-dollar shipment. His lawyer, Jack Briscoe, called them back. "It's not my client, it's that bastard Molt you want," Briscoe told customs. Allen had not disclosed that the animals themselves were smuggled, but it didn't matter: an undervalued shipment was fraud.

Molt decided not to mail his pink price list with its fifty thousand dollars' worth of smuggled animals. It would be smarter, he decided, to drive straight south and sell them out of the back of the car to as many zoos as possible. He invited the Cobra King, a vagabond snake handler who hung around the shop, along for company.

Molt was readying his Oldsmobile for the trip on the afternoon of January 7, a bitter, snowy, rotten day, when the customs agent Joseph O'Kane knocked on his door. "We had a one-line lead from New York on an illegal importation," O'Kane said.

A cordial Molt claimed that all his records were elsewhere. Yes, the placard in his window read "Importers-Exporters," but as a matter of fact, he told O'Kane, he had not imported reptiles in years. He took O'Kane's card. He would call, he said, the minute he had the records.

O'Kane struck Molt as a hard type, "a big, Irish, beer-drinking thug of a guy."

Before becoming a customs agent the year before, O'Kane had flown around the world as a sky marshal for the U.S. Treasury's new antiterrorism unit. O'Kane loved breaking down doors, loved weapons, saw a world filled with irredeemable "bad guys" best dealt with at gunpoint.

Snakes, however, he could not abide.

"I don't like snakes. I don't want to be around snakes," O'Kane said. "Molt had a goddamn snake, a python, up in the transom in the lights. He had deadly snakes spitting at us." A blue hard-sided suitcase, covered in yellow Qantas labels, leaned against a back wall, but all O'Kane could think about was getting out of there. "Nothing registered until I left," he said.

THE COBRA King was an odd sort. He was a childlike little man, but so old that he'd known Frank Buck personally, and he babbled habitually about snakes and about lesbians, a sexual fixation of his, for hours on end. Molt, despite having invited the Cobra King on a twenty-hour road trip, was in no mood to listen. Molt had already consulted with his family lawyer about

O'Kane's visit, and was now phoning him from each rest stop along I-95. Everyone in Philadelphia seemed to know about Molt's customs problem.

The worst of it was that the zoos did, too. In Jacksonville, the curators wouldn't touch Molt's animals, even the rare Australian species. Molt returned to his car, grim and speechless. His silence endured to Miami, where the same thing happened again.

A week after leaving Philadelphia, Molt and the Cobra King, having failed in their mission, unpacked the unsold animals into an apartment Molt had rented just to house them, a block away from the Exotarium. Molt had also failed to call O'Kane about the import records, as promised. When he returned to the Exotarium from the apartment, Molt recognized O'Kane's car. "Molt's face went white," O'Kane said. The Cobra King ran away.

For six hours, Molt tried to keep O'Kane and his partner from opening his files. A drawer marked "foreign" had piqued O'Kane's interest. Molt called his lawyer, but his lawyer was not in. The agents had no search warrant, just copies of some customs statutes. What would happen, Molt asked O'Kane, if he said no? Well, O'Kane replied, he would merely go downtown, get a warrant, and be right back. But he had the authority to search even without a warrant, he told Molt—a bluff he would come to regret.

Finally, Molt's attorney called. Molt assured him he had nothing to hide, though he in fact had much to hide. O'Kane and his partner snapped Molt's picture, and his animals, and late that night, O'Kane carried Molt's filing cabinet out of his humid, snake-filled storefront.

Neither Molt nor his lawyer could be certain about the extent of Ed Allen's cooperation. He'd been interviewed by customs, but what exactly had he told them? Minutes after O'Kane drove off, Molt phoned Allen to tell him about the raid.

Allen "freaks out," said Molt. "He fucking panics."

Allen sped to Willow Grove in his Mercedes convertible. In the dark and the cold, "we drove around and around in circles," Molt said, "trying to figure out a game plan." Molt wanted to stop at a diner to talk, but Allen refused. He was sure they were being followed. Allen had disclosed to customs that he'd undervalued the nine-box shipment, but not that he'd smuggled 150 Australian reptiles in suitcases. The prospect of being found out had Allen terrified: The reptiles must be moved somewhere safe. The apartment Molt had rented to house them was too close—customs would find it, Allen insisted. "By then we'd been driving around for hours," Molt said. It was two a.m.

Removing the Australian animals "was a temporary arrangement," Molt said. "We were looking just to get them out of harm's way that night." Molt and Allen packed them in cloth bags and one of the blue hard-sided suitcases they'd arrived in. Allen drove away with the reptiles, agreeing to touch base in a day or so with Molt.

When they spoke on the phone, two days later, Allen's tone had changed. "I knew then that the Feds had gotten to him," Molt said.

WITHIN DAYS of searching the Exotarium, Joe O'Kane located Steve Levy at Allegheny College, where Levy, under the advice of the family lawyer, told him everything. O'Kane found Bob Udell, a furry bear of a man who laughed like a lunatic when O'Kane so much as looked at him. He found Karl Sorensen in New Jersey. "We had three file drawers full of documents, charts, and maps," said O'Kane. And, curiously, a large collection of au-diotapes. After the Udell-Sorensen burglaries in 1973, Molt had adopted the Nixonian habit of taping himself and others. O'Kane played ten hours of Molt's phone conversations, and they left him more confused than be-fore. Who was the Cobra King? Who were Stefan Schwarz, Mme Schetty, Christopher Wee, and Y. L. Koh? He had obviously stumbled on something meatier than a Tariff Act violation.

In late January, O'Kane returned to the Exotarium for the last time, search warrant in hand. Molt was at home when he received a warning call from O'Kane. He drove straight to the shop, but by then, O'Kane had already broken the glass door and entered. Accompanying O'Kane was John Behler, the Bronx Zoo's assistant curator of reptiles. Molt's price lists had long aroused suspicion in the Bronx Zoo's reptile department. Behler's superiors, old friends and customers of Molt's, kept it to themselves, but Behler had been sharing what he knew with O'Kane's counterparts in New York.

Molt was flabbergasted. Behler and Molt had gotten into a tiff over some snakes once, but nothing too serious, and here was Behler, placing red seizure labels on Molt's cages. There weren't a whole lot of illegal animals in the shop, since most of those had disappeared with Ed Allen, but Behler discovered an Argentine boa from Schetty, and slapped a seizure label on it. He scrawled out another label, for an amethystine python. Except that this was a Timor python, Molt saw. "The great curator of reptiles can't tell one snake from another!" Molt taunted. Behler ignored him. A baby Nile crocodile snapped its jaws as Behler passed a document over its tank. A Nile crocodile: that was illegal. It thrashed violently as Behler restrained it. Behler removed it to the Bronx, where weeks later it died.

WHEN ED ALLEN returned home from Molt's on the morning after their meeting, he had not moved the reptiles indoors, as he'd promised. Instead, he had let them freeze to death in his car. When they were good and stiff, he asked one of his sons to help him bury them in the only spot they knew where the ground remained soft in the winter.

Now, nearly two months later, Allen directed O'Kane to a quiet pocket of the Pine Barrens near Medford, New Jersey. "Eddie wanted this to be over," O'Kane said.

O'Kane, his fellow agents, and John Behler looked on as police turned the sandy earth with spades. Cameras flashed. There, one by one, surfaced the leathery carcasses of Molt's collection of a lifetime. And one blue suitcase.

# 4

## O'Kane and Mellon Fly Around the World

The Exotarium was a ten-minute drive from Joe O'Kane's house, and in the weeks after his final raid, he'd taken to spying on it from his parked car, sometimes in the middle of the night. "Molt had his cronies coming in and out at two or three a.m. They did not keep bankers' hours," O'Kane said. Yet neither did they resemble the hardened drug smugglers he was used to.

"They were goofballs," O'Kane said. "Even their names were funny." The Cobra King? "Like a criminal from a comic book," he said. "Henry Molt—that's right out of Dickens." Bob Udell really weirded O'Kane out— "a big hulking guy with the emotional stability of a fourteen-year-old."

O'Kane's Treasury superiors were not as fascinated. To them, and to the Justice Department, this was fringe stuff.

Only Assistant U.S. Attorney Thomas Mellon felt that a wildlife case was worth the trouble. The photos from the Pine Barrens haunted and sickened Mellon—who, in O'Kane's estimation, was a tree-hugger.

"Rows and rows of reptiles all lying dead," Mellon recalled. "It was very poignant, very powerful."

Mellon had worked on cases with O'Kane before, and liked him. Mellon was a Harvard law graduate with a slight build, long hair, and an affected, WASPy accent. O'Kane was a more straightforward product of North Philly, stout and tough-talking. Mellon liked the idea of trying out the new federal wildlife laws. The only recent endangered species case, against the New York mammal dealer Fred Zeehandelaar, had been based on a technicality. The Molt case smelled more like a multinational conspiracy. Wildlife "was a whole new realm of investigation without any precedent," Mellon said. "Joe came to me and said, 'To hell with drug smuggling, everybody in this building is doing drug smuggling.'"

"Of course, we knew nothing about wildlife," said O'Kane.

"Absolutely, positively nothing," agreed Mellon.

FOR WEEKS after the "Gestapo raid," as Molt had taken to describing O'Kane's search, there was only silence from the government: no phone calls, no letters, no word from Ed Allen or Steven Levy. Silence afforded Molt enough confidence to resume business more or less as usual. "I was half hoping nothing would ever come of it," he said.

The Australian animals were gone, and though Molt had no idea what had happened to them, he had a pretty good sense that they weren't coming back. He managed to sell the Knoxville Zoo four Fiji iguanas and seven Fiji boas. A zoo in Rochester, New York, bought some D'Albert's pythons.

Either the Knoxville and Rochester zoos hadn't gotten the word about Molt's "customs problem" or, more likely, they didn't care. In 1975, only a minority of zoo curators viewed themselves as wildlife conservationists. Even the job description "curator," appropriated from museums, was used mainly by the large elite zoos in San Diego, Washington, and the Bronx. Elsewhere, they were called animal keepers, and they paid little heed to the new federal laws.

The American Association of Zoological Parks and Aquariums was itself ambivalent about the laws. The zoo association had always supported the government's efforts to conserve animals in the wild, and was quick to join the international conservation societies, like the World Wildlife Fund, as they formed in the 1960s. But the Endangered Species Act and CITES had zoos worried that they, too, might be facing extinction.

Scrutiny and bureaucracy became the new norms for zoos. The Centers for Disease Control banned the import of primates to pet dealers, meaning that zoos could no longer casually buy monkeys; they would have to apply to the government for permits. The Animal Welfare Act, an agricultural law, was revised to protect zoo animals from cramped cages and filth. Customs checked shipments of foreign wildlife, and the Department of the Interior's endangered species office issued permits. The Commerce Department's fisheries division monitored the capture of dolphins and whales. By the end of 1975, no fewer than five federal agencies had oversight of zoos and aquariums.

Zoos that professed enthusiasm about this were either extremely progressive or close enough to a major airport to receive animals confiscated under the new laws. The Bronx Zoo was in the rare position of being both. In the late 1960s, Wayne King, its curator of reptiles, began aiding customs inspectors at Kennedy Airport, identifying the mountains of crocodile skins bound for New York's Garment District. King was soon doing the same for the live reptiles bound for New York pet dealers. As the endangered species laws grew in number and scope, so did the Bronx Zoo's cooperation with the government, and the zoo became the permanent repository for many dubious shipments.

On the day Joe O'Kane and his fellow agents raided Molt's Exotarium, King happened to be off, and this was a relief to him, since he had always been friendly with Molt. It fell upon John Behler, King's assistant curator, to ride along in O'Kane's government car and identify any illegal species. Behler had approached the task with relish.

Behler was barely into his thirties then, college-educated and a product of a new and idealistic school of zookeeping. In the 1960s, the Bronx Zoo subscribed to the theory that given the pace of habitat destruction and pollution, zoos would soon serve as earth's last repositories for endangered species. Its president predicted that the Bronx Zoo would become "a Noah's Ark" in the years to come, and it chose its keepers in accordance with this lofty undertaking.

John Behler didn't see the benefits, as his bosses did, of coddling animal dealers and tossing them bonus snakes. Instead he went to work for the government. Behler searched Molt's sales logs for entries that might intrigue Agent O'Kane.

IN MAY 1975, Molt sent out his first price list since his troubles had started. Molt informed his customers that he would be breeding most of his reptiles now, instead of importing them, and he described quite a few, falsely, as "captive hatched" or "captive raised." The whole thing might well have been addressed straight to Joe O'Kane and Thomas Mellon, but lest Molt's customer base lose heart, he advised them to "please remember that we have many, many specimens in stock that are not listed . . . in fact most of the 'goodies' never make it on the list." The Exotarium, he noted in concluding, was now appointment-only. Molt was in no mood for surprises.

In Switzerland, Megot Schetty faced legal woes of her own. The advent of CITES was less than six weeks away. Many of the rare specimens in Schetty's greenhouses would be the last of their kind she would live to hold and feed. The treaty's enactment would instantly eliminate fifty-five reptile species from commercial trade worldwide. Wild parrots would become harder to obtain, monkeys and crocodiles nearly impossible. If you wanted a banned species, it would have to be a specimen imported before 1975, or born of one. "Dear Henry," wrote Hermann Hücker that May. "This is now my last cry for help! Please ship what you have! Do not wait longer for specimens. Ship please a BIG quantity! With 1st July is finished the importation for us. With new laws only few possibilities. Once more: Please Ship!"

Hücker received no response. Molt and the Swiss were finished.

EVENTUALLY, ZOOS stopped placing orders with the Philadelphia Reptile Exchange. There was "a sudden, palpable dropoff," Molt said, as it dawned on the reptile curators that they, too, were being targeted by Mellon and O'Kane. After months of dismal sales, Molt was forced to take a job selling roofing, windows, and siding. As in his Kraft Foods days, Molt was given a territory and sales quotas. His earnings came from commissions, from sitting around kitchen tables all day drawing houses on graph paper. But Molt was thirty-five now, and this conventional job did not cause him the existential angst that he'd suffered at Kraft. A steady income was a huge relief, and he kept the Exotarium going as an evenings-and-weekends affair, with high school kids feeding the animals and cleaning the cages. In the winter of 1976, Molt traded his Oldsmobile for a Cadillac. He expected that he would have been indicted already if he was to be indicted at all.

IN EARLY 1976, Joe O'Kane drafted a plan outrageous enough that he had to go to Washington to sell it to his superiors' superiors at Treasury. He brought along a box of documents—correspondence between Molt and Schetty, Molt and the Asians, Molt and everybody; transcripts of phone conversations Molt had taped, including one in which Molt and Ed Allen mulled their smuggling options out of Zurich; maps of Wau, Papua New Guinea; and forged customs documents. "I gave them the full performance," O'Kane said. "The full song and dance."

That April, O'Kane and Mellon packed their suitcases. They shared a handsome itinerary: Philadelphia–San Francisco–Honolulu–Fiji–Sydney–Port Moresby–Solomon Islands–Singapore–Manila–Hong Kong–Bangkok–Colombo–Bonn–Zurich–Philadelphia. They would complete this travel in six weeks, and for a tidy $5,000 apiece, according to O'Kane's hopeful math.

O'Kane took his service revolver because he suffered separation anxiety without it. But this was mostly fact-finding. O'Kane and Mellon suspected, by now, that much of the evidence gleaned from Molt's filing cabinets would be thrown out by a judge for O'Kane's failure to secure warrants the first time. The upside was that nobody but Molt would have immunity from that illicit search; if Molt's tapes, maps, letters, and ledgers couldn't be used against Molt, they could nonetheless be used against dozens of others, even zoos. O'Kane wanted to go higher up the chain, and then higher still. Who were the suppliers of all this wildlife—who made the real money?

"Had Joe gone in with the warrants, it probably would have been prosecuted as a fraud case," Mellon said. "We had no idea of the scale of endangered species smuggling. By having to look at everything else," he continued, "we began to realize the enormity of it all."

It didn't matter to Mellon that Molt dealt in relatively small numbers of animals. Molt, as far as Mellon was concerned, was part of a global menace, one narrow tendril of which had curled into his jurisdiction.

Molt, Mellon concluded, was an agent of extinction.

PETER SHANAHAN'S coffee farm in Wau, Papua New Guinea, had gone to swamp, and its crop had withered. The old plantation house stood derelict.

Shanahan had emigrated from New Guinea reluctantly. Shanahan's image of America comprised "black-and-white movies, guys with guns, dark cities." He'd lived in Eureka, California, less than two years before O'Kane and his men drove up in a long black car, carrying guns. They showed Shanahan a photo of Karl Sorensen. Hank Molt had tried to kill him, they explained. Shanahan was aghast, and promised to share whatever he knew about Molt. Shanahan's wife rummaged up her old Leon Leopard files, full of doctored documents and fishy permits, and handed them over, too.

It had only been a matter of years since Shanahan had last seen Molt and Leopard, but they belonged, he now thought, to the same lost world as he did. "They hankered for adventures that could only be experienced, by their time, in a handful of isolated places," Shanahan said. "The Wau coffee plantation was once among those places."

O'Kane and Mellon promised Shanahan he'd be hearing from them again. They had several stops to make first.

MOLT HAD no idea that Mellon and O'Kane were retracing his steps. It was May 1976 and by now they'd solemnly photographed the tree in Navuloa, Fiji, that a young man named Epineri had climbed for Steven Levy. The tree matched, to the branch, one in a photo Levy took the day he arrived. The worn nine-seat plane to the island "looked like something from World War II," O'Kane said, and may well have been the same one Levy had flown in on.

O'Kane had canvassed the Asian embassies before leaving, collecting assurances that he and Mellon would be aided by their counterparts on foreign soil. Yet official cooperation, after all the formalities and niceties, proved "tepid at best," said Mellon. The Vietnam War had only ended the year before, and Southeast Asians remained wary of Americans on innocuous-sounding missions. "No one believed we were on a wildlife case. They all thought we were working with the CIA on some covert operation," O'Kane said. Even the CIA seemed to assume as much. The U.S. Embassy in New Guinea assigned O'Kane and Mellon a mysterious attaché, a small man with thick glasses who "took us to a secret compound in the jungle. It had these fancy villas and a swimming pool and restaurant. I don't know why they took us there except to find out exactly what we were doing," said O'Kane.

The attaché was of little aid to O'Kane, and the locals even less. Port Moresby, O'Kane said, "was a scary, scary place. One hour in New Guinea is more than anyone really needs. Their idea of a good time is standing around throwing beer bottles at each other's bare feet."

Australia was friendlier, at least on the surface, with cooperative wildlife officers who drove for hundreds of miles with the Americans. Mellon and O'Kane had watched Ed Allen's home movies of a python hunt in a rainy gorge—they knew what Stefan Schwarz looked like. With the Australian agents, they drove to Cairns, only to be told Schwarz was out of the country. "In those days, several of the wildlife rangers and customs officers were also Germans who had emigrated and were in cahoots with the bad guys," O'Kane said. When O'Kane and Mellon returned to Australia weeks later, they were again told that Schwarz was out of the country.

In Singapore they had better luck—not because the government was any help, but because the Chinese animal traders were eager to snitch on anyone who owed them money, and each other. Y. L. Koh, the bird baron of Singapore, not only granted O'Kane an audience but handed over records, for Hank Molt hadn't reimbursed him on the shipping from Singapore to Schetty's. Koh informed O'Kane that Christopher Wee smuggled not only reptiles but also horses and heroin and jewels. Christopher Wee told O'Kane that Koh ran a cockatoo ring through Qantas Airlines. They didn't care what they told O'Kane—Singapore wasn't going to touch either of them. "Those guys were so comfortable in their environments," O'Kane said.

The farther O'Kane traveled, meeting men like Koh and Wee, the smaller Hank Molt seemed to him. For Mellon, it was the opposite. He couldn't get over the ugliness of the open-air animal markets of Bangkok and Manila—the vast, noisy alleys of parrots, the bars of their cages caked with down and feces; buckets of turtles; sad-faced primates; and next to all these, piles of skins. This was what Mellon felt himself up against, the larger world of cruelty and exploitation that Hank Molt was part of. "This was a lot bigger than we realized," Mellon said.

The Swiss were not helpful to Mellon and O'Kane, either. Only one official offered them any sort of aid—directions to Megot Schetty's Schlangenpark. The town of Maggia "was the most beautiful place I'd ever seen," O'Kane said. "A postcard." But the widow herself eluded him. Everywhere she promised to be, she wasn't. Schetty, despite her advanced age, "kept running away from us, literally," O'Kane said. "She was a wily old bird," he concluded.

O'Kane and Mellon headed home.

MOLT LOOKED forward to the First Annual Symposium on the Captive Propagation and Husbandry of Reptiles and Amphibians.

Zoo people and dealers had long attended annual conferences of the Society for the Study of Amphibians and Reptiles, but they didn't really fit in. The society, started in the 1950s, was made up of university and museum scientists, and the science presented at their conferences was dry. Dealers and keepers napped through talks like "Erythrocyte Count, Hematocrit and Hemoglobin Content in the Lizard *Liolaemus multiformis.*" The dealers and keepers shared two basic interests: how to find more reptiles, and how to breed them. So they decided to start their own, looser sort of symposium. Peer review would consist of nodding and clapping, and there would be beer. People like Molt's old Hungarian friend Joe Laszlo, now a well-regarded reptile curator himself, would be there. The whole spectrum of snake guys—from maniacs like Bob Udell to prigs like John Behler— would be there. Molt hadn't seen Behler's face since January 1975, when he was assiduously seizing Molt's animals; now it was July 1976, and Molt had done his best, in the interim, to broadcast to the zoo community that Behler was a fink. Molt's campaign was effective: "I was basically looked at as a pariah," Behler said. Other curators had cooled to Molt, for obvious reasons, but they weren't about to go breaking into people's offices with federal agents, either.

The symposium was hosted by a small college in Maryland, and Molt and Behler found themselves in the same auditorium. "Behler and his friend were sitting toward the front," Molt said. "I walked down the aisle and sat behind him. I put my foot on my leg and made sure the toe of my shoe just rested on the shoulder pad of his blazer. Everybody was watching. He did nothing."

Behler could live with the insult, for, unlike Molt, he had an inkling of the government's plans.

MELLON AND O'KANE thought about indicting the zoos. By now they'd sifted through 15,000 documents, including seemingly every letter ever sent or received by Molt: It was clear that zoos in Philadelphia; Brownsville, Texas; and Washington, D.C., had conspired with Molt to secure false permits.

In grand jury hearings, Mellon interviewed the curators of the Philadelphia and National zoos, who confirmed what he already knew.

"Were you fully aware of the fact that you did not have nor did Henry Molt have the requisite papers required for securing the protected species either from the country of origin or this country?" Mellon asked Philadelphia's reptile curator, Kevin Bowler.

"Yes," Bowler said.

"And what is your explanation for that?"

"I guess as a zoologist and curator I thought that the law perhaps didn't apply to somebody that was supposed to be interested in wildlife, such as myself, and that I guess I was above the law."

Above the law. Mellon and O'Kane loved it. They had hard evidence on a dozen zoos, and every intention of using it.

When their superiors heard this, they balked. No one minded an indictment against a zoo in Rochester, New York, but the National Zoo—that was too much. Going after the National Zoo "almost got us all fired," O'Kane said. They cooled their rhetoric. They *might* indict the zoos, they said. Mellon and O'Kane summoned Robert Wagner, director of the American Association of Zoological Parks and Aquariums, to Philadelphia. Wagner was not under oath—they just wanted to scare him.

"Supposedly, a maximum number of 11 zoo people will be indicted," a shaken Wagner wrote to his board in May 1977. "Mr. Mellon is of the opinion that the evidence against these 11 and the other more than 20 persons involved is *overwhelming*."

Yet Mellon's boss, the U.S. attorney in Philadelphia, had already barred Mellon from indicting the zoo people. "He was the jerk of the century for that," O'Kane said.

IN MAY 1977, Molt pulled the Exotarium sign out of his window and changed the name of his business to Herpetofauna International. He announced this with a sunny yellow price list. The name "Herpetofauna" had been rolling around in Molt's head a long time. The Philadelphia Reptile Exchange had begun as a fake business, without much thought given to its name. "As the years went by, that started to sound a little parochial," Molt said.

After a yearlong depression, and a subsequent course of medication, "a little more optimism was creeping into my life," Molt said, "an optimism not born of any reason, but chemical," and highly inappropriate in light of a recent *Newsweek* article titled "The Snake Smugglers." In it, Thomas Mellon had leaked his whole game plan for Molt: "As many as 35 indictments are likely to be handed down within the next few weeks. The case involves a variety of traffickers, but is based mainly on one remarkable round-the-world reptile caper."

On August 4, 1977, six envelopes landed on Molt's parents' doorstep. Each contained an indictment. Molt expected one—after all, he'd read about it in *Newsweek*—but here were six separate cases, all naming Molt.

Molt, Udell, Karl Sorensen, and Christopher Wee were targeted over Fiji iguanas and New Guinea pythons. Another indictment named Jonathan Leakey, of Kenya, citing phony invoices and Tariff Act violations. Then came an assortment of smuggling and Lacey Act charges against Molt, Levy, Ed Allen, and Y. L. Koh. One whole case involved the Nile crocodile John Behler had confiscated back in January 1975. "There was no reason for Mellon not to wrap everything into one," Molt said. "It was an intimidation tactic, to make me buckle under the pressure."

Mellon had been barred from indicting zoos, but his office made sure to malign them in the press. REPTILE RING CRACKED, ran the front page of the *Philadelphia Daily News*. WE DON'T BUY HOT SNAKES, ZOO SAYS. Joe O'Kane was photographed for the story, holding an enormous liquid-filled jar. In it floated one of Ed Allen's formerly frozen crocodiles from the Pine Barrens, reconstituted in alcohol. The rest had been consigned to the Philadelphia Academy of Sciences.

Mellon's boss, United States Attorney David Marsten, told United Press International that the Molt indictments would "break the back of a multimillion-dollar reptile smuggling ring." O'Kane did Marsten one better. With rare reptiles, O'Kane informed the *Philadelphia Inquirer*, "the profits are greater than smuggling heroin."

Henry Molt, alleged head of a multimillion-dollar reptile smuggling ring more profitable than heroin, wore his best suit to the U.S. District Court in Philadelphia. He carried a fine-grain leather briefcase. "Where's your client?" they asked him. "I'm not an attorney," Molt said, but it pleased him to be mistaken for one. They took his mug shot and he entered six separate pleas, not guilty to all.

STEVEN LEVY woke up to find his photo on the front page of a Pittsburgh paper. Ed Allen's reputation suffered gravely in Newtown Square.

Molt's lawyer filed to suppress all the evidence O'Kane had collected from Molt's shop, contending that the searches were illegal. Not long afterward, Molt was hospitalized with an ulcer.

Molt's father retired in early 1978 from his job as a chemist and bought a local plumbing-supply business. "Like every man, my dad always wanted his own business," Molt said. Molt quit the siding firm, stopped sending out his reptile lists, shuttered the former Exotarium, and attempted to manage the new company for his father.

Soon afterward, Molt's father had a stroke. Molt's wife had a nervous breakdown.

Molt's mother expressed regret that he had ever quit Kraft Foods.

ROBERT WAGNER, head of the American Association of Zoological Parks and Aquariums, suspected that the government would leave the zoos alone, but no one could be sure. "The Molt case really caused us to sit up and take notice," Wagner said. "We got lawyers after that."

The zoos' new public relations strategy, largely of Wagner's design, was to emphasize their captive breeding and conservation programs. For now, this served to distract from the zoos' more or less constant consumption of wild animals—"a lot of zoos today would be very embarrassed by what they did in the seventies," Wagner said—but Wagner was hopeful that within a matter of years, zoos could end their reliance on animal dealers. Zoos would breed their own animals if it killed them.

Wagner nonetheless maintained close personal ties to the aging lords of the animal trade. Fred Zeehandelaar had willed his fortune to the association; Leon Leopard, another dear friend of Wagner's, was not only dying of cancer, but was being harassed by Joseph O'Kane, who in November 1977 had flown to Texas to find him.

Leopard received the agent coolly. He'd been in and out of the hospital, and his normally lean and angular look bordered on gaunt. O'Kane threatened Leopard with conspiracy charges, but both men knew Leopard would be dead before any of it mattered. Leopard waived his rights and told him all about his fake zoo uniforms, fake permits from Papua New Guinea, and secret arrangements with zoos to deceive foreign governments.

Leopard recalled O'Kane's visit in a bitter letter to Robert Wagner. This whole mess, as far as he could tell, was started by "an unfriendly person" at the Bronx Zoo, and the government was in over its head, he wrote. "I personally believe O'Kane has been grasping at straws trying to justify his bumbling of the Molt case and the large amount of money and time he has spent on this investigation . . . We had all better get our act together and start looking for ways to countersue these dirty S.O.B.'s."

He omitted the fact that he'd agreed to rat out the zoos. But it didn't matter; Leopard's grand jury testimony was postponed by further hospitalizations. Finally it was canceled. The zoo men would remember Leopard as one of their own, whose like would probably never be seen again.

KARL SORENSEN pleaded guilty, receiving probation and a $5,000 fine. Steven Levy pleaded guilty and received probation. Edward Allen pleaded guilty, received probation, and paid $10,000.

Bob Udell went to trial, but behaved so strangely in court that the judge dismissed his case. Udell had shown up high on quaaludes and taunted Joe O'Kane with sexual remarks about his school-age daughter, whose name he had somehow learned. "That's a pretty big breach of etiquette," Mellon said. "Even the drug dealers and Mafia people don't mess around that way." Outside the courthouse, O'Kane lost his cool and pointed a gun at Udell.

Christopher Wee of Singapore was arrested in California. But then Wee was released without explanation. O'Kane would not explain what had happened, except to imply, a bit dubiously, that Wee was under the protection of the CIA.

Y. L. Koh and Jonathan Leakey canceled whatever American vacation plans they might have had, but otherwise went on with their lives.

Megot Schetty and Hermann Hücker died—Schetty of old age, Hücker of cancer.

By the summer of 1979, Molt was the only one still fighting.

# 5

## The Kingpin

From the beginning, Mellon and his people had described Molt as a "kingpin of a multimillion-dollar reptile smuggling ring," who, if that wasn't bad enough, was "engaged in the business of extinction." That was standard prosecutorial slur, and it played well in the newspapers. Privately, Mellon had found Molt sympathetic to a point, "like an art smuggler," Mellon said, "who smuggles because he loves art."

But after hearing upon hearing, Mellon saw someone different. Molt denied ever having read the customs statutes O'Kane had showed him the night of the first search and claimed never to have consented to the searches in the first place; it all sounded weirdly sincere. "We went from thinking of Molt as a victim of his own naïveté and enthusiasm to someone much more calculating," said Mellon.

Mellon offered Molt a deal: three years in prison. But Molt was not interested in a deal. Counts were whittled down; whole cases got thrown out. Only those built on the testimony of Allen, Levy, and Sorensen would be prosecuted. But Molt would be tried.

Steven Levy, by then a first-year law student in San Diego, returned from class to find a U.S. marshal waiting to put him on a plane. Peter Shanahan, too, was quietly flown from California to Philadelphia to be deposed. "Hank never knew I was there," Shanahan said.

Molt relished the thought of cross-examining John Behler. That year Behler had succeeded Wayne King as the Bronx Zoo's curator of reptiles, the office once held by Molt's hero, Raymond L. Ditmars. This offended Molt, who wanted badly to make an ass of Behler. But Behler refused to testify in person. He had a vacation planned, he told the judge, and the timing was inconvenient.

MELLON AND O'KANE'S successes, up to now, had been modest. "The judges were not buying it," Mellon said. "They viewed it as a technical violation about obscure customs statutes that nobody really gave a damn about. We tried to impress on them that it was far, far more than a technical violation."

In wildlife conservation circles, meanwhile, Mellon and O'Kane's work was viewed as nothing short of heroic.

The National Wildlife Federation presented a special falcon-shaped trophy to O'Kane, its favorite tree-hugging tough, though O'Kane's motives had more to do with "giving the bad guys agita," he said, than with saving the planet.

Mellon's fortunes also changed course. His original boss had been fired, and the new U.S. attorney in Philadelphia was keen on wildlife crime. And now so was President Jimmy Carter, who advised the Justice Department to "seek stiff penalties for persons who engage in illegal wildlife or plant trade including jail sentences for principal violators."

MOLT FOUND much to enjoy amid his tribulations. "It was like living in a movie," he said. The *Philadelphia Inquirer* covered his first hearings, and Molt proved a quote machine. The government had spent $2 million on his case, Molt told the paper—"They built a tank to kill a rabbit!"

The government had spent nowhere near $2 million on Molt's case. Molt just made up the figure. He felt it was fair game, though, since the government was making up its own figures about him. They'd labeled him a kingpin of a multimillion-dollar smuggling ring when his best year had netted him $39,000. By now Molt's wife was begging his father for spending money and his mortgage was in arrears.

In September 1979, a jury found Molt guilty of violating the Endangered Species Act. In a separate case, a judge found him guilty of violating the Tariff Act. And there were three more cases to go.

President Carter lauded the verdicts in a press release: "The evidence adduced at a trial of a wildlife dealer in Philadelphia which led to his conviction for felony violations revealed that he purchased one species of reptile for $10 a pair and sold it for $550 a pair."

Such profits, the president added, "are greater than those from drugs."

MOLT'S DELIGHT in the spotlight gave way to the disquieting awareness that he could find himself on the butt end of a landmark court decision. After the Carter speech, Molt deemed it time to exchange his laid-back suburban lawyer for a tougher one. Molt's father, weakened from his stroke but recovering, promised to pay the bills.

Gil Abramson defended white-collar criminals, and righteously. He knew nothing about reptiles or wildlife law. "This was the only snake case I ever had," he said. Molt sold mostly to zoos. This was practically a public service, Abramson felt. "When the kids walk into the Bronx Zoo and see a pair of tortoises, that's a wonderful thing. How many kids have an opportunity to go to Borneo?

"The government tried to portray him as some sort of evildoer who was trying to destroy the ecology," Abramson said. "I always thought of him as quite the opposite. He loved the animals. There's no comparison between someone like him and the guys who deal in animal skins."

Abramson's legal strategy was to bundle Molt's remaining cases into one and plead guilty on most counts, yet reserve the right to appeal. In December 1979, Molt pleaded. All that was left was his sentencing. All the counts together could earn Molt ninety-five years. Mellon's demand for twelve was enough to keep Molt up at night.

Mellon called on the chief of international affairs for the U.S. Fish and Wildlife Service, an Australian customs official, and the head of the Justice Department's new wildlife crimes unit to attest that Molt was an eager agent of extinction. All the evidence that had previously been suppressed—letters to Megot Schetty and Jonathan Leakey, tape recordings of Ed Allen and Stefan Schwarz—was admissible in sentencing. O'Kane and Mellon were sure these letters and tapes would expose Molt as the sociopath they knew, not some giddy man-child whose love of reptiles had gotten the best of him.

Molt had few well-placed allies left. Certainly none among the zoo people. He would rely on his own testimony, mostly, and a few words from his father, his family doctor, and a lady who worked at his plumbing-supply company.

IN MELLON'S opening statement to Judge Edward Becker, he called the case "a grave matter involving the business of extinction, that is, the business that Mr. Molt was engaged in for some 10 to 15 years, and its consequent effect upon the environment, and, frankly, our heritage."

Becker cut him off. He was irked by Mellon's hyperbole. At the same time, he was confounded by Molt. Becker knew what to do with drug dealers and bank robbers. He did not know what to do with reptile smugglers. Was this case about undervalued goods or about extinction, as Mellon and his witnesses emphatically claimed? The chief of international affairs for the U.S. Fish and Wildlife Service said it was about extinction. Using some mysterious algorithm, he calculated Molt to be "public enemy No. 9 in terms of the destruction of our natural heritage."

Judge Becker knew nothing about reptiles. He was flabbergasted to learn that hundreds, maybe thousands, of Americans kept cobras as pets. He asked whether such people also kept mongooses.

A few years earlier, Becker had taken his own children to the Philadelphia Zoo's new reptile house, more than half of which, he now learned, had been stocked by Molt. Molt had impressed Becker at one hearing with the story of climbing a tree in pursuit of an iguana on the island of Ovalau, Fiji. Becker even remembered the native term for the iguana: "voiki."

"I don't know whether Mr. Molt just went up and grabbed the first hundred voikis or whatever they were, or whether he said to himself, 'Well look, these are not rare or endangered species, there are plenty of voikis over here' . . . It is important for me to know whether Molt went over and indiscriminately and callously grabbed voikis because voikis were available without any reference to the impact of such matters," Becker said.

Becker also took an interest in the Bronx Zoo's reptile curator, who was absent from the proceedings. Was it true that Behler bought reptiles from Molt, then fingered him to the government? Yes, Mellon acknowledged, but Behler suffered for it professionally.

The judge wanted to know what pythons and iguanas ate. And whether Molt viewed himself as guilty.

"There is no question, is there," Becker asked Molt, "that you knew the illegal character of the importation?"

"Absolutely, I did know the illegal character."

"You knew you were smuggling, violating the law?"

"Absolutely."

"What plans do you have for the future in terms of reptile activity?"

"Well, I love reptiles. It's something—it's hard to explain to somebody, but I think I will always be interested in them no matter what happens."

"Do you plan down the road to engage in importing or retail sales of reptiles by putting out price lists and so forth?"

"Well at the present time I have, you know, people ask me, and I say I might, I might not. I just don't know."

BECKER SENTENCED Molt to fourteen months in prison. For his three-year probation to follow, Molt was barred from importing reptiles and from traveling to Australia, Switzerland, Papua New Guinea, Singapore, or Fiji.

"I don't think society needs protection from Mr. Molt at this juncture," Judge Becker concluded. "I don't think he is a likely candidate to be involved again."

O'Kane couldn't believe it. "I almost thought he was talking about some vestal virgin, rather than the Molt we've all come to know," he told a newspaper.

Molt, pushing for a reduction of his already minimal jail time, wrote Becker the next week. He'd had some time to think, he said, and "fully recognizing that wildlife dealing was no longer a viable and dependable vocation, and faced with the reality of living in today's world, my father and I sought to establish a small family business." He was through with reptiles, he claimed, for good.

Molt, in the months before he left for prison, kept a low profile at the plumbing supply company, where every week or so arrived parcels marked "Books" and "Photographs—Do Not Bend" from Australia.

# Part II

# Tom Terrific

**After Tom** Crutchfield's second prison term ended, in 2001, he was hired as an ecotour guide in the Everglades. The Web site for the company, Everglades Day Safari, provided Crutchfield with a very flattering biography that, while not untrue, did omit quite a bit of the context:

> Tom Crutchfield is a native Floridian and a world renowned Herpe-tologist. His reptile pursuits have taken him to Africa, Asia, South and Central America, and the Caribbean. He has authored many scientific papers on the captive propagation and social behavior of reptiles. Tom is also very qualified in Ornithology, Mammology, and Everglades History. We were very lucky to find Tom in the jungles of Belize, where he owned an ecotour business. Tom's vast knowledge and his ability to entertain make him a great addition to our staff of professional naturalists.

I took Crutchfield's safari with a couple from Arizona. We were to meet Crutchfield at 7:30 in the morning; he pulled into the parking lot ten minutes later. He was not tall, only five-six or so, but with a torso like a side of beef, and arms that skewed a few degrees at his sides from all the muscle. His legs were completely hairless.

Crutchfield did demonstrate vast knowledge and the ability to entertain, though both traits weren't always on simultaneous display. He had hunted in the Everglades for forty years and knew all its secrets, but was clearly tortured by the rote repetition of the Everglades Day Safari script, and a robotic tone crept into his voice as he narrated and drove. He delivered knowledge in bite-sized chunks of taxonomy, etymology, myth, or ethnography, very often prefacing them with the phrase "Point being . . ." Any foreign words or places he pronounced in an approximated, staccato accent—Haiti was "High Tea," Guatemala was "Gua-tey-ma-LAH," even Africa became "Af-REE-ka," or, alternately, "Af-ree-KA."

So a typical Crutchfield-ism might go like this: "The word 'Sem-in-ole' is from a Creek word, 'simano-li.' Does anyone here speak Spanish? The Creeks adapted it from the Spanish 'cimarrón,' or 'wild man.' Point being, the Seminole was not a true ethnic group but the wild wandering men of several Western tribes, pushed East into the Everglades by Andrew Jackson, who's actually a distant ancestor of mine . . ."

Crutchfield seemed to view the world as an endless string of immutable factoids, wound up like a ball of twine.

"For twenty years I owned and operated one of the largest international reptile concerns in the United States," he explained as he drove, but the Arizona couple appeared not to understand what he meant. Lately, he noted, wild populations of Burmese pythons—snakes he'd imported thousands of in the 1980s—were exploding in the Glades, and he feared they would decimate the ground-nesting birds.

On the trails of the Fakahatchee Strand, where there was wildlife to be found, Crutchfield entered his element, spotting snail kites and roseate spoonbills and snakes concealed in brambles, which he caught with a bare hand and a quick lunging action. We hopped from the trail into a boat for a long ride through a mangrove-lined canal. There Crutchfield fell asleep in the hot sun, a cigarette burning in his hand, letting the captain's jaded narration substitute for his own. It made sense that he was tired. After the twenty years he'd had, anyone would be.

# 6

# I Search for Adventure

The reptile men of the South came up in a different way. No stately old zoos or cathedral-like natural history museums stood to inflame their young ambitions. Instead there were the roadside snake men.

Since the turn of the century, a handful of Southerners had made a living selling snakes and alligators to the zoos and circuses of the North, and to the traveling carnivals that proliferated all over the country until there were three hundred or so by the Great Depression. After the Second World War, the number of traveling carnivals swelled to seven hundred, most of them operating nearly year round, and every single one had a snake show. The Southern snake men could feed this demand only with colossal imports from Latin America; in 1947 one Oklahoman imported 150,000 pounds of snakes from Mexico alone, along with monkeys, Gila monsters, boa constrictors, and iguanas that became "green dragons" behind the curtains of carnival booths. The animals died fast, but there were always more, and as highways got paved and the rural carnivals waned, "free zoos" sprung up on the roadsides as fronts for cons, luring in motorists with the promise of monkeys and snakes, then fleecing them in card games. People grew tired of the cons, but not of the animals, and in the 1950s, when the nation was awash again in money and hope, and families set out to discover the highways in their Buick Roadmasters, the roadside zoos simply charged admission and thrived.

These small zoos were especially concentrated in Florida, which had no natural history museum at the time, only a dank university collection in Gainesville; and of its two public zoos, one was an embarrassment staffed by inmates of a municipal jail. Land was cheap in Florida, tourists were plentiful, and animals could be kept outdoors all year. All you had to do was gather a lot of them in one place, whether you had ten acres or a vacant lot next to a gas station. It helped if you knew how to feed them, but if they died, the snake men would replace them for a pittance with the next shipment from Mexico.

With enough animals, a spot close to a highway, and a decent sign, you had a Wonder Gardens, a Snake-A-Torium, a Gator Land. You could use the snakes and monkeys to sell gasoline. Or you could successfully reinvent yourself as a man of science, interpreter of the world and its mysteries.

One man did this better than anyone else.

In the mossy tourist village of Silver Springs, Florida, Ross Allen wore khakis, tall boots, and a Randall knife on his belt. He was a champion swimmer and a woodsman, who as a young man had served as Johnny Weissmuller's body double in Tarzan films. Allen had begun his career traveling to Honduras and Panama as a snake importer for carnivals. Before the war, he set up a business milking rattlesnakes of their venom. The venom went mostly to the military, which was seeking ways to weaponize it, and in the 1950s, Ross Allen's Reptile Institute came to thrive as a tourist destination, where visitors could watch Allen grapple with an anaconda underwater, or tease a diamondback rattlesnake into popping a balloon with its fangs.

Ross Allen's Reptile Institute was a very strange, very successful hybrid of sideshow and science. Allen had genuine scientific interests, and recruited a local biologist to help him author hundreds of papers and pamphlets on the natural history of Florida reptiles, while in the institute's gift shop, tourists bought live snakes and baby alligators, key chains made from rattles, and canned rattlesnake meat in "special sauce."

Allen had peers all over Florida, fellow snake men who wore lab coats and pushed snake heads into beakers and even injected themselves with venom; others wore safari suits and sat on alligator backs. For millions of tourists in the 1950s and '60s, these institutes and serpentariums were just part of the landscape, experiences quite interchangeable with the Cypress Knee Museum or the Weeki Wachee mermaids.

But for those kids with eyes only for reptiles, who hid their snake books inside their math books and spent their summers searching rock crevices with forked sticks, these highway snake men were so much more.

TOMMY CRUTCHFIELD came from a line of wealthy English adventurers, military men and seamen, the kind of people who like to be in charge and who do not play well with others. The first Crutchfield to arrive in the New World was a sea captain named Thomas, and for two centuries his descendants, many of them also named Thomas Crutchfield, built banks, hotels, and vast plantations from Chattanooga to Dallas. They fought in the highest ranks of the Confederate Army.

With the South's defeat, the Crutchfield fortunes evaporated. Later generations of Crutchfields became vaudevillians: Will Rogers was a Crutchfield relation, and others danced with lassoes or joined the circus. When, in 1949, Bonnie Crutchfield had "Tommy," not "Thomas," inscribed on her newborn son's birth certificate, it was as though all memories of the family's stalwart past had faded beyond recall. Two years later, she would name his brother Bobby.

The Crutchfields were poor even by the standards of the Florida panhandle: no hot water or indoor toilet, much less a telephone or television. As a child, Crutchfield had to visit a neighbor's house to watch *The Lone Ranger.* His father plowed their garden with a mule. When Crutchfield was six, his father left the family. At seven, Crutchfield began penning up wild alligators in the backyard and hunting snakes. Ross Allen's Reptile Institute paid a dollar a foot for rattlesnakes, and half that for rat snakes. There wasn't much work for boys in rural Florida then—"It was snakes or loading watermelons," Crutchfield said—so the young Crutchfield hung on to whatever snakes he'd gathered until he could get a ride to Silver Springs and dispose of them.

When Crutchfield turned eleven, his mother married a man who beat him so badly he stayed out of school a week. Crutchfield sent away for the Charles Atlas bodybuilding course, "thinking that by the time I was fourteen I'd beat the fuck out of him," Crutchfield said, and he did as he planned, which strained relations at home. During the school year, Crutchfield took refuge in the snake books of Raymond Ditmars and Clifford Pope. In the summers, he emancipated himself from his family and went to work for Ross Allen.

In the mid-1960s, attendance at Ross Allen's Reptile Institute had diminished to barely a trickle of what it was at its postwar height, but Allen was still around, wrestling anacondas with a couple of his sons helping out. "Ross was past his prime," Crutchfield said, "but he didn't realize it." ABC-Paramount had recently offered to buy Allen's property, which he ought to have recognized as a bad omen. Walt Disney had just bought 27,000 acres in nearby Orlando; corporations were displacing Florida's quirky home-grown entertainments. But Allen chose to see only opportunity in the new Florida. He set up a second zoo in Panama City called Ross Allen's Jungle Land, where the teenage Crutchfield performed all summer, popping open alligators' jaws with a fish hook, then straddling their backs and forcing them closed.

Crutchfield no longer loved Allen with the sweet, unfiltered love of a boy for his idol, but the old man still dazzled him. Allen had limitless patience for Crutchfield's questions about reptiles, and had more facts at his disposal than anyone Crutchfield had ever met. The two had plenty of time for long chats because Jungle Land was failing, unable to compete with the local Snake-A-Torium, whose owner walked through pits of rattlesnakes wearing sneakers. Allen sold Jungle Land and left for Sarasota, where he performed five reptile shows a day alongside a "Bird Circus" and "Gardens of Christ."

Crutchfield didn't know what he would do with his life, just that he wanted out of the Florida panhandle. A short-lived television show from the 1950s, *I Search for Adventure,* had seared into his psyche images of African leopard men and other exotic dangers, "and I thought Jesus, that's got to be the neatest thing in the world," he said. When he finished high school, Crutchfield made a gift of his alligators to Ross Allen and got his passport. He married Penny, a beautiful girl with waist-length hair who took tickets at the Snake-A-Torium. They moved to South Florida, where Crutchfield registered for biology classes at a community college. "I was gonna become an academic herpetologist," Crutchfield said, and Penny encouraged him, but his adviser warned him that there were barely any jobs in that field, and the few that did exist didn't pay—better to keep your job, he told Crutchfield, and make reptiles your hobby. Crutchfield was working in the flooring department at the Fort Myers Sears then, living in a mobile home and earning $18,000 a year selling carpet and tile. He dropped out of the biology program.

On weekends, the Crutchfields flew from Miami to Hispaniola, the Bahamas, and the Turks and Caicos, looking for rare iguanas and boas. The Caribbean was as far as they could afford to go, but it was as rich in snakes and lizards as anywhere. There were endemic iguanas, each unique to a small island, in a palette of colors and sizes. There were bright red boas in the trees, and ground boas, slim as pencils, hiding on the forest floor. And there were species yet to be discovered. In the Turks and Caicos, Crutch- field, poking around the walls of a crumbling old fort, captured a gecko he'd never seen before. He sent three specimens of this gecko, a holotype and two paratypes, to a famous herpetologist in Miami, and was thrilled to find out that it was new to science. Crutchfield hoped it might be named for him, but the herpetologist named it after a colleague instead.

On another trip to the Turks and Caicos, Crutchfield collected a pair of *Epicrates chrysogaster,* a native boa constrictor. Crutchfield sold the pair of boas, the female bulging with young, to the Jacksonville Zoo. He used the $600 as a down payment on a one-acre home site, the first land he ever owned. When the female boa gave birth, Jacksonville's curators published a triumphant account of its breeding. First breedings were a big deal in the zoo world, and Crutchfield felt he'd been slighted, yet again, by the sci- entific establishment. Jacksonville hadn't bred the snakes—the snakes had bred in Crutchfield's mobile home while he was figuring out what to do with them. He'd even charged the zoo extra because the female was gravid.

In 1980 Crutchfield quit Sears, having sold all the carpet he ever cared to. He dug crocodile pens in his yard. He packed his car for the annual reptile symposium, which that year was being hosted by a zoo in Monroe,

Louisiana. Reptiles would be Crutchfield's whole world, and no sooner had he decided this than the federal government entered his life for the first of many times.

AFTER THE Molt trial, the U.S. Fish and Wildlife Service felt the time was ripe for a reptile sting of its own. The agency, part of the Department of the Interior, had been sidelined during the Molt case, with Joe O'Kane at U.S. Customs taking the lead. This was embarrassing to Fish and Wildlife, whose law enforcement agents were regarded, fairly or not, as a group of glorified game wardens. The wildlife agents spent part of the year in northern marshes surveying ducks and duck nests, then migrating south with the flocks and ticketing poachers. There weren't many of them—fewer than two hundred in the whole country—and they weren't taken seriously by federal prosecutors, or by their counterparts at U.S. Customs, the Drug Enforcement Administration, or the FBI. "They were understaffed, undertrained, and ill-equipped," O'Kane said. "Duck-stamp guys."

The point of the "duck cops," as they cringed to be called, was to prevent illegal commerce in game, a role little changed since the passage of the Lacey Act in 1900. In the 1970s, after the passage of the Endangered Species Act, the beefed-up Lacey Act, and CITES, a few dozen branched out to become wildlife inspectors at the airports. The new laws put reptiles, tropical fish, and parrots under the agency's watch, but to distinguish among tens of thousands of species, legal and illegal, was stretching its abilities.

Within a few years, though, the Justice Department's newfound interest in wildlife crime provided the agency the moral and financial boost it needed to enforce the new laws. Its chiefs started phasing out the old warden types, recruiting agents from U.S. Customs, the FBI, and narcotics enforcement with promises of better pay and rank, and retraining some of their own. In 1979, the Fish and Wildlife chiefs noticed that Bob Standish, a ranger in his early thirties, had a master's degree in zoology. They sent him off to learn about evidence collection and how to shoot a gun, and Standish found himself one of the handful of investigators in Fish and Wildlife's new Special Operations branch.

Standish designed their first operation: a fake reptile business in Doraville, Georgia. He called it the Atlanta Wildlife Exchange, and called himself Bob Stephens. He compiled a list of a hundred people, most of them small-time poachers, suspected of smuggling reptiles. Hank Molt was on the list, for everyone assumed that he was still smuggling reptiles, and so was Tommy Crutchfield.

With a thousand addresses copied from the directory of a herpetological society, Standish mailed out price lists. He bought reptiles from whomever he could, and hired an unwitting teenage keeper away from the Atlanta Zoo's reptile house to care for them. Standish tricked out a van with a snake design along its sides, driving it hundreds of miles and popping in on pet stores. When the timing felt right, he would ask for, or offer, a species that was illegal to sell across state lines, or a venomous snake that was illegal to mail. Dealers sometimes balked at sending snakes by mail, but Standish insisted.

Tommy Crutchfield, like Hank Molt, had a reputation for circumventing federal wildlife laws, and Bob Standish targeted him intensely, sending his teenage intern down to Florida in the snake van, and phoning frequently. Crutchfield offered Standish threatened rattlesnakes, proposing that in lieu of a sale, which would have been illegal, he instead "give" Standish the animal, and that Standish, at his convenience, "give" Crutchfield the money. He offered Standish endangered Jamaican boas under a "breeding loan agreement," with a donation instead of payment.

All these tricks were variants of Molt standbys. Molt frequently "donated" or "loaned" to zoos protected species as a way of avoiding the Endangered Species Act's ban on interstate sales. A donation was a way to disguise a sale, with the price of something else inflated to compensate for it. But it was one thing to offer an animal on breeding loan to a zoo. A breeding loan to a shady animal dealer in Atlanta was pushing it. Crutchfield felt sure it would work. He could even send a shipment of alligators across state lines and feign ignorance of the law, he told Standish—the government had to prove he was aware of the violation. Standish demanded indigo snakes and "swamp lizards," their code for alligators. Crutchfield was always fresh out.

IN EARLY 1980, after only a few months in business, the Atlanta Wildlife Exchange "was booming," said Standish. "It just got totally out of hand. We got another agent to help." One day, he said, "I got 1,500 box turtles out of Oklahoma. We had to take them over to one of the field agents in Atlanta. We put them in his yard in swimming pools—it was a real chore."

For an agency tasked with guarding the nation's biological heritage, Fish and Wildlife was putting an awful lot of it on the market. In a year and a half, some 10,000 illegal specimens, a number of them poached from national parks, were bought and resold by Standish. Fish and Wildlife's feeling was that the operation had to fund itself, and the more animals the exchange moved, the more cases Standish had. Federal prosecutors urged him to close the businesses already and start making arrests. "Even some of our own agents frowned on that investigation—'We're supposed to be protecting ducks and deer,'" Standish said.

Standish agreed to close the exchange down, but first he had to attend to some business in Louisiana.

TOMMY CRUTCHFIELD had known Hank Molt since he was a teenager, enchanted by Molt's price lists. "Then I ordered a baby Burmese python from Hank and it came in with broken ribs, dying. He never did anything for it," Crutchfield said. "He cheated me." Crutchfield chalked that up to his own naïveté, but then, in 1975, Molt had stiffed him again on some iguanas he'd gone out of his way to collect for Molt on a trip to the Caribbean. By June 1980, they hadn't spoken for five years.

Crutchfield had also recently appropriated Molt's business name. At first, Crutchfield had called his import-export business Reptile World, and then Reptile World Research and Breeding Center, though very little research or breeding occurred there. Unfortunately, he soon found out, the name Reptile World was being used already, by a venom farm near Orlando. Herpetofauna, another name Crutchfield liked, was also taken, by Hank Molt. But Crutchfield didn't care what Hank Molt thought—Hank Molt was on his way to jail. Crutchfield's new firm would be called Herpetofauna, Inc., and Molt was helpless to do anything about it. People said he would become the next Hank Molt.

ON THE road to the reptile symposium in Monroe, Louisiana, Crutchfield stopped to take a dip in a clear Florida spring. He emerged with an alligator snapping turtle the size of a woman's palm. Alligator snappers were protected in Florida, but this little one had swum right by Crutchfield's face. The turtle was a certain sale; Bob Stephens at the Atlanta Wildlife Exchange had been asking everyone for alligator snappers.

"Bob Stephens" sat by the hotel pool, drinking whiskey and wearing a wire, his teenage friend beside him. Crutchfield sold the agent the snapper. Later that day, Standish sold the turtle to Hank Molt, whose conviction, imminent incarceration, and unpaid debts to any number of people were not enough to keep him away from a reptile symposium. Nor had those kept him from selling smuggled reptiles—Bob Standish called Molt frequently that summer, seeking Australian reptiles, and Molt was happy to take the orders. Standish had also promised to procure for Molt some nice alligator snappers, the kind Molt insisted on—young, with no blemishes. "He found it necessary to say to me, 'These are illegal as hell but I'll send them,'" Molt said.

By buying the turtle from Crutchfield and selling it to Molt, Standish racked up two interstate wildlife violations in an afternoon. By the end of the weekend, he would have dozens more potential cases; by the end of the year, hundreds.

Molt had not expected a warm reception from Tommy Crutchfield in Monroe. Surprisingly, though, Crutchfield was cordial, for Crutchfield had learned that Molt still had, if not much else, a steady and discreet supplier of Australian reptiles. In the reptile business, "ancient hatreds revert to friendships with the promise of money," Molt said, "and ancient friendships revert to hatred with the first transgression."

Crutchfield and Molt got on like old friends that weekend. Crutchfield remembered Molt, a condemned man, looking delighted as he played with his new turtle by the pool.

"It was a nice turtle," Molt recalled a quarter century later. "A perfect juvenile, flawless."

ON JULY 16, 1981, the U.S. Fish and Wildlife Service arrested twenty-seven people in fourteen states, including the formerly law-abiding kid whom Standish had lured away from the Atlanta Zoo with the help of a snazzy snake van. Tommy Crutchfield's Herpetofauna, Inc., was raided.

More than a hundred agents had trained for the takedown. Goggles were issued in the event of a spitting cobra encounter. Some of Fish and Wildlife's newly minted agents drew their guns for the first time while they banged down pet shop doors in Michigan and South Carolina. By two o'clock that afternoon, the Feds had issued a press release: "A massive illegal trade in protected and endangered U.S. reptiles has been uncovered by a live animal 'sting' that was concluded today by Federal wildlife agents . . . the 18-month investigation revealed that hundreds of thousands of U.S. reptiles are illegally taken from the wild each year for a thriving black market."

Hank Molt was performing his cafeteria job at the federal prison in Allenwood, Pennsylvania—rolling knives, forks, and spoons into napkins—when a fellow inmate called him by his nickname. "Snake man! Snake man!" the inmate yelled. "Come look at this!" Footage of the arrests was playing on the evening news.

At the U.S. Fish and Wildlife Service's press conference in Washington, a pretty secretary handled for the cameras a few of the live, wriggling snakes recovered in the July 16 raids. Later, Bob Standish released some alligators in the Okefenokee Swamp, and set loose his indigo snakes on some property he owned in Georgia. As for the foreign reptiles he'd bought, "some of them may have ended up in zoos," he said. The rest were impossible to account for, shipped overseas or lost to a labyrinth of small-time deals.

Most of the offenders faced only civil penalties. A handful went to jail for a month or two. Hank Molt was ordered to pay $30,000 for selling Australian reptiles to Standish, but never bothered to. Tommy Crutchfield paid his $5,000 fine, assuming this would be the end of it.

ROSS ALLEN'S Alligator Town, a fifty-acre, $800,000 theme park in Lake City, Florida, was set to open in June 1981. Allen had found a wealthy new business partner, and at seventy-three looked forward to his comeback.

Alligator Town would boast all the trademark Ross Allen spectacles, the gator and anaconda wrestling and the rattlesnake shows, but there would be an amphitheater, too, and a turtle garden and "lizard jungle." Lake City itself was sleepy, but at the intersection of I-75 and U.S. 90, Alligator Town could siphon off any southbound traffic headed for Disney World.

In the month before Alligator Town was to open, Allen was hospitalized, sick with cancer he never knew he had. Tommy Crutchfield visited him in the hospital, and found his mentor strangely upbeat, "talking about what he was going to do in the future. I'm sure he knew at that point he had a very short one," Crutchfield said.

Weeks later, Allen was buried at Alligator Town. Crutchfield could not bear to attend the funeral.

# 7

## Golden Pythons

In the summer of 1981, the summer his mentor died and Bob Standish's agents raided his house, Tommy Crutchfield cheered himself up with some highly desirable snakes.

He'd seen the first one that spring in a photograph in *National Geographic:* a big, healthy, golden-yellow snake dangling gracefully around a Thai man's neck. The snake was a Burmese python—not a rare snake, but normally a greenish brown, not yellow. The man in the picture was smiling, holding a cordless telephone. "'Mr. Dang' of Bangkok annually sells nearly a million dollars' worth of pets from Asia," read the caption. "This rare albino python could bring $20,000 in Germany, Japan or the United States."

The accompanying article was a depressing exposé of the international wildlife trade. In it Hank Molt's conviction was mentioned, as a hopeful sign that the trade could be curtailed. The rest of its photos showed cheetah pelts in Hong Kong, bear paws made into soup, disemboweled sea turtles. But Crutchfield, like many of his fellow reptile dealers, saw only the yellow snake. The question was who among them would get it.

Weeks after the article appeared, an enterprising Thai thief broke into Mr. Dang's Bangkok compound and stole three of Dang's golden pythons, and a few months after that, in July 1981, an animal importer in the Bronx was offering the trio for $21,000. "Nobody in those days paid $7,000 for a snake," said Crutchfield, who immediately bought all three.

Crutchfield hid the pythons at his business partner's place, fearing they would be stolen. He quarantined them in new cattle troughs and fretted over them, terrified they would die. Reptile dealers began making pilgrimages to Fort Myers, where Crutchfield's guys would present one of the pythons ceremoniously, then remove it to its undisclosed location. Even Hank Molt, just weeks out of prison, took a break from selling plumbing supplies to drive down and have a look. The pythons were brighter and prettier than they'd appeared in *National Geographic,* yet they were "not something I felt really jealous about, for some reason," Molt said. They were, after all, only mutants of a common species.

The pythons were two males and a female, but they looked like they might be siblings, not the best candidates for breeding. Crutchfield's associates and hangers-on, of whom there were an increasing number as his business grew, recommended that instead of mating them with each other, he should mate them with normal Burmese pythons, invigorating the gene pool a bit and allowing their albinism to show up in later generations. But this would take time, and Crutchfield would have none of it. All he really wanted was a fast litter of little yellow snakes to unload for the price of a house.

Crutchfield's associates were tempted to mate the albino males with their own normal-looking females, but they were too scared of Crutchfield to try. Crutchfield's temper was easy to ignite, his fits of rage so sudden and violent that they seemed to short-circuit his own memory. His friends remember him eating a peach one day when something set him off, and Crutchfield threw the peach pit so hard that it chipped the window of his office. When his friends recalled it to him, he responded with the blankest of looks. They wondered whether Crutchfield might be taking steroids, since he went to the gym daily and lifted obscene amounts of weight. He was short but massive, always keen to get bigger, and hairless— he spread depilatory creams all over his body to make his muscles stand out. The Crutchfields' house was decorated with floor-to-ceiling mirrors, and friends watched incredulously as he would stop to regard himself, with a deadly serious expression, and pop a tricep.

Crutchfield was as hard-working as he was narcissistic. If an order came in at closing time, he'd force his guys to stay late and build a shipping box. He never kept records, but seemed to remember which animals people wanted. Crutchfield hustled the phones, doodling the same aggravated star pattern over and over until his pen ripped through his legal pad. He was an impulsive businessman, but a wonderful salesman, with that dollop of vaudeville in his blood. Every single one of Crutchfield's emerald tree boas was "the greenest I've ever seen." Crutchfield's price lists never matched the eloquence of Molt's, nor did they even attempt to hit the high notes of intrigue and discovery that Molt's did, with some unheard-of Iranian viper and its holotype number in a Prague museum. But unlike Molt's quasi-literary confections, which came out whenever he was in the mood or had money, Crutchfield's plainspoken price lists circulated without fail every month. Customers got Molt's and Crutchfield's businesses mixed up, because of the names, and this irked Crutchfield to no end. As far as Crutchfield was concerned, there was only one Herpetofauna now, and it was his.

IN 1983, when he could afford to fly farther than the Caribbean, Crutchfield bought himself a round-the-world ticket through the Seychelles, Sri Lanka, Thailand, Hong Kong, and Japan. At long last, Crutchfield got a piece of the adventure he craved.

In the Seychelles, he went jogging up a mountain road, only to be apprehended by Creole-speaking soldiers with machine guns and thrown into the back of a military vehicle. Things had been tense in the Seychelles after the Irish mercenary "Mad Mike" Hoare had tried to take over the islands, and Crutchfield always cultivated a soldierly look, though he'd kept himself out of Vietnam by staying awake for three days until his blood pressure was high enough that he failed the physical. At the army station in town, an interpreter straightened things out for Crutchfield, and he shipped home some of the islands' famous giant tortoises.

He progressed to Sri Lanka, where jackals surrounded his bungalow in a national park, and a civil war wore on, just out of sight. "It was nuts of me to even go there," Crutchfield said of Sri Lanka, since it didn't even allow the export of animals. But he pressed the Colombo zoo officials hard, asking whether he might trade them some animals, if he couldn't lawfully buy any.

He thought of his yellow pythons. Albino animals had a mythical cachet in Sri Lanka, just as they did in Thailand. And Crutchfield's albino python breeding program, back in Fort Myers, wasn't going as swimmingly as he had hoped. The first hatch had resulted in ten baby yellow snakes with kinked, deformed spines. He figured he'd just sell his breeders and be done with it. So he promised the Colombo Zoo a golden python, and Sri Lanka let him send home his boxes of reptiles.

Crutchfield stopped over in Bangkok, where it took him two days to find Mr. Dang, the man from *National Geographic*. In his blind search, Crutchfield ended up accidentally at a venom farm, then at a shop where busloads of Japanese men bought snake-blood pills for their sex tours. When a taxi driver finally delivered him to Dang, Crutchfield was surprised to find that Dang knew his name. "You have my snake," Dang said. Crutchfield had three of Dang's snakes, actually, but Dang was only upset about one, the female. She was his pet, and he wanted her back. "It was the first I'd heard of the theft," said Crutchfield. "By then I'd had the snake two years." Crutchfield told Dang he would think about it.

Dang was Crutchfield's first experience of that archetype—the Mercedes-driving, Rolex-wearing, flamboyantly wealthy Asian wildlife tycoon—and he was impressed. "I thought, 'Gee, I could be like that in the United States,'" he said. Crutchfield agreed to return to Dang his pet python. "The difference between me and Hank," Crutchfield said, "was that I actually paid for what I got, and on those trips formed business relationships and friendships that lasted for years."

Crutchfield returned to learn that his shipment of Sri Lankan reptiles had been confiscated at Kennedy Airport and sent straight to the Bronx Zoo, where John Behler was holding it, and not inclined to release it. Crutchfield was livid. He and Behler had been friendly at the last few herpetological symposiums, where Crutchfield endeavored to give scientific talks such as "Territoriality in *Python reticulatus*," an account of snakes mauling one another in his old mobile home. Moreover, John Behler was an occasional customer. After Molt's trial, all but a few zoos gave Molt a wide berth, so Crutchfield had wasted no time taking over the big zoo accounts.

Crutchfield called Sri Lanka, whose consulate intervened for him in New York. "John wrote me a letter after that," Crutchfield said. "Saying, 'I'm like an elephant. I won't forget.'" Crutchfield made so much money on his Sri Lankan animals that he was soon sporting a Rolex President.

HERPETOFAUNA, INC., made its first million dollars in 1986. Some of the money came from zoos, which bought small numbers of high-dollar species from Crutchfield, but more came from the pet store chains, which were starting to devote extra shelf space to iguanas, turtles, snakes, and the stuff to care for them. If a supplier was particularly good to Crutchfield, Crutchfield sent him a Rolex. Penny wore her own gold Rolex, and drove her own Mercedes.

The Crutchfields made Fort Myers a favorite hub for snake people. Visitors got to watch Crutchfield toss baby pigs to his crocodiles, or send his young daughters running along the banks of his ponds—if the crocodiles lunged at the girls, "we knew they were nesting," he said. When a zoo curator showed up to buy a rare tree viper, Crutchfield shot his blank gun at the snake, just to see the curator's anguished face as it fell off its branch. Crutchfield had even been getting into movies. He supplied an alligator, the local game warden, and his manager to the set of the zombie flick *Day of the Dead;* the people played zombies and the alligator played itself.

Hank Molt visited two or three times a year with the Australian reptiles he was getting in the mail from Stefan Schwarz. On every visit, Crutchfield seemed richer, more flamboyant to him. "He went from a vacuum cleaner salesman or whatever to a big house with a pool!" Molt said. And on every visit Molt seemed like more of a joke to Crutchfield. "I thought Hank had weird delusions of grandeur," Crutchfield said. "He still fancied himself a high-flying wheeler-dealer, when he would come down with ten thousand dollars' worth of animals he probably paid $20,000 to get."

Crutchfield brokered Molt's deliveries to zoos—Houston, Dallas, San Diego. "The zoos all knew where the animals were coming from," Crutchfield said. "They just couldn't buy them from Hank." Molt went so far as to supply Crutchfield with a waiver for every zoo sale:

> These animals are not acquired in violation of any U.S. or foreign wildlife laws, and I hereby indemnify and protect the purchaser from any legal claim or evidence which proves the illegal origin of these animals.

"Which of course means absolutely fucking nothing," said Molt.

CRUTCHFIELD CHARMED his foreign suppliers and the zoos, but he was not nearly so beloved by his employees, who suffered his temper regularly. Snake kids flocked to Crutchfield's despite his reputation. At Herpetofauna they could work among more and better reptiles than at any zoo in the country, though Crutchfield would time them with a stopwatch as they cleaned animal cages. The kids lasted as long as they could stand it. Crutchfield's managers, some of whom were also his investors, had to be replaced at roughly eighteen-month intervals.

Hank Molt nicknamed him Tom Terrific, after a little cartoon from the 1950s. Sometimes, with a beer or two in him, Crutchfield would sing Tom's ditty: "I'm Tom Terrific / Greatest hero ever / Terrific is the name for me / 'Cause I'm so clever."

Behind his back, though, people called him the Godfather.

# 8

# Herpetological Research Associates
# of Papua New Guinea

In 1983, when Hank Molt reemerged publicly on the reptile scene, he aimed to distinguish himself from the more successful, albeit predictable, Tommy Crutchfield, with a memorable price list. To illustrate it, Molt clipped and enlarged slightly repellent images from his collection of art books: a bug-eyed toad, snakes coiled menacingly around a decayed tree. "RAISE HIGH AGAIN YOUR EXPECTATIONS," he proclaimed. "WE HAVE THE GOOD STUFF & NOTHING BUT!" A word processor opened up new obsessive possibilities for Molt, who needed something to obsess over. Repeatedly he checked for misspellings, tried various color schemes, stood back to take in the whole effect. "I wasn't down and gone forever. I wanted everyone—the zoos, the Feds—to know that," Molt said. Molt expected no business whatsoever from zoos, but he sent them his new lists anyway, "just to fuck with them," he said. "I wanted them to see what I had."

What Molt had, people suspected, was a fraction of the animals he claimed to have. Everyone assumed Molt was finished. Tommy Crutchfield certainly did after he'd entertained angry Japanese customers who'd marched mistakenly into his Herpetofauna, seeking money Molt owed them. "The decline of Hank's business had everything to do with the rise of mine," Crutchfield said. "Though I would have overcome him anyway. If an animal was on my list, I actually had it, unlike Hank."

As Crutchfield had eclipsed Molt, people figured when they saw Molt's peculiar new price lists, Molt's fantasies had finally eclipsed his reality. Molt's peers made fun of him at the herpetological symposiums, circulating mock ads:

*Herpetofauna Irrational*
*Hank Ecdysis, owner*
*Tyrannosaurus Rex, adults, in our collection two years, the only ones*
*available, eats anything, must sacrifice ......... $10,000,000 pr.*
*226 Horseshit Rd, Horseshit, PA*

But Molt did retain a few assets from his old existence: a scheming, consumptive lust for rare species; Stefan Schwarz in Australia, who kept the good stuff coming in the mail; and young local men not averse to adventure. Already Molt prepared to deploy his latest college kid to the Solomon Islands. The kid got his first passport, then impersonated a researcher, as Molt had instructed him to, and squeaked out scientific permits, succeeding "beyond all expectations," said Molt.

Weeks later Molt announced—in giant letters—"SOLOMON IS-LAND PREHENSILE-TAILED SKINKS (CORUCIA ZEBRATA) *FLAWLESS* HAND-PICKED SPECIMENS. VARIOUS SIZES AND COLOR PHASES AVAILABLE. A UNIQUE OPPORTUNITY TO ACQUIRE ONE OF THE MOST DESIRABLE LIZARDS IN THE WORLD!!! $2500 PR."

Tommy Crutchfield was among the first to buy them.

ONCE THE word got out about Hank Molt's Solomon Island skinks, a young man drove from Cleveland, Ohio, to Horsham, Pennsylvania, with his wife's diamond necklace in hand, hoping to trade it for one. His name was Edmund Celebucki, and he had first learned about Molt in the March 1981 *National Geographic.* "Hank's name always came up attached to some novel form of larceny," Celebucki said. "And his price lists were so imaginative. You always saw something you never thought you'd see alive."

Celebucki was a prison guard, a karate instructor, and a dedicated thief of antiquarian natural history books, which he would liberate from public libraries and sell to specialty dealers. He was well-spoken and personable in a way that belied the wretchedness of his upbringing. When Celebucki was ten, his mother died of a heart attack. Months later, his father died of pneumonia in the mental institution to which he'd been committed. A Catholic Charities case worker rescued Celebucki, an only child, from an aunt who beat him with the cord of her iron. Celebucki spent the remainder of his youth at a Catholic orphanage, where "I got my ass kicked all the time," he said. "I had a big mouth and no muscles."

A teenage Celebucki was riding a city bus with a broken, bandaged nose when he had the good fortune to encounter Mr. Moon, a local karate master. Under Moon's tutelage, Celebucki earned eight black belts. He went on to college and later joined the Cuyahoga County sheriff's department as a jailer.

Celebucki had nothing against his wife; he just needed a Solomon Island skink, he decided, more than she needed her necklace.

Celebucki had no passport, nor, at twenty-nine, had he ever ventured far from Cleveland. Yet he had dreamed, from time to time, about Angola, Namibia, and the island of Komodo. "I saw the movie *King Kong* as a little boy," he said. "The idea of taking a boat ride to hunt mythical monsters—it stuck with me." Lately it was Papua New Guinea that excited him, and particularly the beautiful, iridescent Boelen's pythons that lived in its hills. Molt knew the feeling.

"I think Hank saw me the way he saw everyone, as a potential mule," Celebucki said. Which may have been true, but Molt also recognized Celebucki as a cut above the ordinary reptile thug. "We had good chemistry," they both said of each other. The wife's necklace—it was like something Molt might have tried himself. Molt refused Celebucki the skink, if only because Celebucki seemed to want it so badly. "I knew he'd be back," Molt said.

A SLIGHTLY deranged tone infected Molt's next price list, which featured a Shel Silverstein drawing of a crocodile in a dentist's chair, and a very peculiar message: "SOMETIMES THERE ARE SHIFTS IN THE BALANCE OF POWER: SO, IF YOU WANT A **GOLD** TOOTH YOU HAVE TO PLAY BY THE GOLDEN RULES AND REMEMBER, HE WHO **HAS** THE GOLD **MAKES** THE RULES."

Only Molt had any idea what he talking about, and years later it wouldn't make sense to him, either, but it seemed to refer to Tommy Crutchfield, somehow—gold teeth, gold snakes, gold watches. And however Molt might have felt about Crutchfield and the shifting balance of power, Crutchfield was emerging as Molt's only buyer of significance. He paid fast and in cash, and usually wanted some part of almost every Stefan Schwarz package. Molt took it upon himself to compose special price lists just for Crutchfield, full of nothing but smuggled Australian reptiles:

*DIAMOND PYTHONS (Morelia a. argus) 3½' by 5½'. SPECTACULAR COLOR & PATTERNS—these would give the DeBeers diamond family a permanent hard-on. 100% PURE DIAMONDS have not been around for some time—savage feeders on dead rats—EXTRA - EXTRA NICE!*

IN LATE 1984, Stefan Schwarz did something no one ever had: He hatched Fly River turtles in an incubator. The babies began arriving at Molt's two weeks later, in balsa containers lined with rubber and moist sponges, each one wrapped like a Tootsie Roll in a twist of pantyhose. Schwarz labeled them books.

Fly River turtles are a genus all their own, isolated for seventy million years from their closest relatives, living only in the waterways of southern New Guinea and a short curve of coastline near Darwin, in Australia's remote Northern Territory. They look like miniature sea turtles, with flippers in place of feet and funny piglike noses. Molt and Leon Leopard had each wrangled Fly River turtles out of New Guinea in the early 1970s, but most of those had since died.

Schwarz and Molt had wanted to fake a breeding of this species for years. Schwarz knew someone in the Northern Territory who would help him locate wild Fly River turtle eggs, but he had to hold off on collecting them until Molt's two turtles were of breeding size. Finally, in 1984, they were. Schwarz drove his Toyota pickup to Darwin and dug up five dozen eggs. He drove them a thousand miles back to Cairns, carrying his own fuel across the vacant, hot, dusty northern deserts. Molt sent Schwarz newspapers from Philadelphia, rulers from Carolina Biological Supply, and Budweiser cans, to make any photos of the eggs look like they were taken in the United States. "I was just thinking forensically," Molt said.

After months, though, the Philadelphia newspapers were getting yellow and the eggs weren't hatching. Not a whole lot was known about the turtles' biology then. Schwarz was fiddling with his incubator one evening, removing trays of eggs to pour a little water into each, "when the door on the incubator sort of slammed and [he] hit the pitcher with his elbow and it flooded his tray and the baby turtles started hatching," Molt said. Schwarz realized that the developed eggs must wait in a sort of suspended animation until the rains came to flood the riverbanks. Schwarz now had sixty baby Fly River turtles. He snapped their photos with the Budweiser cans and the Philadelphia newspapers, and got to work making boxes.

"HAPPY NEW YEAR," Molt wrote his customers in January 1985. As always, when he had something really good, he spared them the cryptic talk and baroque illustrations. He typed up a single page with a little sketch of a hatchling Fly River turtle. Molt priced them at $1,500 apiece, many times their weight in gold.

Schwarz's packages kept arriving in the mail, and collectors kept arriving in Horsham until Molt sold out. The final ten or so Fly River turtles—those meant for the zoos—Molt delivered to Tommy Crutchfield that summer, speeding down I-95, fearing that if he stopped, the turtles would die from the heat. "I couldn't even get a sandwich at Wendy's," he said. Crutchfield didn't believe for one moment that Molt had bred his Fly

River turtles, since he'd visited Molt's shop a few years before and seen the supposed breeders. "I knew they were both males," he said.

Molt filed Schwarz's snapshots away, in case the Feds ever made inquiries, but they never did.

MOLT AND Eddie Celebucki began traveling together to the reptile symposiums, drinking and whoring and sometimes getting arrested. Celebucki demonstrated his karate at bars, spin-kicking ashtrays off tables. They kidnapped Tommy Crutchfield, who could be a little self-serious, and dragged him to strip clubs. Celebucki charged hookers to his wife's credit card, and Molt drank Scotch in a bathtub with one, while Celebucki poured a bag of Argentine boas all over another, "and she liked it," Celebucki said.

Celebucki had done much to revive Molt's sense of possibility. Molt's travel ban had expired and his probation period had ended, so there was nothing stopping them from traveling to New Guinea and smuggling back the shimmering black-and-white Boelen's pythons, as Celebucki was gamely suggesting. But to execute their nascent plan for doing so, they would need the backing of a zoo, and this required some finessing.

ZOOS, BY the mid-1980s, were under tremendous pressure to clean up their acts. In 1984 the Humane Society of the United States began taking inventory of the disgusting conditions at even famous zoos, issuing thick reports to the national press. Newspaper editorials began calling for the abolition of zoos.

The American Association of Zoological Parks and Aquariums defended itself in two ways. The first was to force zoos to raise their standards, fast. Modern, clean enclosures and proper veterinary care would be minimum requirements for membership, and without membership, a zoo stood no chance of getting any more giraffes or orangutans—the association by now completely controlled the exchange of large, high-profile mammals. Since the zoos' cozy relationship to the animal trade was another longtime sticking point, the association kicked out the old animal dealers, like Fred Zeehandelaar, who had once been among its proudest and most prominent members. It issued public statements against keeping exotic animals as pets, and sided with the Humane Society in a tough posture against roadside zoos, many of which had also been its longtime members.

The zoo association's second tactic was ideological—to disseminate the idea, long fashionable among elite zoos, that zoos existed, above all, to save endangered species from extinction. Publications like *National Geographic* ran breathless articles about zoo breeding programs as the "new Noah's Ark." So enamored was the zoo association of the concept that it sometimes seemed to take the biblical story literally. "Unlike Noah, scientists piloting the 20th century ark cannot protect endangered animals simply by collecting a pair of each kind," the association gushed in a brochure.

The zoos' bird and mammal departments quickly adjusted to the new politics, but the reptile departments lagged. Many reptiles were challenging to breed in captivity, and the keepers still depended on fresh infusions of wild stock from reptile dealers, with whom they continued to fraternize at the reptile symposiums. Reptile keepers faced far less ethical and financial scrutiny than keepers of apes or giraffes. If a giraffe dropped dead, the Humane Society would surely investigate; if a snake died, no one noticed. If the government confiscated a shipment of protected reptiles, straight to the closest zoo they went. What happened after that—whether they were exchanged, sold, or even quietly returned to the dealer who had ordered them—was anyone's guess.

Still, buying animals from a convicted smuggler like Hank Molt was beyond what most reptile curators could get away with in the mid-1980s. The few zoos that still dealt with Molt did so only because they housed rare and expensive snakes Molt had loaned them before his troubles. Under the terms of his old breeding loans, Molt was entitled to half of any offspring, and the right to sell or recall the parent snakes at any time.

In the 1970s, Molt had loaned the Knoxville Zoo his male olive pythons from Papua New Guinea. Two more zoos, Los Angeles and San Antonio, later moved their female pythons to Knoxville, to try to start a breeding group. For nearly a decade, Knoxville had held all the olive pythons in the country, and they weren't producing offspring. In early 1985, Molt began making noise about transferring his snakes to a zoo or university that might be better able to breed them, and since he owned all the males, the matter was his to decide. Curators wrote sycophantic letters to Molt, begging him for the chance to work with the Papuan pythons. The University of Tennessee's zoology department wrote Molt a three-page letter naming eleven highly credentialed people—including, for some reason, psychologists—who would be charged with the care and breeding of six snakes.

Having whipped the institutions into a frenzy, Molt opted to leave the pythons at the Knoxville Zoo, which redoubled its efforts at breeding them. Within a year, the first Papuan olive python babies hatched. Knoxville received the Edward H. Bean Award, the zoo association's prize for a first breeding. All this meant, of course, that Knoxville owed Molt a favor. Molt already had one in mind.

ON SEPTEMBER 17, 1985, Molt and Eddie Celebucki signed into being Herpetological Research Associates, Inc., a not-for-profit corporation with the sole purpose of defrauding Papua New Guinea of its choicest reptiles. They sealed the deal with a notary's stamp and a $300 money order made out to the state of Ohio.

The plan was for Celebucki to travel alone to New Guinea and establish a fake research institute. "Hank worried they'd arrest him on the spot," Celebucki said. Celebucki would procure whatever lizards and pythons he could through his institute, then consign them to the Knoxville Zoo. All Knoxville would owe Herpetological Research Associates, Inc., according to this plan, was half of any offspring produced, which Molt and Celebucki agreed to split. Molt and Celebucki paid friendly visits to the Knoxville Zoo, hanging out at the reptile house. Knoxville "probably expected we would pull some shady stuff in New Guinea," Celebucki said, but specifics were not discussed.

Celebucki ordered some business cards for himself, illustrated with a Boelen's python, and paid for his plane ticket with the proceeds of stolen library books. Molt and Celebucki commissioned from a Philadelphia sculptor a realistic likeness of a baby Fly River turtle, mounted on a slab of marble. This Celebucki took to the Cleveland firm that produced his karate trophies, and had affixed to its marble base a plaque:

HERPETOLOGICAL RESEARCH ASSOCIATES

AND

DEPT. OF HERPETOLOGY

AT THE

KNOXVILLE ZOO

ARE PROUD TO PRESENT TO THE GOVERNMENT

OF

PAPUA NEW GUINEA

IN APPRECIATION FOR COOPERATION RESULTING

IN THE FIRST CAPTIVE BREEDING

IN THE UNITED STATES OF AMERICA

OF

PAPUAN PYTHON

(LIASIS PAPUANA)

FLY RIVER TURTLE

(CARETTOCHELYS INSCULPTA)

Celebucki planned to present the plaque to some minister or another; he had yet to figure out whom. "They love ceremony, those guys," Molt had informed him. But Molt, who referred to New Guineans in general as "spearchuckers," was never one for cultural subtleties, and so Celebucki took it upon himself to research some manners and customs. "I learned that all the people in agriculture in New Guinea were of the Goroka tribe," Celebucki said. "If you ask them for something, they won't do it. But if you give them something, they're bound to return the favor. That's why the zoos had such bad luck in Papua New Guinea—they didn't have the diplomacy down." Celebucki felt certain that he did.

In November 1986, Celebucki departed for Port Moresby, turtle trophy in hand. Next to him on the Qantas flight from Los Angeles sat a friendly dreadlocked man who introduced himself as Ari Tara, a minister of roads in the Papua New Guinea government. "He had on one of those wool caps—he looked and kind of sounded like a Rastafarian. But he was a minister," Celebucki said. Celebucki and Ari Tara landed in Port Moresby on a Friday. They spent the weekend figuring out how to impress the agriculture minister. On Monday afternoon, Celebucki stood in the agriculture minister's office wearing a dress shirt and a tie, presenting his turtle trophy before television cameras and scrawling reporters. The minister, who'd learned of Celebucki's visit only that morning, had called a press conference. "I would like to give you this on behalf of Herpetological Research Associates, the Knoxville Zoo, the Cuyahoga County Sheriff's Department, and the People of the United States of America," Celebucki intoned, with maximum ceremony.

Celebucki's cultural investigations had paid off. Over lunch the minister asked Celebucki how he could help Herpetological Research Associates, the Knoxville Zoo, the Cuyahoga County Sheriff's Department, and the People of the United States of America. "We would like to continue our work," Celebucki said, explaining that this meant getting export permits for snakes. The minister assured him that something could be arranged; all Celebucki would have to do was collect the snakes.

Celebucki was introduced to Steve Cutlack, an Australian who, before New Guinea's independence, had worked as a patrol officer in the highlands. Unlike Cutlack's old friend, the erstwhile coffee farmer Peter Shanahan, Cutlack and his family had stayed in New Guinea after independence. Cutlack now worked in the mining industry, traveling between the highlands and his home in Port Moresby. Cutlack liked snakes, particularly Boelen's pythons. He offered Celebucki a place to stay, and a hand collecting. Cutlack found Celebucki to be "a nice bloke, friendly and cheery," and got the word out to his friends in the highlands. Snakes arrived on small planes every other day, while Celebucki entertained Cutlack's family with nightly karate exhibitions, whacking the bottoms out of beer bottles.

Package after package of green tree pythons, D'Albertis pythons, olive pythons, carpet pythons, amethystine pythons, and blue-tongued skinks landed in Port Moresby. To Celebucki's grave disappointment, none of the packages contained Boelen's pythons. But every extra day he stayed cost him money and put the animals he'd already collected at risk, so after several weeks, Celebucki chose to return home with what he had. The Knoxville Zoo would be sad not to get any Boelen's pythons—for by now, the Houston Zoo had the only two specimens in the nation, and these were geriatric, imported by Leon Leopard in 1970.

On the day after Thanksgiving, when Celebucki and his crate arrived at the Los Angeles airport, an inspector for the U.S. Fish and Wildlife Service took a look at Celebucki and got a feeling. No one had seen a legal shipment of animals out of New Guinea in fifteen years. After three hours and several phone calls, the inspector had no choice but to sign off on Celebucki's twenty-six snakes and four skinks. The animals were accompanied by proper veterinary and export papers, stamped with New Guinea's bird-of-paradise emblem. There was rejoicing in Knoxville.

ONLY THREE months after returning from New Guinea, Celebucki flew back, hell-bent on getting some Boelen's pythons. This time, Hank Molt came, too. Celebucki had assured Molt that nobody in New Guinea remembered him from the colonial days—the government was now full of Ari Taras and guys who chewed betel nuts in Parliament.

In the years since Molt's last visit to New Guinea, a Rutgers University scientist had discerned the true range of *Python boeleni* and produced a map of it, which Molt and Celebucki studied. The range was huge—nearly a thousand miles over high elevations all the way west through Irian Jaya, on the Indonesian side of the island. In Papua New Guinea, the pythons were black with short, fat white stripes; as their range progressed west through Indonesia, the white deepened into yellow and the stripes lengthened. The pythons were nowhere near as rare as had earlier been supposed, but they were inconvenient to get to, occurring thousands of feet above sea level in rocky, uninhabited forest.

Steve Cutlack knew those forests well, and soon after Celebucki arrived, a few weeks ahead of Molt, Cutlack's miners were loading the pythons, tagged with notes about where and when they were found, onto Twin Otter planes back to the capital. Getting them out of New Guinea was a problem that had yet to be solved, as there had been a shakeup in the agriculture ministry, and Celebucki's minister friend was gone. Having no turtle trophy or anything so inventive in hand, Celebucki considered bribing the new minister with a camera, but Steve Cutlack talked him out of it. Celebucki was starting to think his early success in New Guinea had been a fluke. "That whole turtle trophy thing succeeded in the limited fashion it did because of my naïveté," Celebucki said. "A more seasoned person might not have tried that." Cutlack assured Celebucki he could secure some export permits through the University of New Guinea; all they had to worry about was getting the snakes.

Hank Molt arrived at the Port Moresby airport with his own Herpetological Research Associates, Inc., business cards, matching luggage tags, and a fake gold Rolex. Molt had taken note of Tommy Crutchfield's tendency to gift his foreign suppliers with Rolexes. Molt was more apt to bolt on a supplier than give him a watch, but a fake one was no great sacrifice. At the airport, "Ed was sitting there, sort of glowing," Molt said. "You could tell he'd been successful." Five Boelen's pythons had already arrived from the highlands, Celebucki told Molt, and they stood a chance of getting far, far more if they went to a village called Woitape, which appeared, from the notes, to be the common source of the pythons. On the plane to Woitape, they stared in shock as a young woman clasped a piglet to her nipple and began to nurse it.

Steve Cutlack was not sad to be relieved of Molt, who drank a lot and talked a lot and years back had railroaded poor Peter Shanahan, who never quite got over it. "I did not like him at all," Cutlack said. Molt had presented Cutlack with a nice book on birds of paradise, but then, Cutlack said, "he stole my book on New Guinea snakes."

IN A matter of hours, Molt and Celebucki secured a room and an inter-preter in Woitape, showed photographs of Boelen's pythons to prominent villagers, learned the local name for the species—*manuf*—and set a gener-ous bounty of $120 per live manuf. The "live" specification was important, and a point that always had to be hammered home in the third world; otherwise it was assumed that the collector wanted dead ones. Most snake guys, Molt included, had learned this the hard way.

In Woitape, "you saw a night sky like it was ten thousand years ago, and there were the neatest species, tiny parrots that would eat fungus off the ground at night, all kinds of plants that sting you and kill you," Molt said. He and Celebucki huffed about in hoodie sweatshirts, going for hikes amid giant windblown cedars. After days, though, the manufs had not ar-rived. This made no sense, so Molt and Celebucki confronted their inter-preter. "He told us that no one believed they would pay $120 for a snake, that we were mocking them," Molt recalled. They reduced the bounty to fifty dollars. After that, "People came on word of mouth; some walked two days because they'd heard about it," Molt said. "Within twenty-four hours we started getting the snakes."

Every evening, weathered middle-aged men arrived at the rooming house with burlap bags that they dumped in the grass before Molt and Celebucki, who surveyed the catch, like regents, from lawn chairs. "Back to bush!" they would declare if a weasel or other mammal crawled out. But there were manufs aplenty—nearly twenty good ones by the end of the week, and more on their way. On sunny afternoons, they would arrange the snakes on branches in a big tree and allow them to bask. "Then Ed would go in and get his karate uniform on and do kicks and moves under that tree. It was like a spiritual thing for him," Molt said. Finally Molt, knowing that within a few days they would return to Port Moresby "and had to get permits and go to the university and would have to play the role of assisting the government of New Guinea in the future management of the species and all that bullshit," began drafting his first and only attempt at a scientific paper.

Herpetological Research Associates, Inc.'s "Preliminary Field Report on *PYTHON BOELENI*" was not acutely scientific in tone, omitting citations and most other evidence of scholarship, though Molt did manage to note the stomach contents of pythons that had regurgitated, and arranged into a table the daily rainfall data from the Woitape weather station, enhancing the paper's scientific aura. Molt addressed it to New Guinean agriculture officials, confident that none of them had more than a fifth-grade education.

EDDIE CELEBUCKI thought about using a coffin to transport the reptiles back to the United States. A plain wooden coffin would be a cheap, ready-made container secure enough for the eighteen Boelen's pythons he and Molt had selected from their catch. But when Celebucki and Molt landed back in Port Moresby, three more crates of snakes were waiting for them, filled with animals from the outlying islands. Among them were Bismarck ringed pythons, carpet pythons, and a type of amethystine python that was probably new to science. A coffin would be nowhere big enough: they now had seventy-three specimens. The problem was further complicated when they received their permits from the agriculture ministry and discovered they could take only thirty-nine animals, a mere five of which could be Boelen's pythons.

This was not exactly a surprise. "We didn't want to ask for too many because the venture would have seemed commercial," not scientific, Molt said. The obvious solution was to take home only animals they had permits for, but neither Celebucki nor Molt could bear to do that: the eighteen Boelen's pythons alone were worth nearly $200,000. More tempting was to alter the permits. "Back then they were stupid enough to give you the original copy," Molt said, and no one had bothered to spell out the quantities in words. So, with a stroke of Celebucki's pen, five Boelen's pythons became fifteen. They were still nearly double their adjusted quota, so they would need a custom-built box to conceal the extra animals. Steve Cutlack and Celebucki designed one with a false bottom and hidden compartments.

Once the materials for the box had been paid for, and the shipping costs set aside, Molt and Celebucki were penniless. They camouflaged their rental car under bushes and branches, since Celebucki had paid for it with a dud Visa card, and the rental firm was searching for them. They dined at country clubs and left without paying. "We were trying to spiv everyone we could by that point," Molt said. When a hotel locked their luggage in their room for nonpayment, Molt and Celebucki staged a fight in the hotel lobby. "We pretended to be strangers—that Ed had let me stay and that they locked my stuff in his room," Molt said. The alarmed staff released the bags just to be rid of them.

Celebucki and Steve Cutlack began construction on the box, while Molt "sat there drinking beer as usual," Celebucki said. Molt wasn't taking on much of the legal risk, either. It was Celebucki's name on the permits, and Celebucki who would accompany the box home. When Molt tired of watching Cutlack and Celebucki hammer and sand, he made his way to the University of Papua New Guinea, chatting with the secretaries in the biology department and photocopying his scientific paper.

The finished box was a marvel—furniture quality, wide as a queen-size mattress, but still compact enough to plausibly contain only thirty-odd large snakes. The Knoxville Zoo would get its share—maybe five or six of each species. The rest would be the discreetly held property of Herpetological Research Associates, Inc. "The plan was to take the crate to Knoxville, unload it, and take the crate back with the false bottom," Celebucki said. "Knoxville was greedy. They were getting these snakes for nothing—what did they think we were gonna do?"

Wishing to avoid another three-hour inspection in Los Angeles, Molt and Celebucki had studied the arrivals at the Los Angeles airport, and concluded that a Friday afternoon, between three and six, was the ideal time for Celebucki to land. "There were so many flights, so many passengers then," Molt said, that inspectors would be overwhelmed. "I just hoped they would look at the numbers, look at a few snakes, and rubber-stamp it," Celebucki said. Molt left for Los Angeles a day early; Celebucki would follow with the box.

Before leaving Port Moresby, Celebucki presented Steve Cutlack with an extravagant gift. Cutlack at first refused, but Celebucki insisted. Cutlack had never taken money from Molt or Celebucki, nor did he want any. "I was helping Ed out," Cutlack said. "I befriended him because of his interest in reptiles." Now Cutlack had a gleaming gold Rolex to show for his friendship. Cutlack was deeply touched, for a day or so. Then a friend of his inspected it closely. "A fake bloody Rolex! I have never been so insulted in my life," Cutlack said.

"It was Hank's idea and Hank's watch," said Celebucki, though Molt would years later insist that the idea was Celebucki's, even if the watch was his. They would agree, at any rate, that it was not the smartest thing they'd ever tried.

"Always use a real Rolex," said Molt.

"OUR STUFF looked good, we had the permits and the papers," Molt said. Celebucki landed in Los Angeles at five p.m. When he went to pick up his box, however, "it was the same officer who had been a dick on my previous trip," Celebucki said. "He decided he'd seize the shipment pending verification and send it to the L.A. Zoo." But it was the weekend, and no one in New Guinea would be answering phones until Monday. Herpetological Research Associates, Inc., cooped themselves up in a dank hotel room at the airport, coughing up strategy after futile strategy. "The whole time, our animals were languishing at the L.A. Zoo—it was one of the worst zoos in the country then," Molt said. Celebucki phoned ministers at their homes in New Guinea, begging them to cover for him when U.S. Fish and Wildlife called. "Ed was telling him he changed the permits but he was under a lot of stress because his mother died. That was always the excuse he used when he had nothing else. Ed's mother died, like twenty times," Molt said. But the officials were in no mood to help. Steve Cutlack was not an option either, for Celebucki's wife reported to him that Cutlack had already called Cleveland, in a rage. He had flung his gift into the Brown River.

At midnight, Molt and Celebucki took a taxi to the Los Angeles Zoo, searching for its garbage pile. If their box had been tossed out intact, some snakes would still be inside its secret compartments. But "we found the crate in pieces," Celebucki said.

Molt and Celebucki knew that whenever Fish and Wildlife and Papua New Guinea compared notes, the results would not be good, but they clung to the hope that Los Angeles would forward the snakes to Knoxville before then.

After four wearying days, Molt flew back to Philadelphia. He knew better than his younger friend when a mission was beyond salvaging. Celebucki waited in Los Angeles awhile longer, still hoping for a miracle. "I just wanted to see how it would pan out with the zoo," he said. "I knew I was screwed when it was on the TV news."

The Los Angeles Zoo is said to have used the wrong deworming treatment on the pythons, killing all eighteen.

# 9

## Fijis

By 1988, Tommy Crutchfield's Herpetofauna, Inc., had been through five managers and was grossing close to $2 million annually. Zoos and private collectors counted on Crutchfield for rarities, and the pet store chains for the common, crowd-pleasing baby iguanas and Burmese pythons that he imported by the thousand. Crutchfield turned golden-brown by the side of his pool, read weight-lifting magazines, and accumulated collections of Haitian folk art and expensive, custom-made Randall knives.

Crutchfield liked the word "prosperous"—it had a nice tone to it, something Oriental and gentlemanly. He used it all the time on price lists, as in "We wish you a happy and prosperous New Year," or in letters to his contacts in Bali and Bangkok: "I hope you and your family are prosperous and well." But Crutchfield's ego, already formidable, had swollen with his prosperity, so much that he felt free to belittle federal wildlife inspectors at the Miami airport when they threatened to cause him grief. "Your problem is when five o'clock rolls around, you're gonna check your Timex watch and start your Toyota, while I'll be looking at my Rolex and driving my Mercedes," he told one. "You're gonna go back to your apartment, while I relax in my pool, *and you know it.*" His longtime acquaintances, accustomed to his fits, were nonetheless taken aback by this sort of display. "'Failure' was not in his vocabulary," said Molt, who had the habit of hanging around the Herpetofauna compound for days after making a delivery. "Then again, 'caution' was also not in his vocabulary."

IT WAS largely thanks to Crutchfield's short-sightedness and impatience that in 1988, when a golden python stared back at him from the first cover of *The Vivarium,* a new magazine for reptile enthusiasts, he could not take credit.

Five years earlier, a frustrated Crutchfield loaned his last albino Burmese python to a Bob Clark, an Oklahoma City clothing-store manager who'd also lusted after the yellow snake since the March 1981 *National Geographic.* For years Clark had tried to buy one from Crutchfield, but Crutchfield refused him. "He was impossible," Clark said. Crutchfield had sent two of the snakes off to Sri Lanka and Thailand but eventually, after protracted negotiations, agreed to loan Clark the remaining one, for $10,000 a year.

Bob Clark was a new kind of snake guy, more snake farmer than hunter. "I remember having a lightbulb go off in my head one day, thinking, 'You can make these things at home,'" Clark said. "That was not the way we looked at animals then—it was all about acquiring them." But pet birds and tropical fish were already being mass produced for commercial sale, and Clark was discovering that some snakes, especially some pythons, reproduce well under controlled conditions, in floor-to-ceiling racks of breeding drawers and incubators. When the first of his yellow Burmese pythons hatched, in 1986, Clark said, "I didn't know how much I could sell them for because nobody sold anything like that." Normal-colored Burmese pythons, imported from Asia, were twenty-five dollars apiece. "I wondered, 'What if somebody paid $2,000?' And it turned out they would pay $4,000." Tommy Crutchfield, when he learned of Clark's success, immediately demanded that Clark return his python, only to turn around and sell it to a Cuban drug lord in Miami. "He sold the golden goose!" Clark marveled. Clark negotiated with the Cuban for the snake and resumed his lucrative breeding project. He soon quit the clothing store; his first hatchlings had earned him the equivalent of a year's salary. He wrote up his triumphs in *The Vivarium,* making sure to detail Crutchfield's extortions.

Breeders like Clark had a new word for their trade: "herpetoculture." If breeding birds made you an aviculturist, and breeding plants made you a horticulturist, then breeding reptiles made you a herpetoculturist. Herpetoculturists bred reptiles like fruit flies, bringing out striking genetic aberrations: yellow snakes, orange snakes, white snakes with blue eyes, striped snakes that were supposed to be spotted. To keep oddball genes prominent, they mated siblings sometimes, or bred snakes back to their mothers. They gave their creations romantic-sounding names: Sandfire, Tangerine Dream, Pastel, Ghost, Creamsicle.

Herpetoculture threatened to make the old argonauts of the snake trade obsolete. Why risk your life in a malarial backwater when you could make millions of dollars in your basement? And yet Tommy Crutchfield wanted nothing more than to be back in the world, searching for adventure. "That was far more exciting," he said. "Breeding stuff was so fucking boring."

CRUTCHFIELD CONSIDERED himself something of an Asia hand by now. He had become close enough friends with Mr. Dang of Bangkok that he and Penny were invited to a cremation ceremony for Dang's parents. The party lasted a week, "with so much pageantry, so much food, people dressed as albino monkeys dancing. I'm not sure what it all meant," Crutchfield said. When the party was over, he and Penny hunted king cobras in the Golden Triangle, where they sat in a hut and smoked opium with an old Hmong woodsman. They stuffed a king cobra in one of Penny's suitcases, and filled her purse with lizards.

Not long after their trip, Dang suffered a debilitating stroke. Crutchfield sought a new Asian supplier, and he found one, soon enough, in Anson Wong, a young Chinese-Malaysian animal dealer who operated out of a drab storefront in Penang. Wong's father had been a live-animal and hide dealer, with a network of animal trappers from Vietnam through Manila, and in some ways Wong, who was only thirty, resembled the Singapore bird barons of his father's generation, Christopher Wee and Y. L. Koh, both of whom he knew well.

Bespectacled and slender, Wong impressed foreigners as erudite, since like most Malaysians, he spoke several languages, including a very fine British-accented English. He was actually something of a stoner and a dropout, who had left school as a young man to work as a zookeeper in Johor, where he trained dolphins until he could no longer stand the water splashing his glasses, then transferred to a zoo in Kuala Lumpur, where he taught parrots to play tiny pianos. That zoo was then full of Western curators, whom Wong would accompany on parrot-buying trips to Y. L. Koh's in Singapore. Singapore was one of the few wealthy nations that had yet to join CITES, and "we just drove [animals] across the border—I mean palm cockatoos, scarlet macaws, in the eighties you could do everything," Wong said. The zoo was poorly run, and its curators on the brink of mutiny, when an escaped-chimpanzee fiasco caused them all to quit. Wong quit, too, and moved back in with his parents. But he kept in touch with his curator friends who'd returned to Europe or the United States or Australia, and they tapped him for any rare reptiles he could find. This was not hard: In Malaysia's wet markets, even the CITES-listed species were routinely sold for food.

Wong called his fledgling business Exotic Skins and Alives. The skins part was short-lived; he never had his father's taste for it. But he kept the name and continued to use the letterhead, which was illustrated with a crocodile that appeared to be in the early stages of rigor mortis. The tribesmen who trapped for his father began trapping for him, and so, in time, did their sons. Wong grew rich, infuriating his well-heeled neighbors when his escaped cobras turned up in their yards.

When Crutchfield first ventured to Malaysia and met Wong in person, he found Wong to be nothing like Dang. For an Asian wildlife tycoon, Dang had been a gentle soul. "Dang wasn't nasty. He tried to keep the animals really well," Crutchfield said, and Dang for the most part avoided illegal schemes. Wong positively delighted in illegal schemes, always finding ways to slip something extra into a box, and his animal husbandry was proportionately lacking—on one visit, Crutchfield noticed a seedling palm sprouting from the body of a dead tortoise in Wong's yard.

Crutchfield enjoyed Penang, a mean slice of Asia full of motorboat pirates and Chinese Tong gangsters with whom he was sure Wong was connected, despite Wong's Brooks Brothers aura. When Wong was late to meet him one night at a restaurant favored by the gangsters, Crutchfield felt their stares from the surrounding tables. "You could have heard a pin drop. Those were bad motherfuckers. Then Anson showed up and everything was okay," Crutchfield said. He made a mental note to buy Wong a Rolex.

Crutchfield bought an enormous number of animals from Wong, including thousands of baby Burmese pythons, which were a staple of the pet trade until Thailand banned their export in the 1980s. Wong got around the ban by driving the babies—hundreds at a time—across the Thailand-Malaysia border in trucks and exporting them as Malaysian. The deal allowed Crutchfield a lucrative monopoly, for a time, on all the baby Burmese pythons coming into the United States. The catch was that he had to accept whatever other animals Wong sent him, the tens of thousands of fifty-cent lizards, beat-up turtles, and snakes that died shortly after arrival. Wong's shipments arrived every two or three weeks through Miami—twenty crates at a time, enough to fill a van. When they contained too many junk animals, Crutchfield just faxed Wong and claimed half the shipment was dead.

The Wong connection narrowed the already fine legal line Crutchfield treaded. For eight years, Crutchfield had ingratiated himself with the nation's best zoos. Thomas Schultz, the celebrated curator of reptiles at the San Diego Zoo, had become a major customer of Crutchfield's and an increasingly close friend who visited for days or even weeks at a time. Crutchfield funded a local sea-turtle research group and joined the IUCN–World Conservation Union as a crocodile consultant, donating thousands of dollars and traveling all over the world for meetings.

Yet the U.S. Fish and Wildlife Service had been keeping an eye on Crutchfield ever since the Atlanta Wildlife Exchange, and his habit of berating agents didn't help. His shipments, particularly the big loads from

Wong, were getting heavier inspections. Crutchfield could not escape the government's sanction forever, and in the spring of 1988, the agency confiscated several of Wong's boxes for prohibited animals and bad documents. In response, Crutchfield forwarded Fish and Wildlife a fax from Wong, handwritten on his weird Skins and Alives letterhead and laughably transparent in its intentions. "Mr. Crutchfield," it read,

> *I have arrived home today in the middle of all problems!!! My secretary tells me you called and there was much confusion. I have to tell you that there has been a terrible, terrible mistake. Because during my absence the packer that I hired two weeks ago not only packed and sent more animals than he had on the permit but the stupid fellow sent you my prized collection of the six heads desert pythons and worse my one and only striped island monitor which I have had since 1977. Please see if there's any way of sending back my six heads desert pythons and one head island monitor which are both pre-convention animals. As for the extra monitors, do anything you want with them. They're meant for cobra food.*

The agents were not impressed. Crutchfield was assessed $4,000, and the government kept the animals. A month after that "terrible, terrible mistake," Wong sent Crutchfield a crate containing banned turtles from India; these, too, were discovered and confiscated. "In hindsight I would never have dealt with Anson—it was fun at first when he would put stuff in there," Crutchfield said. But the penalties were starting to add up.

In May 1989, an employee of Crutchfield's returned from Miami International Airport with a Toyota minivan filled with eighteen crates from Wong. It was late, ten o'clock or so, when the employee turned into the Herpetofauna driveway and backed up to the warehouse. Crutchfield and two more workers were waiting in the dark, drinking beer, in a good mood. Unpacking a shipment was one of the highlights of the job, a break from the relentless snake bagging and cage cleaning.

Crutchfield seldom handled boxes personally, preferring to stand by and bark instructions. With this shipment, though, Crutchfield glanced at the packing list and made for one box himself. He removed his fifteen-inch Randall knife from its sheath on his waist and ran it under the crate's wooden lid, popping off the tiny nails that held it together. The box contained green water dragons, little iguana-like lizards that got sold in bulk to the pet store chains of the world, nothing special—each tucked into a cardboard tube. Crutchfield tossed the tubes aside. The dragons escaped and scattered as he dug to the bottom.

At the bottom of the box, immobilized with packing tape, were two rice bags, and from them Crutchfield gently pulled out four Fiji banded iguanas, a species that would have been tough to explain to the Fish and Wildlife office in Miami.

The lizards emerged from their bags healthy and flawless and seemingly docile, if a little shell-shocked. Crutchfield cradled one in the crook of his arm and began "prancing," recalled the employee who'd driven the van. "Walking around talking about how beautiful they were and how rare they were and how valuable they were and that kind of thing. Was almost like a carnival."

# 10

## Colette

Hank Molt's Herpetofauna quietly died. Molt had fallen into a depression after the disastrous New Guinea trip with Eddie Celebucki. The aquarium shop above his reptile store flooded, and "one night I just vacated," Molt said, moving the reptiles that remained into the warehouse of the plumbing supply company, whose assets he was now selling off. His price lists ceased.

With both businesses collapsed, Molt hoped to reinvent himself as an itinerant reptile collector, but he was mostly just itinerant, spending a lot of his time with Celebucki in Cleveland. Their failure in Los Angeles had put Molt in a rut, but Celebucki was fixed on future success in New Guinea. There was too much money at stake not to try again. A Boelen's python was fifty dollars there, and $7,000 here. Bismarck ringed pythons were $3,000 on Tommy Crutchfield's price lists; Celebucki could dig one out of a trash heap for free. Celebucki's other options were limited anyway. He had quit his job as a prison guard because it was making him paranoid. Teaching tae kwon do at the YMCA didn't cover the bills.

Molt, having little better to do, lent his faculties to Celebucki's cause. This time, they decided, there would be no messing with phony research institutes, government officials, false-bottom boxes, or zoos. It was back to basics: Celebucki would smuggle snakes home in his suitcase, and together they would sell them to Tommy Crutchfield. This presented one problem. Since not a whole lot of snakes can be carried in a suitcase, the trips would have to be frequent to garner significant profits, and both New Guinea and United States officials were well onto Edmund Celebucki. They would have to train mules.

Their first recruit was Kevin O'Donnell, a janitor at the Cuyahoga County jail. O'Donnell was legally blind as a result of a childhood reaction to penicillin, and "we thought there would be enough sympathy for a blind man to prevent him from being overly scrutinized," Celebucki said. During a dry run at the Cleveland airport, as Molt and Celebucki watched, their theory was proven. O'Donnell wore the most outlandish clothes he owned, "a Hawaiian shirt when it was like February," said Molt. "Flower pants that clashed with the shirt. The most bizarre outfit. And then we put a ten-inch bowie knife under his belt. He went through security just fine." Molt termed the operation Blind Man's Bluff.

O'Donnell left for Rabaul, a town in the island province of East New Britain, in late 1987. He returned with two suitcases full of Bismarck ringed pythons. The next year Celebucki, feeling more confident, made several trips to New Guinea himself, reasoning that if he could avoid Port Moresby he could avoid detection. He flew straight from Sydney to Rabaul, where he taught karate for weeks on end. "On my visa form, I put that I was a volunteer to train the Olympic team in tae kwon do," Celebucki said. "It was a convenient truth. I did train the team. The team members paid for their lessons by hunting ringed pythons." On his returns through Sydney, Celebucki would dress as a businessman, in suit and tie, carrying a briefcase and a bottle of duty-free Scotch. After each trip, he turned the snakes over to Molt, who sold them to Crutchfield.

On one return through Sydney, the suited-up Celebucki bought his bottle of Scotch and walked through security, only to set off a metal detector. "I had reptiles in my pockets and a six-foot diamond python balled up in the small of my back," he said. "They're running the wand over me and hit the python," Celebucki said. "The guy's squeezing it—it's in a little tight bag. The guy said, 'What is this?' and I didn't know what to say, so I said, 'It's a tumor.'" Celebucki was allowed to proceed.

On his next pass, however, Celebucki's luggage was discovered to contain fifty mangrove monitors and six pythons, and Australian authorities arrested him.

Celebucki, who was sensitive to cold, had trouble sleeping in jail. He had no clothes with him, because he'd traded everything for snakes in New

Guinea, so Molt wired him money for long underwear and blankets. He got on well with his jailers, since he'd been one himself. Soon, they allowed Celebucki to live in a parole-like arrangement. For three months he taught karate and awaited trial.

THE LAST thing Hank Molt expected, given the general trajectory of that summer, was to fall in love.

Colette Hairston worked as a reptile keeper at the zoo in Brownsville, Texas, just across the Rio Grande from Mexico. It was rare enough for a woman to be a reptile keeper, much less a woman with fine cheekbones and long legs. The reptile curators of North America had a collective crush on Hairston, who, it was reputed among them, sunbathed in a bikini on the roof of the reptile house.

Hairston had left home at seventeen and landed in Brownsville with a drug-dealing boyfriend. She dumped him and married another drug-runner, who then branched into people-smuggling. But Hairston's real interest was reptiles; all her young life she had chased snakes and lizards. In 1976, after a year of trying, she got a job at the Gladys Porter Zoo, where she maintained the reptile terrariums, and those small worlds provided her some badly needed asylum. "The zoo pretty much raised me," she said. "It was really a source of stability through years of insanity." She still drank and did drugs and fought girls in bars, but by her late twenties Hairston had also made a name as a serious, published keeper, an expert on reptile diets, and a very good breeder.

Molt had first encountered Hairston years before at a reptile symposium, where she was sitting on the floor of a Dallas hotel with a parrot perched on her shoulder. "It was hard to forget that sight," Molt said. Shortly afterward, he made a stop in Brownsville, ostensibly to visit Hairston's boss. Molt found Hairston—just as he'd hoped to—in the reptile house, feeding flowers to her rhinoceros iguanas. She did not seem unhappy to see him. "You keep some bad company," she joked to her boss.

"There was just always something there, always something between us," Molt said. Every year Hairston attended the reptile symposium; every year, it pricked at Molt's heart to see her. Once she turned up pregnant, "looking very radiant and beautiful in her pregnancy," which just made Molt sadder.

Hairston was divorced, sober, and a mother of two by the summer of 1989, when she attended the reptile symposium in Phoenix. Molt was still drinking and still married, facts he downplayed to the best of his ability.

"The minute I got there she put her hands around my eyes," Molt said of Hairston. "I had a rental car and she drove with me to the zoo. We sat together under a tree. We were everywhere together." At midnight, she knocked on his hotel room door with news: Her endangered Philippine crocodiles, animals that Molt had bought in 1973 from a leather farm in Manila, smuggled back, and sold to the zoo as tiny babies, had hatched out babies of their own! "The next day at the bar, she had her legs draped on my lap," Molt said. Everyone knew, and everyone was, to Molt's delight, flabbergasted. "John Behler, all those guys couldn't believe it," Molt said. Tommy Crutchfield couldn't believe it. "I was shocked," Crutchfield said. "I thought she was an idiot. She could have done so much better."

Before the weekend in Phoenix was over, Molt got a phone call from a friend of Bob Udell, Molt's bearish former compatriot from Philadelphia. Udell had died of a drug overdose in an Ohio house crowded with fire-arms and reptiles. The timing of it all—the death of Udell, the birth of the crocodiles, this improbable romance—struck Molt as eerie and wrenching, a movie happening to him, again.

MOLT STARTED to divide his time among the Crutchfield compound in Florida, Colette Hairston's place in Texas, and his own home in Philadel-phia. He told Hairston that he was divorced and staying at a YMCA when in Philadelphia. "I never knew who he was living with. I never knew where his money came from. I never cared to know," she said. "Most of the information I got about him came through back channels." As Hairston suspected, Molt was not divorced, and his wife had no clue about most of his doings. "She never asked me where I was at any time in my life," said Molt. "My family had nothing to do with anything—it was two different universes."

In Brownsville, Molt bought Hairston's young boys bikes, and told them bedtime stories. "Hank would sleep until noon, then come into the zoo with his coffee, wearing these jean shorts that showed his knobby knees. He'd sit around for hours telling stories," she said. "Everyone got used to him and liked him," except for the zoo director, who had some misgivings about an unrepentant smuggler loitering in the reptile house. On weekend nights, they left Hairston's sons with a babysitter and drove the empty country roads together, looking for rattlesnakes.

Molt never stayed in Brownsville for longer than two weeks. He could only take so much of Hairston's boys, and wanderlust was his dominant emotion anyway. Molt would hole up in Philadelphia when the weather was mild enough to get snakes through the mail, and open packages from Stefan Schwarz. Then he would drive the animals to Crutchfield's, and drink himself to sleep in Crutchfield's living room. Then it was back to Texas.

EDDIE CELEBUCKI faced the prospect of a very long prison sentence in Australia until, days before his trial, the zoo in Sydney came to his aid. "The curator made a deal that if I was willing to sign the snakes over to the people of New South Wales or whatever, he would speak in my defense," Celebucki said. Hours after his trial, Celebucki was deported.

When Celebucki returned to Ohio, he was penniless and facing divorce. His wife was not only mad about the Australia debacle, but also "in love with another guy who was remodeling the house every time I left on a trip," Celebucki said. Hank Molt suggested that he and Celebucki open a business together—a travel agency–cum–coffee shop–cum–reptile store in downtown Cleveland. They would call it the Adventurers' Gallery, and it would get Celebucki back on his feet. Celebucki rented a storefront, next door to a taxidermist's. But "Hank didn't have any money to contribute," and was spending most of his time in Florida and Texas, so the Adventurers' Gallery became a place for the single, destitute Celebucki to house his reptiles and lick his wounds.

Then Molt accused Celebucki of cheating him out of the proceeds from some lizards. Celebucki thought Molt could forgive this, since he'd taken one for the team in Australia, but Molt demanded his share. Molt had a peculiar way of accounting that tended to deny his compatriots any profit whatsoever, and "I never made more than beer money with Hank," Celebucki said. They stopped speaking.

EVEN IN his best years, Molt's success had depended on Stefan Schwarz and his Australian reptiles. In 1989, when Molt was living out of his car, running to Texas and Florida, Schwarz was all Molt had left. Schwarz was Molt's product line, his solvency, his sole source of adventure, and his hope.

Their constant challenge was getting animals that nobody else had. By the late 1980s, a huge number of Australian species had already been smuggled into the United States, or imported quasi-legally from animals smuggled to Europe, and were being bred. Snake people in California had ruined the market for smuggled Mexican reptiles by breeding the ones they'd already smuggled; now the same was happening with Australian reptiles. Any species Molt received had to be new and fantastic, which meant that Stefan Schwarz had to risk more and travel farther.

In 1989, Schwarz hatched his first Woma pythons. These were big, splendid white-and-honey-colored snakes, with burnt-orange heads and a black sunburst pattern around the eyes, colors that dissolved them into their austere desert habitat of red rock ledges and crevices. No zoo in the Western Hemisphere possessed a Woma, and Schwarz had taken his usual pains to catch wild adults of the most beautiful strain he could find, then set them up in a breeding group. This alone took two years, and two years after that the first finger-sized hatchlings arrived at Molt's, curled tightly inside cassette tape cases.

Molt paid Schwarz $1,000 for each hatchling; Crutchfield paid Molt $4,000, then sold them for $12,000. The day Molt delivered the first Womas to Crutchfield, he was startled to find a young assistant keeper from the San Diego Zoo awaiting him there, sent by Crutchfield's friend and customer the reptile curator Thomas Schultz. "Needless to say there was no discussion of permits," said Molt, and the young keeper trembled so much holding the Womas that Crutchfield forced him to sit down, lest he drop them.

Schwarz had an even better project in the works. This involved a massive green python that lived in ancient sandstone caves within the well-defined boundaries of the Kakadu National Park, near Darwin. Oenpelli pythons were first described in 1977, when an Australian herpetologist spotted one crossing a road. The Oenpelli python grew to eighteen feet, and it was incredible that a snake so huge could have eluded science for so long. A pair of Oenpelli pythons could have commanded far, far more than what Crutchfield was asking for Womas. Of course, one could not easily snag an Oenpelli python. In the Kakadu National Park, "there was only one road to come in on, no food, no water, mosquitoes everywhere, and the Aboriginals would know you're there; they're like ghosts," Molt said.

No one, least of all the scientist who had discovered the species, believed Stefan Schwarz when he said he'd captured two Oenpelli pythons outside the boundaries of the park. Schwarz had caught the snakes in caves well within it—one of them as it was struggling to eat a wallaby. But Schwarz stuck to his story, and the Australian government miraculously issued him permits to keep two Oenpelli pythons. By then Schwarz had caught four. They were constant trouble—one would only eat birds, another had problems laying eggs. But in time, babies hatched. Schwarz invited Molt to Australia to come have a look, and bring along the money he still owed for the Womas. In early 1990, Molt, newly flush from selling the Womas to Crutchfield and high on his affair with Colette Hairston, flew to Cairns, cash in suitcase.

At the airport, an Australian customs officer greeted Molt a tad more warmly than Molt expected, or homed in on him—Molt couldn't quite tell. On his immigration card, Molt had written that he was in the window business. "Is the window business any good?" the customs officer asked, a bit smirkingly. Molt was so surprised by the question, and the officer's tone, that he did not reply. "That comment haunted me for days," Molt said.

Schwarz's young Oenpelli pythons looked fantastic, spotted olive drab miniatures of their parents, healthy and feeding. The usual postal treatment would not do for Oenpelli pythons. Molt and Schwarz needed a plan to smuggle them, but Schwarz would not talk about plans in the house, and Molt was still on edge about the "window business" comment. So Molt and Schwarz put on their swimming trunks and talked amid the rushing waters of a river. Schwarz's paranoia was not unfounded—the Australian government was onto him, for sure, but what they knew was hard to say. "All the reptile people called him the biggest smuggler in Australia," Molt said. "But he was disciplined. Not even his family knew his business. He was always on my shit for not being as secretive as him."

AFTER A few weeks, Molt was starting to miss Hairston. He sent her post-cards and aerograms and called her from the pay phone across the street from Schwarz's house, as Schwarz had suspicions that his own phone was tapped. Molt had not filled Hairston in on the objective of this Australia trip, "and I had given her the vague general impression that my smuggling days were behind me," he said. Hairston sent letters to Molt in Cairns, and he kept them in the inside pocket of his new jacket from Banana Republic, which sold safari clothes in those days. It was called a smuggler's jacket, and it featured all kinds of folds and zippers and hidden pockets. Molt couldn't resist it when he saw it.

By the eve of Molt's departure, he and Schwarz had a plan for the Oen-pelli pythons. "We were gonna have a college girl courier them from Darwin to Hong Kong to Turkey, then by train to Germany," Molt said, where the young snakes could be exported to the United States, labeled captive-bred. Tommy Crutchfield would be ready to buy the pythons—that went without saying—and the San Diego Zoo would be their likely destination.

Molt wore his smuggler's jacket on the ride to the Cairns airport. On the way, he and Schwarz stopped to mail a diamond python to Philadelphia. Schwarz was paranoid, but habitual. He had placed the python in a mailing box inside a pillowcase, his usual procedure. Then, as Molt waited in the passenger seat of his truck, Schwarz emptied the bag into a mailbox. "We stupidly did it while I was in the country," Molt said, and agents were right behind them.

Molt was drinking a beer at the airport bar when two agents came for him. They took him to baggage, where his suitcases had been pulled from the pile. "I better not get bit by anything, mate," said one as he opened Molt's bag, but it contained only natural history books. They opened another, but it contained only clothes. "Then they strip searched me—naked," he said. "They asked me about Eddie—'How's your friend Cele-bucki?' they asked, pronouncing it 'Celebussy.'"

The agents opened every pocket on Molt's jacket. He winced as they read his letters from Hairston.

"Are you pinchin' fauna, mate?" one asked.

Molt couldn't understand him through his accent.

"You got plenty of time to learn the language in jail, mate," he said.

Molt demanded that the agents charge him already. But they had nothing to charge him with. Stefan Schwarz had mailed the package, and it was Stefan Schwarz they wanted. Schwarz returned from the airport to find wildlife officers in his driveway. "They had been following us since the day I arrived," Molt said. "They'd videotaped [Stefan] dropping the snake in the mailbox. That pay phone that I thought was so clever to be using—they probably bugged it."

Molt returned to the United States unscathed, but Schwarz was ruined. Within weeks, all of Schwarz's animals, even the legal ones, were confiscated. The Oenpelli pythons were taken to a zoo, and, being rather high-maintenance, died shortly afterward. Schwarz sent Molt a letter announcing his retirement from smuggling.

"I was devastated," Molt said. Schwarz was "my juju, my kryptonite. No one else could get this stuff anymore."

# 11

# Conservation thru Commercialization

The legal status of the Fiji banded iguana had been less than clear in the 1970s, when Hank Molt smuggled his. The species was protected in Fiji then, but by a statute that was too ambiguous to trigger the Lacey Act, and Molt was never convicted on the charges related to Fijis. By May 1989, however, when Tommy Crutchfield took his Randall knife to Anson Wong's box, Fijis were among the most illegal reptiles in the world, falling under the unambiguous protections of the Endangered Species Act and CITES.

The Fiji iguanas that Molt had imported in the 1970s were all dead, to the best of anyone's knowledge. Outside Fiji, the only legal colony of Fiji iguanas lived at the San Diego Zoo, cared for by Crutchfield's friend Thomas Schultz. San Diego had kept Fijis since the 1960s, when the king of Tonga sent three as a gift, but by 1987 the colony had dwindled, forcing Schultz to make three trips to Fiji to eke out more. Fiji gave Schultz six, and Schultz, a very skilled breeder, turned these into a thriving colony of forty. All of them were still, technically, the property of the Fiji government, to which Schultz was obliged to send annual reports.

Very few reptile enthusiasts had ever laid eyes on a live Fiji iguana, except in San Diego. Even Anson Wong had only ever seen a Fiji iguana in the San Diego Zoo, until a Swiss guy showed up in Penang one day with a bag of them. Wong called to share this news with Crutchfield, who was, Wong said, "ecstatic."

Crutchfield had told friends that the iguanas were a surprise, that he didn't know a thing about them until Wong phoned on the night of the shipment, telling him to open one particular box first.

Wong said it was no surprise. "Sure—send a $7,000 animal and risk him not accepting it, no way. He wanted them from the word go."

"We did flirt with the idea," Crutchfield acknowledged. "But when he actually said, 'I want to ship them,' I said no, then quite some time passed and these came in. Originally there were supposed to be six or eight," he said, and he agreed to send Wong some rhinoceros iguanas in exchange. Later, he said, he thought better of it and changed his mind, but by then Wong had sent four.

Crutchfield soon realized there wasn't much you could do with four Fiji iguanas. Fiji iguanas were CITES Appendix I, and one of the few foreign reptiles listed by the Endangered Species Act; in the United States, only the San Diego Zoo had permits for them. In hindsight, Crutchfield said, he wished he had simply called Fish and Wildlife and reported the lizards the minute they came in, but he knew it would cost him. "I didn't want to pay another $4,000 fine," he said, much less face the criminal charges the agency had so far spared him. And the iguanas, so beautiful with their turquoise bands and red eyes and yellow nostrils, would surely be confiscated, and that would be a waste.

Crutchfield turned to the only person in any position to help: Thomas Schultz. Schultz and Crutchfield shared a close bond. Schultz, like Crutchfield, was short but powerful, and an autodidact in a world that increasingly valued degrees. Both men talked fast, with high, wound-up voices that people found incongruous with their tough looks. "I always admired people who kept in shape and people who weren't wussies," Crutchfield said, and Schultz was no wussy. Schultz had dropped out of high school in the 1950s and served in the Panama Canal Zone as a trainer for the army's jungle warfare school, teaching soldiers which animals to eat and how to catch them, and how to escape ambushes, camouflage themselves, machete their way out of a fix. In 1960, Schultz was back in the United States, serving in the army reserves, when he crushed his elbow, broke his neck and knees, and dislodged his heart in a parachute accident. Schultz took three years to recover, spending long stretches at a hospital across the street from the San Diego Zoo, which he visited almost daily. When Schultz was well enough, the zoo hired him as its gorilla and reptile keeper, though he knew little about reptiles, and nothing about gorillas.

The San Diego Zoo was among the wealthiest zoos in the country. It was famous for its rare reptile collection even in the 1960s, and twenty years later, as Schultz and Crutchfield got to know each other, it was erecting a cluster of new reptile buildings and eager to fill them. The Bronx Zoo was San Diego's only real rival as far as reptiles were concerned, and Schultz had little patience for John Behler. "It was a personal thing that we couldn't get along, and the philosophy of the institutions was different," Schultz said. "In San Diego we were looking to get things that no one else had. And you had to be willing to get them." Schultz absolutely was. He traveled to Fiji and Komodo and New Zealand, striking deals for iguanas and dragons and tuataras, deals that Crutchfield suspected involved substantial bribes. Some of Schultz's trips were funded directly by Crutchfield, who wrote his checks out to Schultz whenever he bought animals from the zoo. That way, Schultz could bypass the zoo's general fund, and spend the money in his reptile department, or spread it around Southeast Asia— whatever he had to do. The practice "was pretty much sanctioned by the zoo," Crutchfield said. "Lots of curators did the same thing back then."

Crutchfield could obtain for Schultz animals that the San Diego Zoo could not, by dealing with people the zoo would rather avoid, like Hank Molt. "I bought animals from Tom that I knew came from Hank. I would not buy them from Hank," Schultz said. In 1989 alone, Schultz spent $60,000 on animals from Crutchfield.

Such wheeling and dealing was "marginal" behavior for a zoo curator, Schultz acknowledged. "It wasn't that we couldn't get permits," he said. "There is no animal in the world that the San Diego Zoo couldn't get permits for. It comes down to money. What is it gonna cost to send a keeper to Australia for two months, then try to get a permit, then pay for the shipping and the bonding and hope the animals are healthy? Tom made a lot of money. The San Diego Zoo had the best collection ever in its history. We both profited."

The Schultz connection also gave Crutchfield access to animals he might not otherwise have had, animals Crutchfield liked to list as "zoo-bred" on his mailings. So prolific were San Diego's breeding programs that the zoo often had surpluses of animals, even endangered ones; Schultz sold some of his best to Crutchfield. And since Crutchfield never had the heart to kill an animal, particularly a rare one, if he found himself with something too hot to sell he tapped Schultz to give it a home. Once, he sent Schultz back to San Diego with an endangered black caiman in his luggage that another Florida dealer had imported by accident.

Schultz was not entirely comfortable with the way Crutchfield operated; many times, he said, he warned Crutchfield not to have blatantly illegal animals around the shop when he visited. When Crutchfield offered him a gold Rolex, Schultz balked. "It just seemed too much like a bribe," he said. But then, "Penny convinced me to take it because Tom was very hurt. I sold it after two days and bought a computer."

"Hell yeah, he took it," Crutchfield said. "He also took a handmade Randall knife."

The illegal Fiji iguanas, however, Schultz refused to take. "Hiding a Fiji would be like hiding a panda bear," said Schultz.

And this left Crutchfield in a pickle.

SCHULTZ HAD not refused the iguanas outright.

What happened was, not long after their arrival, two of the iguanas died. Crutchfield had been keeping both pairs in rolling cages on the pool deck, and the kids who worked for him were charged with rolling them in and out of the sun. The kids left one of the cages in the sun too long, and one pair baked. Crutchfield wasted no time putting the surviving pair on a plane to San Diego, where Thomas Schultz had agreed to take them in, Crutchfield said. "He knew exactly where the Fijis came from, the whole story."

Schultz claimed Crutchfield sent him only one Fiji iguana, a female, ostensibly to find out whether it was gravid, which it was not.

Schultz hadn't seen a Fiji iguana in private hands since the 1970s—though it was hardly for lack of searching. He'd tried for years to find the remnants of Hank Molt's storied Fijis for his breeding colony; it was a lot easier to buy one of those than to glad-hand every minister in Fiji. But his effort was in vain; the original Molt Fijis were all dead, as far as anyone knew, and there was no evidence of any progeny. "I had no idea where it came from and didn't ask," Schultz said of Crutchfield's Fiji. "By that time I probably had forty-five young. Why would I want an illegal one?"

Schultz claimed to have returned Crutchfield's iguana the day after receiving it, but Crutchfield said it was at least a month later. "Another keeper started asking why there were two more Fijis," Crutchfield said, which forced Schultz to return them.

Crutchfield never did bother to apply for federal permits for the Fijis—he stood no chance of getting them, and he knew it. But he had to explain the iguanas' presence to his friends and customers, so weeks after Schultz sent them back to Florida, Crutchfield continued to maintain that they were earmarked for the San Diego Zoo. Curators all over the country heard that Crutchfield had imported Fiji iguanas for San Diego, and berated Schultz for snapping them all up, when he had so many already.

Schultz was furious—Crutchfield couldn't keep his mouth shut about anything. He phoned Crutchfield and chewed him out.

Crutchfield found himself stuck with two rare and exquisite animals that he couldn't really keep, and couldn't easily sell. It occurred to him that the smartest thing to do would probably be to kill them, but that was out of the question.

THAT FALL, the Crutchfields decided to go into business with some very wealthy friends. The decision came suddenly, almost impulsively.

The Crutchfields and the Dietleins had known each other for more than a decade. Don Dietlein had been general curator of the National

Zoo in the 1960s; Nora Dietlein was a Canadian-born biochemist with a vast oil inheritance that she liked to spend on the most extraordinary animals—lemurs and Galapagos tortoises and a clouded leopard that walked freely around her home. In the 1970s and '80s, the Dietleins had run an art gallery on Sanibel Island, just across the causeway from Fort Myers, and, since animal people tend to find each other, had gotten to know the Crutchfield family well. They'd traveled with the Crutchfields to Haiti once, and Nora Dietlein was among the first of the Crutchfields' friends to view the new Fiji iguanas from Anson Wong. Penny had invited her to take a look at some "highly illegal" lizards one afternoon, "the most beautiful animals you've ever seen," she promised. Nora was impressed.

Not long after the iguanas arrived, the Dietleins announced that they were moving. Their animal collection had become too big for Sanibel, so they'd purchased a pristine, 120-acre plot in the town of Bushnell, in central Florida, and were just deciding what to do with the rest of it. They considered raising ostriches or catfish, or starting a mushroom farm, but had yet to settle on anything until they joined the Crutchfields for a farewell dinner in Fort Myers. The Dietleins parked their car in the Herpetofauna lot and piled into Crutchfield's Mercedes.

Crutchfield, Nora Dietlein recalled, was in a horrible mood. "He was very emotional. Very depressed. He said the business was getting to be too much for him. He couldn't handle it. He needed more time for his family." Crutchfield drove erratically, unnerving the Dietleins by looking into the backseat at them while he drove, but they said nothing.

It had been a lousy week for Crutchfield. Anson Wong had flown in from Malaysia more or less unannounced in an attempt to collect some $100,000 Crutchfield wasn't paying. Crutchfield had told Wong he was withholding payment because too many of Wong's animals were dead on arrival, but Wong wasn't having it. "About five minutes after I arrived," Wong said, "Tom opened his freezer and all these dead frogs came out." But then Crutchfield put business aside and treated Wong as his guest. He took Wong on a road trip to Silver Springs, home for decades of the late Ross Allen. "Tom was being the ever-gracious host, buying meals, tickets, getting to go behind the scenes and stuff, and it was making me feel guilty bringing up the topic of money," Wong said. "We did the Silver Springs thing Tuesday or Wednesday, and we returned on a Thursday, and I said, 'Tom, about this little money you owe me.' He says, 'Yes, I'll have Penny do it,' but on Friday the subject hadn't come up, and I was leaving Monday. It hit Saturday and I've got nothing." Wong was by now sick of the Crutchfield experience, sick of "the knives in the bathroom and guns in the bedroom. It was all so uncivilized," he said. Crutchfield, Wong concluded, "is loud, basically empty, and when I got stiffed for that $100,000 I decided I'm just not going to make an issue about it because he doesn't have it." They would never do business again.

Now, at dinner with the Dietleins, Crutchfield was an emotional wreck. The Dietleins claimed that Crutchfield offered them his entire business, then and there, begging them to take it over. Crutchfield said the Dietleins made the offer to him, relentlessly and insistently. One way or another, they decided to go into business together.

When the two couples returned to Crutchfield's from the restaurant, an alarm was flashing in the warehouse. Dozens of Crutchfield's boa constrictors had escaped from a holding cage and were hanging spookily from the rafters. The Dietleins and the Crutchfields caught every last one of the snakes. They were in this together now.

IN JANUARY 1990, long lists of assets were exchanged and a contract was signed. Don and Nora Dietlein now owned 50 percent of Herpetofauna, Inc. Crutchfield owned half the Dietleins' art collection, a third of their 120-acre parcel in rural Bushnell, and had use of an incredible structure in which to build the business of a lifetime. The building, which everyone called the barn, straddled the line between the two couples' properties. It was no ordinary barn, but the size of an airplane hangar and wired to the hilt because it had been constructed to conceal a previous owner's marijuana farm. The barn would house all of Herpetofauna's lizards and turtles and snakes. The property's naturally swampy grounds were perfect for crocodiles, so Crutchfield decided to expand into crocodile farming as well. Crutchfield dug crocodile ponds, and sent up trailers for himself and Penny to live in, another for Penny's mother, and one more for an office.

Just before their final move to Bushnell, Penny packed up the two Fiji iguanas into pet carriers and handed them to their veterinarian for safekeeping. She didn't want them getting jostled around during the move, she explained, but she never called to ask for them back, either.

THE DIETLEINS had no children, but somewhat curiously supported a twenty-five-year-old man named Adamm Smith, whom they were taking with them to Bushnell. For two years, Smith had lived rent-free on the first floor of the Dietleins' Sanibel home. The Dietleins had recently paid off all Smith's credit cards, deeded him twenty acres of their new property, provided him the engagement ring for his new wife, who was moving along with them, and changed their wills to make Smith their sole heir. Already, Smith owned a tremendously valuable art collection, given to him by the Dietleins. Smith would renovate the barn and help Crutchfield manage the business.

Crutchfield hired a number of new employees, from handymen to crocodile keepers. For the first time in his life, his budget was nearly unlimited. The only hitch, for Crutchfield, were the Dietleins themselves. Don Dietlein was effeminate and timid, but Nora Dietlein was tough, demanding, as much of a control freak as Crutchfield. In the past, Crutchfield's managers and partners had been his stooges, but now all of Crutchfield's decisions had to be made in consultation with Nora, a situation neither of them ever really adjusted to.

IN THE winter of 1990, the Crutchfields' veterinarian called to say he could no longer care for the Fiji iguanas. He drove the iguanas up to

Bushnell, where the Dietleins agreed to keep them as the compound was being assembled.

The Dietleins technically owned half the iguanas, since two Fijis had been listed among the Crutchfields' assets when their business plans were drawn up. They kept the lizards in a large aquarium, feeding them fruit and adjusting their heat lamps all winter. They knew the iguanas had come from Anson Wong, but were still unaware, they claimed, that Crutchfield had failed in his plan to legalize them through some sort of arrangement with the San Diego Zoo.

That February, state wildlife officers stopped by on a routine inspection of the Bushnell property. Only Adamm Smith was there at the time, and he knew to make sure the iguanas were hidden.

WHEN HANK MOLT and his girlfriend Colette Hairston showed up in Bushnell in the spring of 1990, on their way to a crocodile conference in Gainesville, they were amazed by Crutchfield's new place. Reptile people did not generally live on pristine 120-acre estates, but rather crammed themselves and their animals into whatever space they had, resigned to the omnipresent musky smell of snakes. Crutchfield's new Herpetofauna compound was, by comparison, "fucking paradise," Molt said. "There were flight cages and sprinkler systems and lemurs. Horses and crocodile ponds. The kind of industrial kitchens they have in zoos for feeding animals." To get around the grounds, you had to drive golf carts.

It was important to Crutchfield that his compound be finished within six months. The first-ever National Reptile Breeders' Expo was coming up that August. The expo was a new concept, a showcase for the commercial reptile trade at a time when the zoos' changing politics had forced the reptile dealers to seek new markets.

It had all begun at the 1989 reptile symposium in Phoenix, when the symposium's board voted to ban sales of live animals at the event. This caused bitter feelings among the reptile dealers. Ever since the reptile symposiums had started, in the 1970s, dealers had arrived with live animals to sell—it was part of the fun and half the point. Wayne Hill, an Orlando snake and turtle breeder, was so infuriated by the ban that he decided to start a convention just for the trade. The rising class of reptile breeders, the herpetoculturists, had already turned away from the zoos, looking to private collectors instead for their high-end animals. The expo would formalize the switch. Hill worked all year to publicize the expo, determined that it be a triumph, the biggest gathering of snake people under one roof, and, he hoped, a comeuppance to the zoo community.

Crutchfield hoped to make a big impression at the expo, and planned a grand opening party for the Thursday before it. Now, with six months to go, he was scrambling, intermittently apoplectic, and sweating so much that a salty white residue covered his skin. Some of his crocodiles had escaped from their new ponds into neighboring yards, and a few had yet to be found, adding to his miseries. Crutchfield complained to Molt that he was doing all the work, while the Dietleins played with their lemurs, and Molt noticed that Crutchfield and Nora Dietlein had the same sort of bossy, haranguing, dominant personality. "One or the other of them was always demanding a meeting," Molt said. The two would disappear into a trailer, from which Crutchfield would emerge red-faced, his eyeballs and neck veins protruding.

CRUTCHFIELD FINISHED his compound on time and his grand opening party was a success, though tensions with the Dietleins had hardly subsided. There were visitors from Japan and Germany, "barbecues and music, phones ringing off the hooks, everyone in golf carts," said Hank Molt, who showed up with Colette Hairston on his arm.

In the middle of the party, Molt remembered that the last time he and Hairston had visited Crutchfield's compound, early that spring, he had forgotten to show her Crutchfield's Fiji iguanas, and she was curious about them.

Before, the iguanas had been in the barn. Now Crutchfield directed Molt and Hairston toward the woods, a stand of magnificent, mossy live oaks. The iguanas sat atop a freshly cut tree stump in a cage covered with shade cloth, as though they were being concealed. "I thought, 'That's kind of weird,'" Molt said. "Colette looked at them and thought they were nice, and the next day we all left for Orlando, for the expo."

The expo, too, was a success. The Howard Johnson's ballrooms were packed so tightly with visitors gawking at deli cups that it was hard to move around. "With this convention, the breeding of reptiles as exotic pets, which has become a multimillion-dollar industry in recent years, has finally come of age," the *Miami Herald* reported. For one glorious weekend, it was Tommy Crutchfield's industry.

IN THE middle of the two-day reptile expo, the Crutchfields and the Dietleins stopped speaking altogether. The ill will between the couples, building gradually over months, had reached the point where Crutchfield now suspected the Dietleins of harboring a secret agenda to ruin him, to sell him out to the Feds, "and maybe turn the whole business over to Adamm Smith." Crutchfield planned to pocket the cash sales from the expo, just in case they thought of trying anything. The Dietleins were planning to pack up all the art they'd brought to the business and move it someplace where Crutchfield couldn't touch it, as soon as the expo was over.

Few noticed what was going on besides Hank Molt and Thomas Schultz, who were helping Crutchfield out that weekend. Schultz detected something strange and surreptitious in Nora's behavior, for during the expo she'd began to grill him, awkwardly and out of nowhere, about Crutchfield's Fiji iguanas. She wanted to know the whole story, and she was, unbeknownst to Schultz, concealing a tape recorder under her clothes.

Something weird was going on, something bad was about to happen; Molt, Crutchfield, and Schultz could all feel it. Before the expo was over, Crutchfield turned to Molt for a favor.

That summer, Molt had delivered thirty thousand dollars' worth of animals—the last of his Stefan Schwarz stock—to Crutchfield. Would Molt draft a document to look as though the opposite had happened, as though he had just *bought* thirty thousand dollars' worth of animals from Crutchfield? The fake sale was a way for Crutchfield to hide inventory in case things went south with the Dietleins. Molt said he would. The expo ended on Sunday. Crutchfield departed for Bushnell, and Molt spent Monday with Colette Hairston, then put her on a flight back to Texas. He promised Crutchfield he'd meet him in Bushnell Tuesday to notarize the phony bill of sale. But by Monday, Herpetofauna Inc. was in civil war.

It started when Nora Dietlein and her husband were pulling out of their driveway in their van, and Crutchfield sped up to them in his golf cart, cutting them off. "Get up to the barn!" he screamed. "I want to talk to you now!" The Dietleins had filled their van with art that belonged to the business and were about to abscond with it, Crutchfield said. He jumped out of the golf cart, and the Dietleins got out of their van. Crutchfield blasted the Dietleins with obscenities, then jumped back on his golf cart. "He drove it towards me and I jumped back and he drove over my foot," Nora said.

Crutchfield disputed the foot part of the story—if it were true, he said, Nora Dietlein would surely have had him arrested.

Hank Molt pulled up the next afternoon to pandemonium. A mountain of gravel sat on the drive linking the Dietleins' and the Crutchfields' properties, gravel the Dietleins had hired someone to drop there. Crutchfield's daughters hurried to remove animals from the barn, while a Jamaican friend of theirs guarded it with a rifle. All the phones, computers, fax machines, and files in the Herpetofauna office were missing—stolen, the Crutchfields said, by the Dietleins. Sheriff's deputies were on their way, and Crutchfield's friends searched the yellow pages for a storefront, a warehouse, any available air-conditioned space that could be used to store Crutchfield's animals. It seemed as though an aging strip mall in the neighboring town of Lake Panasoffkee would have to do, and Crutchfield, his family, and Molt began hauling the animals there.

The joint venture between the Crutchfields and the Dietleins—worth millions of dollars in animals, art, and real estate—had imploded four days after its grand opening.

Somehow, in the middle of all this, Molt managed to get notarized his fake $30,000 receipt, and Crutchfield pulled Molt aside with another, stranger, request. Since Molt knew how to take care of Fiji iguanas, would he mind taking Crutchfield's pair back to Philadelphia with him, until things calmed down in Florida?

Molt walked to the woods behind the barn, carrying snake bags. The iguanas' cage was locked, and Crutchfield had been too frazzled to provide a key, so Molt popped the hinges with a screwdriver, and bagged up the iguanas. He arranged them in his station wagon and headed north.

THE DIETLEINS filed suit against the Crutchfields in county court, and the Crutchfields filed a countersuit. A receiver was appointed to divide whatever was left of Herpetofauna, Inc. Adamm Smith fled Bushnell, afraid of being caught between the Crutchfields and the Dietleins. The two families retreated to their sides of the 120-acre parcel, barred by restraining orders from interacting. But neither Nora Dietlein nor Tommy Crutchfield was finished with the other.

For weeks, Nora sifted through the boxes of records she had appropriated, figuring there would be something in them to compromise Crutchfield.

She discovered the double-invoicing Crutchfield and Anson Wong used to avoid import duties on shipments. Nora had discerned by now that Crutchfield and Wong were estranged, and she called Malaysia, figuring Wong might have some more items of interest, and perhaps hate Crutchfield enough to send them.

Wong sent her a fax he had originally sent to Crutchfield in early 1989. At the top was the contorted-crocodile logo of Exotic Skins and Alives.

*Dear Tom,*

*I want to confirm with the exchange of my 7 hds Fiji against your 14 heads RHINO. Can you let me know roughly when I can expect the shipment? Meanwhile here's real total of invoice 12/89 . . . $6,669.00. Pls try to send 5-6000.00 this week.*

*Thanks.*

*Dr. Wong*

Nora Dietlein mailed the fax to the Tampa office of the U.S. Fish and Wildlife Service. With it, the criminal investigation of Crutchfield began.

"SOMETIMES BAD, bad things happen to you and it makes you become mentally unbalanced," Crutchfield said. "I thought of Herpetofauna kind of like a baby, like my son, which I created from nothing. Losing it was like a child dying."

Late one night, a few weeks after the death of Herpetofauna, Crutchfield walked quietly across the woods to the Dietleins' house, carrying his Ruger Mini-14. Crutchfield raised the rifle to the Dietleins' bedroom window. He held it there, unable to shoot the sleeping couple, unable to put the gun down. "I really wanted to kill them," he said, "but I thought about my family. I thought about having that on my conscience for the rest of my life. I came closer than they ever knew."

The Dietleins sold all their animals and moved to Canada.

CRUTCHFIELD REOPENED shop in Lake Panasoffkee, Florida, as Tom Crutchfield's Reptile Enterprises. He was calling himself Tom now, not Tommy, though it took a while for everyone to adjust, including him. Crutchfield had managed to get his shop in order remarkably fast—it was

September 1990, only six weeks since the meltdown—but not his emotions. He hired a private detective to locate the Dietleins in Canada, and had taken to phoning them at four a.m., saying things like "Hi, Nora. This is Tommy. You can never get away from me." Nora Dietlein would reciprocate with sexual allegations about Penny on the Crutchfield family's answering machine.

Crutchfield still maintained the crocodile farm on his half of the Bushnell estate, but the barn stood locked, by order of the court, and the Dietleins' house was now empty. He bought fax machines and computers to replace those the Dietleins had stolen, and came up with a trendy new slogan: "Conservation thru Commercialization."

The slogan borrowed the self-serving ideology long in vogue at the zoos: Grab the animals while you can because they're going extinct anyway.

As Crutchfield looked at it, he wasn't exactly Jane Goodall, but "a lot of the animals I smuggled would have been killed in their countries," by logging, road building, or the skin trade, or for food. Conservation thru Commercialization, cynical though it sounded, "was something I actually believed in," he said.

"If I'd succeeded with the Fiji iguanas, there would be millions of them in the U.S. right now," Crutchfield said. "There would never be another smuggled again."

# 12

## Waffle House Days

Tom Crutchfield decided to send Hank Molt on a collecting trip to Indonesia, all expenses paid. It was the fall of 1990, and if Crutchfield's new business was to succeed, he needed a new supplier in Asia. He was lately cultivating Mohamad Hardi, Anson Wong's rival in the region. Hardi lived in Jakarta, and it was fortuitous that Crutchfield's brother, Bobby, a merchant mariner, had just married an Indonesian woman and moved there.

Molt's assignment was to fly to Jakarta, stay with Bobby, travel to Hardi's farm every day, and select nice, healthy specimens for Crutchfield, putting together shipments that rivaled Anson Wong's best. Molt, who lately had an abundance of free time but few resources for adventures, was all for it. He left for Jakarta by way of Texas, where Colette Hairston helped him pack. She chose his traveling clothes, fussing over him "just like a wife," said Molt, which unnerved him slightly.

Molt prepared for himself a cheat sheet of some forty Indonesian words and phrases, which he encased in a plastic sheath and studied:

Blalok Kiri = Turn Left
Beehunti Disini = Stop Here
Saya Mau Lagi Ini = I Want More This
Kuri Kuri = Turtle
Buaya = Crocodiles
Ular = Snake
Kandang = Cage

In Jakarta, Molt spent his days at Mohamad Hardi's farm and his nights at Bobby Crutchfield's house. Bobby was half a foot taller than his brother, two years younger, and even more pugnacious. He had spent most of his adult life in the shipping lanes of Asia and the Persian Gulf, where he'd been jailed and tortured for spinning around his ship as his crewmen tried to pray to Mecca. The Crutchfield brothers would spend years out of touch, then get together for weeks at a time in Florida, visits that often ended with them beating each other senseless. After one fight, Tom had left Bobby buried alive in a ditch, knocked out, only to have Bobby show up an hour later, covered in blood and dirt, at the bar where Tom was recovering. "Can I buy you a drink, mate?" said Bobby, menacingly, and then they were back to grinding each other's skulls into the floor. They were both in their late thirties then.

Bobby had injured his back and received a large settlement from the merchant marines before moving to Jakarta, and now he was land-locked, a state that did not agree with him. His solace was in war toys and miniatures—like his brother, Bobby was a collector. "Bobby was really good. He'd find little tiny German tanks from 1917 still in their boxes," Molt said. Together they drove all over Jakarta, picking through shops.

Bobby had also contracted hepatitis around the time of Molt's visit, and was rapidly getting sicker. "Hank was so scared of catching what I had that he never ventured into my room," Bobby Crutchfield said.

Molt said it wasn't merely the sickness—he found Bobby Crutchfield just plain scary. "He had that Crutchfield temper," Molt said. "That instant, volcanic, blood-reddening craziness that was Tom's downfall."

AFTER A few weeks, Tom Crutchfield began to sense that Molt was doing a less-than-stellar job in Jakarta. Some snafu accompanied every shipment, some baroque excuse every fax.

Molt blamed the setbacks on Mohamad Hardi, who "was busy down-town playing tennis, driving around in his Mercedes and wearing Ralph Lauren sweaters. When it came to actually making a shipment, he delegated it five times removed," he said. "The guys on his farm were like serfs. They didn't know a snake with a bad eye or a broken tail. If they got the species right it was a home run."

All Molt was interested in, it seemed to Crutchfield, was drinking and smuggling Boelen's pythons. Hardi had permits for four Boelen's. Molt wanted to ship twenty-six. "THINK about it . . . Serious money potential!!!!" he implored Crutchfield in a fax. Crutchfield chose not to chance a high-risk venture with Molt. "Hank would have found some way to fuck it up," Crutchfield said.

Molt, who used a fax machine as if it were a Teletype, sent Crutchfield weekly updates, and they continued to get worse.

TOM—SITUATION HERE VERY NEGATIVE. BROTHER BOB STILL SICK. MIGHT HAVE TO GO TO HOSPITAL IN SINGAPORE—PERMITS FOR A SECOND SHIPMENT HAVE NOT BEEN SIGNED—OFFICER IN BOGOR WHO MUST SIGN THE PERMITS IS NOW AWAY FROM COUNTRY ALSO—PRESENT STOCK AT FARM NOT VERY GOOD.

Molt's Indonesia trip ended in failure. He had managed to get some shipments off to Crutchfield, but the last one—the biggest—got held up at the Miami airport, where part of it was confiscated by the U.S. Fish and Wildlife Service. He blamed Hardi's serfs.

WHEN MOLT returned, he drove to Colette Hairston's in Texas, only to be dumped.

Molt's drinking had been bothering Hairston for a long time. "She made me go to AA meetings," Molt said. "She had a very gradual program to change me, but I wasn't alerted to it until fairly late in the game. I wanted to drink and hunt rattlesnakes. I wasn't ready to be that good."

For the remainder of the fall, Molt made no contact with Hairston. But as winter took hold, Hairston began to receive hostile letters. "He'd mail me pictures of people with no eyes," she said, and the letters "would always be postmarked from someplace unlikely, someplace that made no sense." Molt was living out of his car when he sent the letters to Hairston, driving around the country, in the freezing cold. His depression, which he had always struggled to control, had returned.

It had been an unlucky few months for Molt. The disastrous trip to Indonesia, followed by getting dumped, was then capped off by Tom Crutchfield's Fiji iguanas dying in his care. Molt froze the iguanas for Crutchfield, to prove he hadn't sold them, but when Crutchfield learned that they were dead, he seemed relieved, which mystified Molt.

Then Crutchfield started calling Molt at home in Philadelphia, demanding that he destroy the carcasses. "It just kept getting worse and worse," Molt said. "Tom's calling and calling, saying, 'You gotta make those things disappear.' I thought, 'There's something bad going on here.'"

Molt assured Crutchfield that no trace of the iguanas remained. He then removed them from his freezer, filled two empty instant coffee jars with alcohol, dropped an iguana into each, photographed the jars, and hid them in the wheel well of his station wagon, which he was now driving around the country.

"I didn't know they came from Anson Wong, or anything about them," Molt said of the iguanas. "I just wanted to keep my options open."

MOLT, MISERABLE, decided to hole up at Crutchfield's awhile and regroup.

For eighteen months, Molt had shuttled among Texas, Florida, and Pennsylvania. During that time he had lost Eddie Celebucki, Stefan Schwarz, and Colette Hairston.

Molt did have a friend left in Tom Crutchfield, even if Crutchfield vowed never to send Molt abroad again. "I felt sorry for Hank," Crutchfield said. "I fed him and I housed him. He'd drink Heineken that I bought, go to Catfish Johnny's and eat food that I paid for." It seemed to Crutchfield that Molt spent at least half of each day at the Waffle House. "All Hank did was sit around and talk," said Crutchfield.

Back at the reptile expo the previous August, Crutchfield had written Molt a phony bill of sale for thirty thousand dollars' worth of animals, to fool the Dietleins. But actually, Crutchfield owed Molt the exact same amount for some snakes he'd bought earlier.

So Crutchfield paid Molt in increments of a few thousand dollars at a time, and that was enough to keep Molt in waffles indefinitely.

CRUTCHFIELD'S LITIGATION against the Dietleins wore on. Determined to avenge himself against them, Crutchfield was starting to use his price lists as a soapbox, not unlike the way Molt once had, except that Crutchfield's style was more mafioso. He published the Dietleins' address in British Columbia, tacitly inviting his customers to go settle his scores.

Crutchfield knew of the nascent criminal investigation into the Fiji iguanas, but had no good sense of where it was going, if anywhere. He focused instead on his new business, which he was bent on making a success. He created a new logo for it, a sort of tribal-tattoo snake design, which he slapped on everything. He brought on two old friends to help him. The first was Dwayne Cunningham, a reptile enthusiast and former Ringling Bros. clown who'd been trained by Crutchfield's uncle. Cunningham became the new manager of Tom Crutchfield's Reptile Enterprises. Crutchfield's other new partner—his investor—was Jack Constantine, an old-school sideshow owner with traveling acts such as Fat Albert, an 856-pound man, and Little Eddy Taylor, a midget pianist. Sideshows had made Constantine rich, and Crutchfield persuaded Constantine that reptiles would make him richer. With the legal bills he now faced, Crutchfield needed capital.

Hank Molt held no official title at Tom Crutchfield's Reptile Enterprises, but took it as his duty to make life unbearable for everyone.

AT FIRST Molt lived with the Crutchfield family, and when that arrangement grew tiresome, Molt moved into a rental house with Dwayne Cunningham. Cunningham had grown up in Philadelphia, where he had worked in the zoo's reptile house. He knew of Molt because the curators talked about him in mythical tones. Cohabiting with Molt proved impossible, though. "Dwayne and I were always arguing," Molt said. "Tom always had to break it up. Every day there would be a meeting. Then Tom would be in Colombia or Haiti, we'd have snakes loose in the room, and we'd be coming close to fistfights. I don't know why we hated each other so much."

Crutchfield's contempt for Molt mounted. "I was nice to Hank in spite of what I knew he was," said Crutchfield. "But until he lived with me I had no idea how twisted he really was." Crutchfield was livid when a terrified Colette Hairston sent a parcel from Texas, returning all of Molt's gifts, lest he continue to bill her for them. And then there were Molt's unexplained absences, which lasted weeks. He was visiting his family in Philadelphia, usually, but never bothered to inform anyone before he left. "He would just be gone and we never knew where he went," Crutchfield said. "You never knew what he was gonna do."

Molt thought no better of Crutchfield after those months in close proximity. "Tom called Saturdays 'J & A' days at his shop. 'J & A' stood for 'jerks and assholes,' which is what he called his own customers!" Crutchfield was intense and hard-working in some ways, pathologically lazy in others. He neglected to pay his electric bill for months, "and would freak out and go nuts on the electric company when they shut it off," Molt said. "Meanwhile, he had $100,000 in the bank." Crutchfield's truck was repossessed one day outside a restaurant, while he and Molt were having lunch. "Tom was fuming—the usual high blood pressure and muscle pumping. I said just go to the bank, take out the money, and get it back," Molt said, but Crutchfield refused.

"His Mercedes was a moving trash can. His house was a stationary trash can. Every surface in the kitchen was filled with dirty dishes and refuse, even the oven. He and Penny were real Florida people, no education, happy to live in a little town with a Piggly Wiggly," Molt said. It drove Molt crazy to watch Crutchfield stuff his face with energy bars and study muscle magazines, grunting with approval at every picture. "He was just like a fucking caveman."

TENSIONS WERE further exacerbated when Eddie Celebucki started showing up in Lake Panasoffkee. After a two-year hiatus from smuggling, Celebucki suddenly had hundreds of fresh New Guinea reptiles that he was selling directly to Crutchfield, instead of using Molt as his middleman, as he'd done before. Molt, Celebucki felt, had given him no choice. "I never made any money until I started selling directly to Tommy," he said. Crutchfield felt bad for Celebucki. "Hank used to cheat Ed, though Hank had me convinced it was the other way around," Crutchfield said. "Hank would take the lion's share and the right sexes, leaving Ed with what was left. Meanwhile Ed was doing all the work. It took me a while to realize that Ed was truly the nice guy and Hank was the asshole." In the summer of 1991, Molt walked into Crutchfield's office to find Celebucki in the process of a delivery. "It wasn't outwardly hostile," Molt said of their meeting. But neither was it friendly. Crutchfield was really getting to like Celebucki, and had it in mind to groom Celebucki to run missions for him, to do the kind of work that Molt had proved unfit for. That fall, Crutchfield and Celebucki traveled to South America together, while Molt sat around the Waffle House.

A CANAL ran adjacent to the house Dwayne Cunningham and Hank Molt shared. Molt liked spending his evenings on the porch, drinking beer and listening to the alligators bellowing in the canal. One night Molt was sitting on the porch when "I see these guys with binoculars in the driveway across from me, looking around," he said. "Then they pull into our driveway." Vance Eaddy, a special agent with the U.S. Fish and Wildlife Service, introduced himself and asked, politely enough, if he could take a walk through the house. Eaddy seemed fixated on a large birdcage behind the house, half shaded with tarps, that housed some African chameleons, smallish green lizards that, from a distance, looked a little like Fiji iguanas. Cunningham wouldn't let him near it.

A grand jury had convened in the Crutchfield case. Molt and Cunningham received subpoenas shortly after Eaddy's visit, instructing them to bring to the Tampa courthouse the green lizards in their yard. By the date the two were scheduled to testify, though, the agents had already determined that the lizards weren't Fiji iguanas after all. Don't bother with the lizards, they instructed Molt and Cunningham, who would have none of it. After making sure to notify the TV news, they loaded the cage full of chameleons into a car, then hauled them, with great feigned effort, up the courthouse steps.

Back in Lake Panasoffkee, Crutchfield bought beer and threw a little party. "He thought it was great that we made assholes of the Feds," Molt said. "He was absolutely sure he was gonna win."

Crutchfield's enterprise, meanwhile, was quickly unraveling. Jack Constantine pulled out of the business partnership, leaving Crutchfield heavily in debt. Employee paychecks bounced. Dwayne Cunningham quit. Hoping to avoid another subpoena or worse, Molt departed for Philadelphia, promising he'd be back. Crutchfield hoped it would be a good long while.

Federal agents were coming around Lake Panasoffkee so much that they started lunching at Catfish Johnny's.

On November 6, 1991, Tom Crutchfield, Penny Crutchfield, and Anson Wong were indicted for conspiring to violate the Endangered Species Act and CITES. Wong elected to blow the whole thing off, under-standably. Malaysia wasn't going to extradite him over lizards.

Crutchfield decided that he and Penny would fight the charges with every cent they had. Molt thought Crutchfield was out of his mind. "With a case like that, you either did it or didn't do it, and if you did it you cut your losses and make a deal," said Molt, who had some experience in these matters. "But there was nobody around him with a brain."

MOLT RETURNED to Lake Panasoffkee several months later, seeking money. Crutchfield had just sold off the last of Molt's consignment of snakes, most of them to the Columbus Zoo. He now owed Molt $5,000, by Molt's calculations. But Crutchfield had lawyers to pay; he had already paid Molt some $25,000 over the past year, and that last $5,000 suddenly seemed like a lot. When Molt arrived at Crutchfield's, keen to collect, Crutchfield told him that the snakes died only days after being sold, that he hadn't been paid for them, and that he therefore wouldn't be paying Molt. This did not sit well with Molt at all.

Crutchfield was in remarkably high spirits for someone facing a major federal court battle, Molt thought. Eddie Celebucki was in the shop again when Molt arrived, helping Crutchfield pack a shipment of Bismarck ringed pythons bound for Germany. The pythons had been smuggled from New Guinea, as usual, but Crutchfield and Celebucki had just falsified CITES papers alleging that the snakes were the product of a breeding pro-gram in Ohio. Crutchfield was in such a good mood about all this that he spontaneously burst into his theme song: "I'm Tom Terrific / Greatest hero ever / Terrific is the name for me / 'Cause I'm so clever."

Molt did not think that falsifying government documents in front of a room full of people, with a federal trial pending, was clever. "But that's how Tom did things," Molt said. "He never had the worst-case-scenario conversation with himself."

Before leaving Lake Panasoffkee, Molt gave Crutchfield a ride from the shop to the crocodile farm, because Crutchfield had accidentally locked his keys in his trunk. In the privacy of Molt's station wagon, Crutchfield's spirits subsided. The indictment was weighing on him more than he let on.

"I hope those iguanas are history," he said to Molt. "Ashes to ashes. Dust to dust." Molt assured him that they were. In fact, they were still in the wheel well of Molt's station wagon, and Crutchfield was sitting on top of them.

# 13

## United States v.
## Tommy Edward Crutchfield, et al.

Tommy Crutchfield had rarely ever worn a suit, and his friend Thomas Schultz thought he resembled John Gotti in one. Not once during Crutchfield's two-week trial had he taken the stand, opting instead to influence proceedings thorough a silent display of aggression. He'd blown kisses to the prosecution's key witnesses, Don and Nora Dietlein, and slapped their lawyer on the back, hard. It was June 15, 1992, and Assistant U.S. Attorney Michael Rubinstein wrapped his closing argument with a synopsis of Crutchfield's persona:

> Mr. Crutchfield is a person who, his good friend Mr. Schultz says, can't keep his mouth shut about anything. He's not a shy person, he's a flamboyant person. He's an extrovert. He is a short person who lifts weights every day until he has a bad back. He's a person that tells other people that I can beat the you know what out of you. He's a person that goes around wearing a big knife all the time on his waist. He's a show off. Mr. Crutchfield is the kind of person that wants to be number one. He wants to be the biggest and the best and the first with the most. That's his psychology . . .
>
> My God, he can get things and does get things and daily possesses things that no zoo in the world has ever got. And he knows more about these animals than any zookeeper.

So what does Mr. Crutchfield do? He gets, he does the impossible. He gets the Fiji banded iguana. The hottest thing there is. One lizard that nobody can get.

MICHAEL RUBINSTEIN was a reptile enthusiast—not the type to remortgage his house for a snake, but someone who would understand the temptation to do so. Rubinstein kept lizards and attended monthly meetings of the Tampa Herpetological Society. As a kid in New York, he'd spent many weekend days in the dark and humid corridors of the Bronx Zoo's reptile house, nose against glass. All this made him either the best or the worst person to prosecute the Crutchfields. The Crutchfields deemed him the worst: Rubinstein, they protested in pretrial motions, had not only toured Herpetofauna with the Tampa Herpetological Society in 1990, he had purchased a pet lizard while he was there. Rubinstein acknowledged to his superior and the judge that he had indeed visited Crutchfield's place and bought a forty-dollar savannah monitor as a pet for his son. They allowed him to proceed with the case anyway. Rubinstein wanted the case because of, not despite, his interest in reptiles. "I couldn't have prosecuted the case without it!" he said. "You have to know about the industry you're dealing with. I know a lot about drugs, I know a lot about money laundering, I know a lot about medical malpractice, Medicare and Medicaid fraud—this happened to be something that I was interested in since childhood."

The Crutchfields retained for their defense Fred Ohlinger, the lawyer they'd used in their civil suit against Don and Nora Dietlein. Ohlinger had brought to that litigation a rash, aggressive personal style not unlike that of his client. At one point, he'd even likened wildlife officials' ticketing and inspections of Crutchfield's facility to Nazi persecutions. This only endeared him to Crutchfield. When the Dietleins sold off a herd of Herpetofauna's Galapagos tortoises, in violation of their receivership agreement with Crutchfield, Ohlinger persuaded the county judge to issue warrants for their arrest. Crutchfield published the warrants on his price list.

No sooner had Crutchfield's indictment been issued than Rubinstein was forced to defend himself against an outrageous rumor, circulated by Ohlinger, that the forty-dollar lizard Rubinstein bought from Crutchfield had died, that Rubinstein had not been refunded, and that he was now retaliating with a federal case against Crutchfield.

"An aura of menace hung over this case," Rubinstein said. "Here was this lizard case that was being conducted under the aura that could have been a Mob case." Rubinstein was notoriously excitable, and Crutchfield enjoyed winding him up. "I tried to fluster him so that he hated me so much," Crutchfield said, and Ohlinger did nothing to stop him.

"Believe me, if he had come and said, 'Let's work this out,' we could have made some kind of deal, and that would be it, but it's the ego thing," Rubinstein said of Crutchfield. "I thought he was an asshole."

RUBINSTEIN EXPECTED Fred Ohlinger to come up with one of three possible defenses for Crutchfield: "One, that some goon in Malaysia packed the box by accident. Two, that they were the progeny of pre-CITES animals, that he didn't import them. And three, they're not Fiji iguanas, they're something else—there's a million green lizards out there." Ohlinger surprised Rubinstein by employing all three arguments at once, along with some even less plausible ones. At one point he floated the notion that the entire case against Crutchfield was a plot to distract attention from the George H. W. Bush administration's abysmal environmental record—in particular, its support of logging interests in spotted owl habitat.

Ohlinger didn't have a coherent defense, but he was good at trashing Rubinstein's witnesses, most of whom "didn't have degrees of any kind, they were all kids—they were all smart but they were kids—who'd quit, been fired, hated Crutchfield, this kind of thing," Rubinstein said. "So Ohlinger could say these are pot-smoking drifters." Rubinstein identified with them. "These were kids like I was a kid, who would love to have worked in a place where there were all these exciting things coming in," he said. "Most people may not appreciate that but to them it was the most exciting place in the world you could be, and they were there. The only problem was that Crutchfield was there, too, threatening them. So that was the downside. The only people who were experts were the Dietleins, and they had their motives."

Rubinstein also identified with Don and Nora Dietlein—too much, he would later come to think—and hoped the jury would see the couple as he did: scientists and art dealers, wine and cheese people caught up in Crutchfield's cracker world. "I was very impressed with their love of animals and the fact that he had been a zoo director," Rubinstein said.

The Dietleins may have been wealthy and accomplished, but, like most middle-aged couples who share their homes with leopards and young men, they could hardly be called normal, and Nora Dietlein created nearly as many problems for Rubinstein as she had for Crutchfield. "I eventually got a feeling that there was something going on psychologically with her. Something that I didn't really know," Rubinstein said. He forced Dietlein to repeat before the court an evil phone message she had left for the Crutchfield family, accusing Penny of having an illegitimate child. It was a preemptive move—"I thought, 'Oh shit, [Ohlinger]'s got the tape and he's gonna play the tape to show this crazy lady is so vindictive that she will do anything to attack Crutchfield," Rubinstein said, but the move backfired, causing a furor in the court and accusations that Rubinstein was painting the sweet, churchgoing Penny Crutchfield as a slut.

It got worse for Rubinstein when Adamm Smith, the young man who had lived for years as the Dietleins' ward, testified for the defense with enough vitriol toward the couple that he seemed to be using the trial as an opportunity to break up with them. Nora Dietlein, Smith testified, was an alcoholic and a drug addict. Every day, Smith said, she would take "about three or four Darvocet or Percodan, whatever we had at the time, at night. With some Scotch." Sometimes Nora's lemurs escaped, Smith said, because she was so addled. Nora, Smith testified, was a woman "very much in charge. Having control of everything that was going on around. That kind of thing," Smith told the court. And what she wanted above all, he said, was "to ruin Mr. Crutchfield and steal from Herpetofauna." Rubinstein, furious, probed Smith about his relationship with the Dietleins, hoping to make him seem a freeloader and a parasite. If the Dietleins were such terrible people, Rubinstein chided, why had they been so generous to a nobody like him? "We loved each other" was Smith's odd answer. "Supposedly."

THOMAS SCHULTZ of the San Diego Zoo testified for the prosecution, though much of what he said seemed designed to aid the defense. About the only way Schultz actually helped Rubinstein was by establishing, once and for all, that the animals in question were Fiji banded iguanas, and not some other green lizards, as Ohlinger had first tried to claim. Schultz said that though he had received a Fiji iguana in a package from Crutchfield, he never asked about its origins because he "didn't want to know." And Schultz said he couldn't rule out the possibility that Crutchfield's Fijis were not, in fact, progeny of iguanas Hank Molt had imported in the 1970s.

Hank Molt was not called as a witness, though Rubinstein brought up Molt's name a lot, keen to establish that Crutchfield was very friendly with a convicted criminal who had also smuggled Fiji iguanas, many years before. But Fred Ohlinger got the judge to bar any mention of Molt's convictions. This drove Rubinstein crazy enough that he tried, underhandedly, to elicit the real story on Molt from witnesses. "Have you heard about a bunch of bodies of lizards that were found buried in the New Jersey Pine Barrens near Philadelphia?" Rubinstein demanded of Thomas Schultz, who didn't get a chance to answer over the yelling and gavel-banging that ensued.

"THEY EAT the animals over there," Fred Ohlinger, who had never been to Fiji or anywhere near it, told the jury. "If you go out as the sun's coming down and you look up in the trees around the islands, you can see them fluttering. The chickens of the trees fluttering around. The natives eat them. They don't protect them."

It was closing arguments, and Ohlinger was determined to use whatever he had, including this nonsense about Fiji iguanas as food. Ohlinger had already recapped his claims about spotted owls and the many other ways in which the stars had aligned against the Crutchfields through no fault of their own.

Yes, the Crutchfields did have Fiji banded iguanas, and no, they didn't have permits for them—that much Ohlinger finally conceded. So, if the Crutchfields had Fiji iguanas and no permits, why shouldn't they be convicted?

Very simple, Ohlinger told the jury: the Fijis were Hank Molt's.

"Hank Molt, he was at the beginning of this case, and he was at the end of this case; in fact, he is the beginning and the end of this case as far as Fijis are concerned. There is no way that you can exclude the reasonable doubt that those are captive bred progeny from Hank Molt."

Ohlinger said it again: "There are animals out there that Hank Molt had and the case started with Hank and that's where it comes back to and the progeny would still be alive today."

On June 16, the jury returned its verdict in *United States v. Tommy Edward Crutchfield, et al.* Penny was found guilty on half the counts, and Tommy on all of them.

# 14

## Chambers Not So Distant

Two days after his conviction, Tom Crutchfield tried to phone Hank Molt in Philadelphia, but instead reached Molt's wife, who was disturbed by what he had to say. The four Fiji iguanas he had been convicted over "were your husband's property, and that's the truth," Crutchfield vowed before hanging up.

When Molt returned, his wife played the answering machine. She had accidentally recorded the conversation. "I thought, 'What the fuck is this shit?'" he said.

Molt called Crutchfield back, incensed. They hadn't spoken since March over the $5,000 Crutchfield owed, and now Crutchfield wanted to buy Molt a plane ticket to Florida. It was urgent that Molt, Crutchfield, and Fred Ohlinger meet as soon as possible, Crutchfield said, and Tom Schultz would be flying in from San Diego, too. Crutchfield informed Molt that the Feds were looking to arrest him, a fate he might avert by cooperating.

Molt figured he might be vulnerable to arrest in the Crutchfield case. Much as he would have enjoyed testifying against Crutchfield in federal court, presenting his pickled iguanas in their jars, he did not volunteer his services to Rubinstein, for fear of being slapped with a felony violation for transporting an endangered species across state lines. And now it had happened.

MOLT TOLD Crutchfield he wanted his money first. Then he'd think about flying to Florida.

The next day, Fred Ohlinger called. Molt, who hadn't taped a conversation since 1974, let the answering machine record. Molt told him the same thing he told Crutchfield: he would not consider a meeting unless he was paid first. Ohlinger promised to put $5,000 of Crutchfield's money in escrow until Molt's cooperation could be assured. If all went well, Ohlinger said, Molt would receive it, perhaps even more.

It took several more conversations over several days before Molt figured out what, exactly, Ohlinger and Crutchfield were scheming. Ohlinger and Crutchfield planned to file a motion for a new trial, based on the premise that the four Fiji iguanas had been Hank Molt's lizards all along. "That was the rusty nail they were gonna hang their weak hat on," Molt said.

Obviously the San Diego Zoo fit into this scenario, too, if Tom Schultz was involved, and it would all have to be hammered out fast—they had only a few weeks to file.

CRUTCHFIELD AND Ohlinger nervously awaited an answer from Molt.

"By now I am thinking that these guys are totally nuts, totally out of control," Molt said. "We're crossing the border from wildlife violations into perjury, obstruction of justice." It was so reckless a scheme, he thought, that it might not be real. Crutchfield and Ohlinger could be trying to entrap him, hand him to Mike Rubinstein in exchange for a lighter sentence for Crutchfield.

But if Ohlinger and Crutchfield were serious, Molt realized, he could do the reverse—hand them to Rubinstein and get his own charges reduced, or even dropped. He had to decide quickly: Rubinstein's office had just contacted Molt, demanding he show up in Tampa for processing on his felony charge.

Molt phoned Ohlinger. He'd thought it through, he said, and he was ready to help, but only if Ohlinger came to Philadelphia, alone. Ohlinger balked, but Molt insisted.

Crutchfield's attorney arrived the next day on a flight from Tampa, dressed in golfing clothes. Molt sat waiting for him at the gate. Ohlinger refused to talk at the coffee shop in the airport; instead, he rented a room at the airport Econolodge, where he patted Molt down for recording devices.

Ohlinger, a heavy smoker, lit cigarette after cigarette as he talked. He proposed that Molt sign an affidavit swearing that the four Fiji iguanas were his reptiles, and that he had delivered them to Crutchfield on March 13, 1989. It was a day that Molt had actually been at Crutchfield's. He'd been delivering smuggled Woma pythons from Stefan Schwarz, but no one needed to know that. The point was that credible people, including the deputy curator of reptiles at the San Diego Zoo, could testify that they had seen him there.

Molt would have to fabricate receipts for a sale of the iguanas, Ohlinger continued. Molt said he thought it would be awfully hard to convince people that any of his Fiji iguanas had survived since his round-the-world collecting trip in 1973, which would have been the last time Fiji iguanas were legal. But Ohlinger said no, these lizards were to be called the offspring—or offspring of offspring—of the original iguanas. He had something in mind to help establish this, he said, that he'd explain later.

Molt assented to everything. "I said, 'Yeah, that's a really good idea, Fred'—it was the dumbest thing I'd ever heard of. And seriously dangerous shit, fabricating evidence."

Ohlinger's return flight to Tampa was at six o'clock that evening. By now it was four, and Ohlinger had one last item of business, a thick packet of papers that he tossed onto the bed "with a great dramatic gesture," Molt said. It was the San Diego Zoo's entire file on its storied Fiji iguanas— some eighty-eight pages in all, including feeding data, clutch laying dates and hatch dates, zoo association awards, and a long, meticulous series of studbook entries. The file, Ohlinger explained, contained all Molt needed to know to create four Fiji iguanas on paper. The idea was for Molt to claim that he'd held on to some iguanas since 1973, and secretly bred them.

Molt could use the zoo records as a model to create his own records. Oh-linger left the file with Molt to study.

Years later, Thomas Schultz claimed that Ohlinger must have obtained the copies of the San Diego Zoo records some other way—that whatever papers Molt saw could not have been the original file. Both Molt and Crutchfield insisted otherwise. The file "looked like someone took it out of a drawer and handed it over," Molt said—entries were handwritten in ink, older papers were yellowed, and the whole thing was shot through with separator pages and colored tabs. "Schultz gave them to me," Crutchfield said of the records. "How the hell else would you get them?"

At 4:30, Crutchfield called the Econolodge. Ohlinger assured him that they had a deal. Molt and Ohlinger had drafted an affidavit, which Ohlinger would have typed and faxed to Molt the next day. Molt would sign it, notarize it, FedEx it back to Florida, and receive the $5,000 he'd been trying to collect for the better part of a year. Crutchfield and Ohlinger would file a motion for a new trial.

Ohlinger handed the phone to Molt. Crutchfield, on the other end, sounded happy and relieved. He asked Molt what he thought of the San Diego Zoo file. "Tom thought it was just fantastic, a magic bullet," said Molt, who was finally certain that Crutchfield and Ohlinger were not setting him up, but crazy enough to believe they would get a new trial out of all this. Instead, "they handed me their ass on a golden platter," Molt said.

The next morning, Molt's fax machine spit out the false affidavit from Ohlinger's office in Florida. In March 1989, Molt claimed, he'd delivered four Fiji banded iguanas to Crutchfield in Fort Myers. The iguanas were, he went on, "captive-bred progeny of my founder stock of Fiji banded iguanas which I personally collected in the Fiji islands and imported to the United States in 1973, not subject to the provisions of CITES nor the Endangered Species Act permit requirements."

Molt did not sign the affidavit or return it. Instead he packed it up, along with the zoo files, his answering machine tapes, and two jarred iguanas, and drove straight to the U.S. Attorney's office in Tampa.

MIKE RUBINSTEIN found Hank Molt more likable than he'd expected—
cerebral and businesslike, a refreshing contrast to Crutchfield's huffing and
puffing. He spared Molt the drama of being fingerprinted and photographed at the Tampa courthouse, which Molt appreciated. Molt surrendered himself with a signature, and sat on the other side of Rubinstein's
desk like a colleague.

The reality, though, was that Molt was looking at some prison time.
A year, Rubinstein insisted. "For babysitting a couple of lizards?" Molt
scoffed, and Rubinstein thought that was funny. Molt said he would not
agree to any deal that involved prison, and for good reason—he had something interesting to offer. Molt presented Rubinstein with Ohlinger's false
affidavits, the San Diego Zoo files, answering machine tapes of his conversations with Ohlinger, and color photos of his pickled Fiji iguanas, in their
jars. The actual iguanas were in the car, he explained—he didn't think the
security guards would want him bringing them in.

Rubinstein was not entirely surprised. "Crutchfield and Ohlinger
seemed to be doing stuff behind the scenes and we were sort of aware
of it," he said. Molt informed Rubinstein that Crutchfield and Ohlinger
were waiting for a FedEx containing the signed affidavit. They had only
four days left to move for a new trial, and they were increasingly desperate,
Molt said. Maybe they could be lured to Tampa to discuss and sign the false
affidavit in person—and be caught in the act?

Rubinstein called the U.S. Fish and Wildlife Service, and a plan
emerged to arrange a meeting and to bug a hotel room. "We went to Wal-
Mart and bought a baby monitor," said Eddie McKissick, one of the agents
working with Rubinstein. "I thought it was so funny—I'm a brand-new
agent and I thought we had all this surveillance technology." But Fish and
Wildlife was not the FBI, and McKissick found himself in the nursery aisle.

Adjoining hotel rooms were rented and prepared—one for Molt, another
for the wildlife agents. Molt helped them scratch for places to conceal their

device. From his room Molt placed the first call to Ohlinger, who accepted his explanation that he had flown to Tampa and had issues to discuss in person. Crutchfield and Ohlinger agreed to drive to Tampa the next morning.

That night, Molt hit the Tampa strip clubs and drank himself into a stupor. When Molt's alarm went off at six a.m., he had a terrible hangover and a strange woman in his room, "a homeless chick," he said, whom he kicked out.

The wildlife agents came on time, but Ohlinger and Crutchfield never showed. They'd been edgy about the plan from the start, and with a whole night to think about it, they had changed their minds. Something about Molt's behavior struck Crutchfield as weird. Why had he come down on his own, without so much as calling?

"After a while it became clearer that it was a setup," Crutchfield said.

Crutchfield sat in Ohlinger's office, unsure what to do next. And then Molt called. "I got Tom on the phone," Molt said. "Tom was getting nervous and at some point I made a slip of the tongue to one of the agents. He said, 'Are you alone?' and got off the phone."

After that, Crutchfield said, Molt "kept calling and calling in that soothing Hank voice." Crutchfield let Ohlinger handle Molt's calls. "I said, 'Tell him we're not fucking coming,'" Crutchfield said. "He kept calling and calling and finally we quit answering the phones."

After several hours, the agents retrieved their baby monitor and informed Mike Rubinstein of their failure. They walked Molt to his car, where he handed over his jars of iguanas.

It was by no means the triumphant unveiling he'd envisioned, but "there was no point in running around with them in my car anymore," he said.

RUBINSTEIN NEVER sought criminal charges against Ohlinger and Crutchfield for their scheme. He did manage to quash their motion for a new trial, a motion that—not surprisingly, given the time frame they had—was hastily cobbled together and a total mess.

Molt, undaunted and still bitter about the $5,000 Crutchfield owed him, launched his own, extrajudicial campaign against Ohlinger and Crutchfield.

That August, Molt stormed into the reptile house of the Columbus Zoo, claiming certain of its snakes were rightfully his—Crutchfield had not paid him for them, he explained, and the zoo could expect to hear from Molt's lawyers if they didn't come up with a plan. The zoo, spooked enough as it was by Crutchfield's Fiji iguana affair, cut its ties to Crutchfield. "Hank ruined all my accounts there," said Crutchfield, who was discovering how it felt to be a zoo-world pariah.

A week later, a thirteen-page fax arrived at the San Diego Zoo's reptile house, addressed to Thomas Schultz. Molt had sent it in the middle of the night "so that in the morning it would be like toilet paper all over the floor," he said.

*Tom,*

*The purpose of this communication is to make you aware of a potentially very dangerous situation which is ongoing at this time. There could possibly be serious consequences involving you and the San Diego Zoo. This matter concerns Tom Crutchfield and his recent court case involving Fiji iguanas. Let me begin by saying that I realize you and Tom are very close friends and it is not my intent to have any influence on that. I am just going to report to you a series of FACTS, ABSOLUTE COLD, CLEAR FACTS and you can decide how you need to handle this information.*

Molt went on to describe his series of calls and meetings with Crutchfield and Ohlinger. Most curious, wrote Molt, was the San Diego Zoo's eighty-eight-page Fiji iguana file, which Ohlinger had tossed onto the hotel room bed. It seemed remarkably authentic, Molt said, and he still possessed it—or rather, the government now did, and "I intend to fully cooperate with the US government in any investigations or legal proceedings," Molt informed Schultz.

"I knew Tom Schultz, how to push his buttons. I wasn't out to get him,

I was out to get Tommy," Molt said. "I knew that by going through the San Diego and Columbus zoos I could."

AT CRUTCHFIELD'S sentencing hearing that fall, Rubinstein presented letters from scientists attesting that Fijians do not eat Fiji iguanas, as Fred Ohlinger had boldly and repeatedly claimed. Three local Baptist pastors sent letters on Crutchfield's behalf, but not one zoo came to his aid, which hurt his feelings.

Crutchfield was sentenced to seventeen months in prison and two years' probation. Penny received a year of house arrest and probation. Crutchfield, not humbled by any of it, announced that he would appeal the verdict. Since Hank Molt was not going to cooperate, his appeal would have to be based on something else. Crutchfield focused his ire on Rubinstein.

*Dear Customer,* Crutchfield began his January 1993 price list. *I would like to thank all of you for your patronage in 1992. It was our most successful year yet. My staff and myself wish all of you a very Happy and Prosperous New Year.*

*At this time I would like to explain some of the details and circumstances of the problems we had in 1992 and dispel many rumors. First of all I am not in jail and have not been in jail. It is true that I was convicted for 4 wildlife violations in 1992. I am not guilty of the crimes I am charged with committing. Early on I could have engaged in a plea bargain of substantially less penalty than I received but I cannot plead guilty to something I did not do . . .*

*The first person that played perhaps the most important role in this persecution was the Asst. U.S. Attorney Michael Rubinstein, a customer of mine dating back to the late 80s. Mr. Rubinstein probably has a great future in politics as he has all the major qualifications. This trial incidentally was conducted at the exact same time the Earth Summit was being held in Brazil. The U.S. is the only country in the world that did not sign the agreement. I believe that our persecution and prosecution was as much politically motivated as inspired by our heinous criminal behavior . . .*

*In the next few months we will be updating you on the facts about the case so stay tuned next month for another episode of "As the Stomach Turns." You Reptile Dealers might want to check your mailing list and see if Mr. Michael Rubinstein at 510 Bosphorus Ave., Tampa, Florida, is on your list.*

HANK MOLT'S wife and daughter moved to Atlanta. They didn't consult with him extensively before doing so. If he chose to come along, his wife said, he could sleep in the garage.

The garage was fine with Molt. There he had plenty of time to ruminate. Molt's lingering bitterness over Crutchfield's $5,000—money Crutchfield had zero intention of paying—had swelled into an all-consuming vendetta.

Years later Crutchfield would wonder whether money was really the source of Molt's fury. "I was perplexed why he even got mad," Crutchfield said. "My whole life I never did anything except help him. He never did anything but cheat me since I was a kid." All Crutchfield could think—the only thing that made sense—was that Molt had been secretly envious of him for years, and now saw his chance to destroy him.

Molt stepped up his cooperation with the U.S. Fish and Wildlife Service and Michael Rubinstein, making frequent trips to Tampa. Rubinstein was coming to like the wildlife-prosecution genre, and appreciated Molt's tutelage. In meeting after meeting, Molt lectured Rubinstein on reptile smuggling in general, adding a few specifics "against people that I had a personal bitch with," Molt said. "I wasn't just gonna rat anyone out."

Molt provided Rubinstein the full story, complete with names and dates, on Crutchfield's illegal exports of Bismarck ringed pythons to Germany. The story implicated Molt's old friend Eddie Celebucki, but Molt didn't care. "My goal was to get that ringed python thing turned into another indictment for Tommy," Molt said. "Ed and those guys were collateral damage."

EDDIE CELEBUCKI was surprised to see Molt.

Celebucki was remarried with a new baby, and had just bought a pet store called Jungle Friends, on the east side of Cleveland, when Molt walked in from the cold. It was mid-January 1993, and Molt told Celebucki that he was in the process of moving his stuff from Philadelphia to Atlanta, and thought he'd stop by. Celebucki knew Molt well enough to know that "he never just stops by. There is always a secondary motive," Celebucki said, "and Philadelphia is seven hours away."

Molt stood and talked while Celebucki cleaned cages. Suddenly, a large glass aquarium broke in Celebucki's grasp. A shard of glass had cut Celebucki's hand deeply enough that he needed stitches, and Molt accompanied him to the hospital. In the emergency room, while Celebucki waited, they talked, and Celebucki let slip the name Kevin O'Donnell, the blind janitor they'd trained together years before.

Molt insisted on a generous cut of any scheme he'd helped design, in perpetuity. Molt had designed, and contributed some money to, Blind Man's Bluff, the plot to have O'Donnell suitcase snakes out of Rabaul, New Guinea. So for years, Celebucki had made a point of never mentioning O'Donnell, or the fact that the blind man was still running snakes for him. When Celebucki had shown up at Crutchfield's with a cache of Bismarck ringed pythons, and bumped into Molt there, he claimed to have smuggled the ringed pythons himself. Molt believed Celebucki then.

This time, "something about what Ed was telling me wasn't jiving," Molt said. Celebucki's cut hand was throwing him off. Celebucki, not having the energy to persist in a lie, blurted out the truth: It was O'Donnell making the trips, and he would leave on another by the end of the week.

A month later, Kevin O'Donnell was arrested in Los Angeles with twenty-six Bismarck ringed pythons in his luggage. "We had information that if we checked his bags we would find the snakes," said Marie Palladini, the arresting agent. Palladini said the tip had come through Tampa, by way of the U.S. Attorney's office.

Celebucki suspected a Molt hand in O'Donnell's arrest. "Hank had called me and said, 'You should have your guy get rid of the stuff.' But by then he'd already tipped them off," he said. "It was the typical Hank m.o., covering his ass."

O'Donnell told Palladini everything he knew about Eddie Celebucki. Five years earlier, when one of her colleagues had confiscated Celebucki's shipment of Boelen's pythons at the L.A. airport, Palladini had opened an investigation into Celebucki that went nowhere. She regretted shelving that case, particularly since it involved the Knoxville Zoo. Unlike some of her colleagues at Fish and Wildlife, Palladini had no qualms about going after zoos, and felt they weren't targeted frequently enough.

Palladini located her old Celebucki files—she figured they would be of use, someday.

MOLT AND Rubinstein agreed that Molt would plead guilty to a single misdemeanor for having transported an endangered species across state lines. For this he would receive two years' probation, during which he was to stay out of the live-animal business; serve a hundred hours of community service; and pay a twenty-five-dollar fine.

While waiting to be formally sentenced, Molt resumed the vituperative letter-writing campaign that had begun with his fax to Thomas Schultz. After that, Fred Ohlinger had shot Molt a letter accusing him of libel, which only spurred Molt to further extremes. In the sanctuary of his wife's garage, Molt cut out and photocopied ghoulish images—a vomiting rat, detached eyes, frogs clutching desperately to a log—onto the same pastel-colored, legal-size sheets he had once used for his price lists. These made for creepy visual prologues to the invective that followed. Crutchfield, he was sure, would be terrified by the images, for Crutchfield had spent time in Haiti and was taken with voodoo and magic and symbols. On a word processor, Molt drafted his letters in a Gothic, quasi-Victorian style marked by acute thesaurus abuse. "It was my poor man's fantasy of being a writer," he said.

> *Mr. and Mrs. Crutchfield:*
>
> *I am aware of the threats, rumors, and innuendos you have been spreading about me. Also, I understand that you are telling people that I am "CRAZY" because of the letters I have sent out. It would seem to me that simply telling the truth, reporting accurately events that really did take place, would be far from "CRAZY." Leaving aside the subtle epistemological issues that can always be summoned to cloud the obvious, I hold that the 88 pages of San Diego Zoo records are real. You can feel and touch them as well as see them. They are not a figment of my imagination. Likewise your idiot lawyer's visit to Philadelphia last July to see me and the resulting false affidavit are also real facts, as is all the additional evidence. All the money you have spent is real. Likewise the 3-177 form, the CITES export permit for 7 ringed pythons and the invoice for same, as well as the Lufthansa air waybill and customs export applicable to that transaction are real, tangible, existing items. There is no alchemy in the universe that can make those documents magically disappear . . .*

Molt continued at length.

"Tom," he concluded,

> *You are a man who in your prime used fear as your instrument of personal satisfaction. The satisfaction of your reputation, so carefully cultivated, led to the culmination of all that has now befallen you, where, I am sure, your life consists of many frustrations and few satisfactions. But planning was never a feature of your work. It is not apparent that the SIMPLE TRUTH, by impartial plenojure, will soon render its hard verdict and you*

*will soon harvest the bitter seeds you have sown in the cold and acrid cup that awaits you at the end of your rainbow. The truth remains the truth no matter how loud the clamor of your denial.*

*Anon, when your appeal is denied, nobody will accuse you and Fred of perspicacity. And then it will be time for a new song. "I Am Tom Terrific" will no longer be appropriate. A Medieval threnody may be more suitable for the imprecation you have brought upon yourself . . .*

*I realize it is never over until the fat lady sings. However, if you listen carefully you can hear her rehearsing the stygian dirges in chambers not so distant.*

Enclosed were photos of two Fiji iguanas, preserved in alcohol.

MOLT COMPOSED letters similar in tone and intent to Fred Ohlinger and Eddie Celebucki, and on April Fool's Day 1993 sent copies of all the letters he had written over the previous three months, reprinted in a palette of pastel shades, to all parties involved, complete with cover art and a table of contents. It was a courtesy, he explained, to keep everyone from having to fax the stuff around. "Most importantly, this saves paper, and since Tom was so concerned that President Bush did not sign the Rain Forest Treaty, I thought I would do my small part to save our ecosystem. Thank you all very much and have a nice day."

Shortly after sending the packages, Molt headed off to the Chattahoochee National Forest to serve his sentence of a hundred hours' community service. There, in the cool mountain creeks, he conducted trout surveys with foresters. "They were worried about the dust and silt and runoff from highway construction and whether the trout could lay their eggs," Molt said. "We slept in tents. We had electric shockers with gasoline generators on our backs and we'd net off a hundred yards of river at a time. We stuck these things in the water and all these fish would float to the surface and we'd record how many species came up." This was fine with

Molt, who loved to be out in the woods. He was invited to serve as the project's herpetologist, identifying the stunned frogs and salamanders that floated up with the fish.

No one heard from Molt again for years. "He just sort of dropped off the face of the earth," said Crutchfield.

THE NEXT year, Tom Crutchfield fired Fred Ohlinger, and his new attorney successfully appealed his conviction on the basis of prosecutorial misconduct. Crutchfield had yet to serve any prison time.

Michael Rubinstein, the appeals court ruled, had been out of line for eliciting any mention whatsoever of Penny Crutchfield's sexual history and for his "countless irrelevant inquiries seemingly designed only to display to the jury his own expertise in the reptile field," among other offenses. Crutchfield was free to pursue a new trial. His new attorney counseled Crutchfield to accept a plea agreement instead. Crutchfield pleaded guilty to a single charge of receiving, concealing, and facilitating the transport of Fiji iguanas. It would mean five months, not seventeen, in jail.

"I felt avenged," Crutchfield said.

Rubinstein felt humiliated. Tampa newspapers ran his photo, with news of the reversal, on their front pages. Rubinstein had wanted badly to prosecute more wildlife cases at a time when, he felt sure, bigger ones would be coming. Crutchfield had killed that hope.

IN MAY 1994, federal prosecutors in Ohio indicted Eddie Celebucki for crimes committed on six separate smuggling trips to New Guinea—some on his own, some using Kevin O'Donnell—dating back to 1986, when he'd shown up in Port Moresby with a turtle trophy for the agriculture minister.

O'Donnell faced only misdemeanor charges. Molt, who had a hand in several of O'Donnell's trips, was not charged. The Knoxville Zoo, the designated recipient of so much of Celebucki's contraband, was not even mentioned. Six months later, Rabaul, New Guinea, was buried by a volcano.

Celebucki spent much of his prison term reading Buddhist texts, though he thought about Molt more than he would have liked to. "I've been abandoned by virtually everyone in my life," Celebucki said. "Hank knew more about me than anyone else. Having him turn on me didn't help my abandonment issues."

Celebucki asked prison officials to transfer him to a boot-camp program as a way to shorten his term. There he was beaten up by fellow inmates who didn't believe anyone could get fifteen months for snake smuggling.

In Atlanta's financial district, a youthful crew of Starbucks employees met their new manager: Hank Molt. He took to the job well, as he had a talent for bossing around teenagers.

With the proceeds from Starbucks, Molt hired a carpenter to build a small, apartmentlike enclave in his wife's garage. This allowed him to live more comfortably.

# 15

## *Sanzinia*

The reversal of his conviction hardened Tom Crutchfield's abundant natural cockiness into the stone righteousness of the vindicated. Friends of Crutchfield's considered the reversal a pyrrhic victory; Crutchfield saw it as a moral one. Though he still had a five-month jail term to serve on the one charge he couldn't escape, he chose not to obsess over it. Hank Molt had stopped shooting off his terrorist tomes, and never again would Crutchfield squander a brain cell ruminating about Molt, the Dietleins, Anson Wong, Fiji iguanas, or Mike Rubinstein. "Prosecutorial misconduct"— the very sound of it delighted him.

Crutchfield was in a celebratory mood, and in August 1994, just before the annual reptile expo in Orlando, he ordered two Rolex watches from his customer and friend Frank Lehmeyer, a jeweler with an elegant shop in the Rhine River city of Speyer, Germany. Crutchfield had established a tradition of entertaining guests in the days leading up to the expo—a tradition he kept up even in the summer of his conviction—and Lehmeyer was always among those guests, often with his family in tow. Lehmeyer "always wanted really rare stuff," Crutchfield said, including the Bismarck ringed pythons fresh from Eddie Celebucki's suitcases. Legal formalities never much concerned Lehmeyer, who would put a snake in his own luggage and take it back to Germany if it saved paperwork. Lehmeyer paid on time, sometimes in jewelry. Once he brought Crutchfield a gold, snake-shaped belt buckle with emerald eyes, which Crutchfield cherished.

The year before, Lehmeyer had arrived complaining of some lingering ailment, a fever he'd caught in Madagascar. He had been arrested, on his very first trip there, trying to smuggle tree pythons and radiated tortoises back to Germany, and spent a week in jail. Lehmeyer's Madagascar story impressed Crutchfield, who had regarded his friend, until then, as a connoisseur, not a smuggler, and certainly not someone tough enough to withstand such an ordeal.

"If you want a good snake, you have to get it yourself," Lehmeyer explained.

IT HAD been years since Crutchfield wore a Rolex. Gold Rolexes were once his personal trademark and corporate calling card, to the point where rival reptile dealers started wearing them to keep up, but legal bills had forced him to go without. Frank Lehmeyer's watches were steel, not gold, but they were duty-free at least. Crutchfield kept one for himself. The other he gave Adamm Smith, his number-two and his increasingly close confidant.

Smith was the young man who had lived for years with Crutchfield's enemies, the Dietleins, then redeemed himself to Crutchfield by humiliating them in federal court. He showed up in Lake Panasoffkee a month or so later, and Crutchfield rewarded him with his own business. Or rather, Crutchfield led Smith to believe that Tropical Fauna, Inc., was his own business; Smith never saw the incorporation papers, which made no mention of him. Tropical Fauna was indistinguishable in every way from Tom Crutchfield's Reptile Enterprises—same storefront, same mailing address, same phone and fax—but for its name, and that it was a licensed importer and exporter of wildlife. Crutchfield furnished its Lake Panasoffkee offices with a big, glossy new conference table and a towering leather chair that his employees called "the throne." The license was Smith's; the throne was Crutchfield's.

Crutchfield—after a very brief period of circumspection—was back to welcoming visitors with suitcases. His old friend and manager Dwayne Cunningham, who had a new job as a juggler and comedian on cruise ships, was returning from the Caribbean with island rarities he'd hide in the cabins until his ship cleared customs, and Crutchfield had always been weak for island rarities. Thomas Schultz of the San Diego Zoo was coming around Lake Panasoffkee once more, too, for days at a time, and was swapping animals with Crutchfield again.

Years before, Schultz had bought from Crutchfield some baby Woma pythons that Hank Molt had received in cassette tape cases from Australia. Now Schultz was trading Crutchfield the offspring of those same Womas, which Crutchfield listed as "zoo-bred" on his mailings. Frank Lehmeyer took a few of these zoo-bred Womas back to Germany as payment for the Rolexes. It was beautiful, the way it all worked out.

AND YET the reptile trade was expanding faster than Crutchfield could keep on top of.

Some two million American households now kept reptiles, according to the American Pet Product Manufacturers Association, and the figure would nearly double by the decade's end. Reptile conventions imitating Wayne Hill's Orlando expo popped up in civic centers and school gymnasiums around the country. Species that were easily bred—leopard geckos, bearded dragons, ball pythons, and green iguanas—the herpetoculturists were breeding commercially, and these were becoming as standard in pet stores as gerbils. They were a better product than the imported reptile pets of the past, since they were free of parasites and not beat up from long journeys. After the 1993 movie *Jurassic Park,* cheap, farm-raised green iguanas, with their little velociraptor faces, emerged as a fad pet, and pricier snake morphs began to make their way into pet store chains, too, as did specialty books, specialty foods, frozen mice, and all kinds of products for lighting, watering, and disinfecting reptiles. The popularity of pet reptiles necessitated a different type of reptile business, and in the vacuum left by a weakened Crutchfield a new class of superdealer emerged.

Strictly Reptiles was a volume dealer on a scale the trade had never before seen. Strictly's proprietor, Ray Van Nostrand, was of the same generation as Crutchfield and Hank Molt, with roots in the freewheeling animal trade of the 1960s. But the Van Nostrand family, unlike Molt or Crutchfield, put business before personal prestige, zoo accounts, or rare specimens. Strictly's bread and butter was farm-raised green iguanas, which it imported from Central America in lots of thousands and wholesaled to chains like Petco and PetSmart, which were expanding aggressively throughout the 1990s. Strictly also received all manner of wild reptiles from Mohamad Hardi and from Anson Wong, who after parting ways with Crutchfield sent his massive, miscellaneous shipments to Strictly.

Crutchfield could only stand by and watch as Strictly ballooned, dubbing itself "the Iguana King" and moving into hangarlike new headquarters. "They didn't mind the losses and the huge quantities and selling cheap," Crutchfield said. "Morally, I did mind that, I really did." Sick and dehydrated ball pythons got tossed into Strictly's Dumpster, only to be salvaged by neighborhood children. When local veterinarians complained about school kids marching in with listless, half-dead snakes, state wildlife officers padlocked the Dumpster. In Crutchfield's best year, he'd sold two million dollars' worth of reptiles; the Van Nostrand family sold $8 million.

Reptiles were becoming a commodity divorced from science and zoos. To a younger generation of reptile buyers, accustomed to morphs and mutations, the color of an animal mattered more than the species; its natural history was a distant afterthought. The trade magazines changed with the times. Where *The Vivarium* had taken pains to establish a lofty, scientific tone, the newest magazine on the pet store stands, *Reptiles,* had no such pretensions. *Reptiles* went for neon-colored headlines—THINK SKINK!—and glossy lizard centerfolds. Its articles were full of grammatical errors. Eventually, *The Vivarium* folded, leaving *Reptiles* to dominate the Petco checkout.

GIVEN THE size of the reptile market, it was all too foreseeable that the U.S. Fish and Wildlife service would ponder another reptile sting. After the Atlanta Wildlife Exchange, in the early 1980s, the reptile dealers never lost their fears of one, and continued to assume that the Feds were always near. Any strange telephone call, inquiring into a species of dubious provenance, had to be a Fish and Wildlife agent. Anyone snapping pictures at the expo—a Fed for sure. But the dealers allowed greed to trump caution. Novel snake morphs were starting to fetch new-car sums, making the $7,000 apiece Crutchfield had paid for his albino Burmese pythons, back in 1981, seem quaint. There was simply more money in the system, so much money that it made the old snake men's jaws drop.

The agents suspected that all the captive breeding, all the expensive morphs and mutations, were not making smuggling obsolete, as dealers frequently claimed. Rather, they created a larger, more lucrative market for reptiles in general, including illegal ones. In the mid–1990s, the reptile trade remained "almost unregulated," said Rick Leach, a Fish and Wildlife agent who had helped out with the Atlanta Wildlife Exchange, and later investigated parrot smugglers in an elaborate three-year sting. "Reptiles were still coming into the country by tens of thousands and not only were common things coming in for the pet trade, but some of the rarest species," Leach said. Wildlife was trickling out from previously unknown conduits in Africa, Eastern Europe, the former Soviet Union, and Madagascar.

Madagascar was particularly worrisome. Its endemic animals were both coveted and highly endangered, and after decades of isolation, it was becoming a target for foreign opportunists. In 1993, some Germans had been shot and killed there while removing reptiles from a northern forest. The circumstances of the shooting were extremely murky, and the agents had never heard of anyone being shot dead over reptiles. "That certainly got our attention," said Leach's colleague, agent Ernest Mayer. Then, the agents started noticing huge quantities of Madagascar's CITES-listed animals on price lists like Crutchfield's.

Leach proposed to his bosses an undercover reptile operation. George Morrison and Ernest Mayer, both veteran agents, signed up immediately. "I mean, did we really want to do another elk case?" said Mayer. They chose the West Coast for their base, since so many of the questionable reptiles seemed to be entering the country from Asia.

As "PacRim Enterprises," the agents rented a 5,000-square-foot warehouse in Livermore, California. Mayer had recently seized a shipping container full of shells and corals for bad paperwork, and sent the container to PacRim. Corals and shells weren't what the agents had in mind, but they were wildlife products, and PacRim had a warehouse to fill.

The agents felt sure PacRim would work. It had been fifteen years since the Atlanta Wildlife Exchange, and there were so many newcomers to the reptile market that another was unlikely to incur suspicion. And as an investigative strategy, a front business was an oldie but a goodie. It had worked magnificently against the illegal parrot trade, and "it's the only way profit can be dumped back into an investigation," said Mayer. "If we were wholly dependent on the government, we'd never be able to do it."

For eight months, the agents bleached the shipload of corals and tried to hatch some sort of plan, when all they had were names. "We asked ourselves, Who were the biggest reptile dealers? Anson Wong, Hardi, Van Nostrand, Crutchfield," Mayer said. Ken McCloud, another agent working with the team, had been following the German jeweler Frank Lehmeyer. "We looked at Hank Molt, too," said Mayer, but left him alone when they found him working at Starbucks.

PacRim accumulated reptiles gradually. Wildlife inspectors at the ports sent over animals they'd confiscated for bad paperwork. When PacRim had amassed a respectable number, it introduced itself to the world, fittingly enough, in the classified pages of *Reptiles* magazine.

ATTENTION JOBBERS: West Coast Import/Export company
looking to establish long-term business relationships with jobbers

in all 50 states. We import mostly high-end herps from around the world. Terms available.

UNLIKE STRICTLY Reptiles and the newer dealers on the scene, Tom Crutchfield still cared deeply about his relationships with zoos, and about restoring his reputation among them. After the reversal of his conviction, he enticed Randal Berry, a reptile keeper who'd bounced around Texas and Arkansas zoos, to move to Florida and work for him. Crutchfield noted boldly on his price lists that a card-carrying member of the American Association of Zoological Parks and Aquariums had joined his business. "He had my name on that list a month before I even got there," Berry said.

Hiring Berry was a coup for Crutchfield, since zoos, at the time, were going ever further out of their way to avoid associations with the animal trade as they strained to deal with their newest public relations mess: surplus animals. Zoo breeding programs had begun in the politically charged 1970s and '80s as a way for zoos to end their reliance on the commercial wildlife trade, and then, ostensibly, as a way to save species from extinction. But many zoos had since overbred their stock, even their endangered species, to attract a public that, it turned out, loved nothing more than to see baby animals every year.

So, having little choice, zoos quietly offloaded extra animals onto the same animal dealers, hunting camps, and circuses that they had so publicly cut ties with before. In the 1990s, even the National and San Diego zoos were exposed for selling off highly endangered species to ranches and circuses. The ark—long careening—had finally sunk. The zoo association needed an entirely new rationale for zoos' continued existence, and it now had tough constituencies to appease—vocal groups such as People for the Ethical Treatment of Animals, a fiercer, more radical organization than the Humane Society of the United States had ever been. PETA had huge budgets and mailing lists and strident slogans, the most disturbing of which was "Never Visit Zoos."

The zoos' answer was to position themselves as part of the broader conservation community. They began sponsoring conservation efforts in the field, some serious and others trivial. Some changed their names: The Bronx Zoo's parent organization, the New York Zoological Society, became the Wildlife Conservation Society in 1993. Everywhere, zoo visitors were deluged with information about endangerment, biodiversity, global warming, and the evils of the wildlife trade, and asked to donate spare change to gorilla projects in the Congo. Keepers were encouraged to publish scientific papers on the diets or behavior of their charges, whether or not they had ever published a paper in their lives.

In 1994, the American Association of Zoological Parks and Aquariums changed its name to the American Zoo and Aquarium Association, finally excising the word "parks" and its historic affiliations with amusement and recreation. This was serious, this conservation stuff; there was nothing fun about it.

CRUTCHFIELD ALLOWED Randal Berry and his wife to squat in the Dietleins' old house in Bushnell, which stood half derelict now, its electricity siphoned from Crutchfield's across the way. A few of its rooms were closed off, and there were mysterious giant holes in the drywall. Next door to it was the old Herpetofauna barn, and that was permanently locked under some sort of court order. Crutchfield forbade anyone to go near it.

For Berry, the whole appeal of moving to Crutchfield's was to work with rare reptiles, and he was not disappointed. "I saw better snakes and reptiles and amphibians than ever in my zoo career," he said. In that sense, Crutchfield was still the top dealer around. Strictly Reptiles was richer, but "Strictly was in the middle of the green iguana craze, zillions of iguanas," said Berry. Crutchfield had things like albino alligators, which looked as though they were carved from soap and sold for $125,000 each. It thrilled Berry just to hold one.

Berry soon learned, however, that his exalted status as a zoo guy afforded him no protection against Crutchfield's rages. Berry and Adamm Smith had to replace cordless phones all the time because Crutchfield hurled them at walls when they lost their charge. "Just the way Tom would talk to you, it was like Gomer Pyle and Sergeant Carter, nose to nose. He was very manipulative and intimidating and talked in that mean voice. He'd make you want to go shoot yourself," Berry said. Smith wore a Crutchfield Rolex, but he feared his boss as much as Berry did.

The climate of fear was mitigated by Crutchfield's generous gifts to his employees, including guns and knives that "we never used," said Berry. "We just liked to pretend we were Clint Eastwood all day." Often, without warning, Crutchfield doled out cash bonuses. "Put that in your shoe," he'd say on a Friday evening, and slip Berry $600. On his best days, the tyrant pranced about the shop, filled with a child's enthusiasm, grunting happily to himself. Berry could not help but be charmed.

RANDAL BERRY was not so charmed by Crutchfield's German friend Frank Lehmeyer, who came around once or twice a year as he gained customers fast for the snakes and tortoises he was moving out of Madagascar. Lately Lehmeyer was bringing along a companion on his visits to Florida, a younger man named Wolfgang Kloe, whom Berry liked even less. Berry couldn't put his finger on what was sleazy about Lehmeyer and Kloe. It wasn't the way they looked or dressed so much as the way everyone acted around them.

Crutchfield usually told Berry what happened after every closed-door meeting, but not meetings with these two Germans. Adamm Smith was equally clandestine about Lehmeyer and Kloe. Smith was several layers closer to the boss than Berry, and Berry was starting to notice Smith's lies and obfuscations. Smith had recently flown to Brazil for Crutchfield, collecting Amazon tree boas that he shipped, falsely labeled, out of Suriname. "Adamm told me the snakes had been collected on the Suriname side of the river—that they'd swum across from Brazil. Then I looked at a map and saw the river was like ten miles wide," Berry said. In April 1995, when Crutchfield dispatched one of his low-level employees to Manhattan and put him up for two nights at the Waldorf Astoria hotel, Berry was roiled. But Adamm Smith cautioned Berry that he didn't want anything to do with this trip.

When the employee returned from New York City with a bag full of Madagascar tree boas, *Sanzinia madagascariensis,* Berry understood what the problem was. "I knew they were [CITES] Appendix I and illegal as hell," he said, and the whole thing stank to him of Lehmeyer and Kloe. Crutchfield insisted the snakes had been bred in Germany, and had all the accompanying paperwork. "I had a heart-to-heart with him," Berry said. "Tom denied any illegality. He pretended to listen to me. He said he had learned his lesson with the Fijis."

CRUTCHFIELD WAS thrilled with Lehmeyer's baby *Sanzinia* when he saw them. Few reptile enthusiasts had ever laid eyes on Madagascar tree boas. Usually they were brown. These, though, had notes of bright orange and red along their entire bodies. "Every single one was absolutely gorgeous," Crutchfield said. He called Lehmeyer to say so.

Lehmeyer informed Crutchfield that his checks totaling $14,000 from the Waldorf Astoria meeting had bounced. Crutchfield insisted it must have been a bank error, though it was more likely just his usual negligence; the electricity at his house had been shut off again, and Randal Berry had to plead with Florida Power & Light to get it turned back on.

Every day, sometimes more than once a day, Lehmeyer called Lake Panasoffkee, demanding his money. Wolfgang Kloe would call on Lehmeyer's behalf, or Lehmeyer's wife called, appealing to Penny. Kloe and Lehmeyer had yet to be paid when they arrived for the Orlando expo that August, with fresh Madagascan snakes and tortoises for their now-myriad customers, including, unfortunately for them, the undercover agent Ken McCloud.

McCloud knew more about reptiles than anyone else at Fish and

Wildlife. He styled himself as the snake guys did, with a ponytail and a goatee, and worked under one of those insipid pseudonyms the wildlife agents always seemed to pick: "Mark Phillips." Over dinner, Kloe and Lehmeyer complained about the $14,000 Crutchfield owed them. McCloud took note. McCloud had been following Lehmeyer for two years, but was only just starting to understand the Crutchfield connection. Hank Molt had informed Fish and Wildlife of that connection years before, in a valiant effort to get Crutchfield reindicted, but the agency had no central computer system then, and the information was missed.

CRUTCHFIELD HAD more on his mind than paying Kloe and Lehmeyer. He was about to serve his truncated sentence for the Fiji iguanas, a prospect that caused him to do the unthinkable—cancel his August pre-expo festivities. Foreign guests wouldn't be toasted at Catfish Johnny's this year, or get to throw dead rats to his crocodiles. But Crutchfield forced himself to attend the expo as a matter of pride, and since he could not avoid the two Germans there, he finally paid them. The following Monday, Penny Crutchfield drove her husband to the federal prison camp in Jesup, Georgia, where for five months he taught English to Mexicans, lifted weights, and read nature books in the library.

THE NEXT summer, in Madagascar, some seventy-five young plowshare tortoises were stolen from a British zoo's conservation post less than a mile from where the group of Germans had been shot three years earlier. This heist was spectacular and greedy and immediately big news. Plowshare tortoises, a golden, high-domed species, numbered less than a thousand in the wild, and maybe only a few hundred. Outside Madagascar there were just two in captivity, both of them ancient and one of them sterile. No form of paperwork could cover a plowshare tortoise; it was worse than a Fiji iguana.

Neither the Feds nor the reptile dealers had any idea who'd engineered so egregious a heist, though there were rumors about one Dutchman, and vague suspicions about Anson Wong. Crutchfield hoped no one would think he had stolen the tortoises—it was just too evil. Crutchfield wondered if Frank Lehmeyer had done it, since Lehmeyer had phoned a month before the theft, asking about the "market value" of plowshare tortoises, a species that hadn't been on the market since 1972. The plowshare theft was a mystery, but it was widely assumed, in the summer of 1996, that at least some of the tortoises would make their way to the Orlando reptile expo that August.

FRANK LEHMEYER elected not to attend the expo. After the plowshare incident, the expo would be swarming with Feds, and Lehmeyer was already starting to wonder whether one of his customers, the ponytailed Mark Phillips, wasn't one of them. He voiced his suspicions to Phillips in a phone call. McCloud and his colleagues hoped it was just Lehmeyer's nerves. "These guys get a heightened state of paranoia when they think something isn't right," said Ernest Mayer. "And remember, you've got this whole thing going on with plowshare tortoises. Everybody who was a possible suspect was running a little scared. A whole hornet's nest had been stirred up."

Lehmeyer said it was McCloud's behavior that had begun to alarm him—his "Mark Phillips" persona had been cultivated a little too enthusiastically in the reptile-rogue mold. "He had this long hair, cowboy boots. He would smoke in the nonsmoking section and then tell the waitress to fuck off," Lehmeyer said. "We started to make fun of him because he was asking for crazy things from Madagascar—'I need four aye-ayes, all wild caught.' We said, 'Oh yeah, Mark, okay.'"

Lehmeyer's anxieties prevented him from traveling to the 1996 expo, but not from sending animals. He and Kloe had collected so many by now that there was really little choice. Kloe was willing to travel to Florida and sell the animals, but not to carry them. So Lehmeyer hired a courier, a twenty-five-year-old Briton named Simon Harris, who insisted on being paid in snakes. At his house in Speyer, Lehmeyer supervised as his wife removed Harris's underwear from his suitcase and repacked it expertly with sixty-one *Sanzinia* and four baby radiated tortoises. The Lehmeyers drove Harris to the airport.

Wolfgang Kloe awaited Harris in Florida. Kloe had come early with his wife and daughters, and planned to take Harris's delivery at the Best Western Bushnell, the hotel closest to Crutchfield's place. He would sell what animals he could to Crutchfield and bring the rest to the expo. As smuggling plans go, it was all very simple and workable, but when Simon Harris reached Orlando on the evening of August 12, a customs inspector felt something wiggle.

Agent Ernest Mayer was in the airport when Harris was stopped. Mayer wasn't targeting Harris—he had never even heard of him. He was looking for reptile smugglers in general. "The only time these clowns would come into the country was at the reptile show," he said. What Harris confessed—that he had come to deliver Lehmeyer's animals to Wolfgang Kloe in a hotel right near Tom Crutchfield's place—"was like a gift," Mayer said.

SIMON HARRIS agreed to wear a wire and make his delivery to Kloe. If all went as the agents hoped, Kloe would drive the animals straight to Crutchfield's, and everyone would be arrested. In the morning, Ernest Mayer drove Harris to the Best Western Bushnell. Two teams of agents followed. Instead of finding Kloe, Harris found a note taped to Kloe's door telling Harris he'd left for the Waffle House, because the kids had gotten hungry. Mayer changed his mind then and there about tailing Kloe to Crutchfield's. "He's at the Waffle House for breakfast, with all these people there, and you've got family members involved. We had no guarantee he was going to go to Crutchfield's—are we gonna try to follow this person around for days?" The agents sent the wired-up Harris inside the Waffle House. They would arrest Kloe on sight.

Harris refused to sit down with Kloe's family, demanding instead that Kloe come out to the parking lot. There, the agents pushed Kloe to the ground. Kloe, said Mayer, "didn't seem to be too bad of a guy." He was a smallish man with feminine features who acted passive and cooperative, and the agents, who felt awful arresting Kloe while his daughters looked on, cuffed his hands in front of his body, for his dignity and comfort. Mayer took off toward Crutchfield's place, leaving the remaining agents to load Kloe and Harris into separate cars and drive them to Orlando. Many hours later, Mayer heard what happened next.

Kloe escaped his police car at a tollbooth, still handcuffed. He ran across ten lanes of the East-West Expressway, jumped over a railing, scrambled down an embankment, and found shelter in a plumbing-supply warehouse. He might have succeeded, had the warehouse workers not mistaken him for a thief. They seized him and held him, blue lights and sirens approaching. The newspapers noted that Kloe wore a T-shirt with an iguana on it, an iguana lounging on a beach chair.

CRUTCHFIELD KNEW he would be indicted the moment he heard about Kloe's arrest, but kept it to himself. His employees pressed him to tell them what he knew. "Tom was saying it had something to do with Madagascar tortoises, not us," said Randal Berry, but the truth became obvious hours later, when Tom Crutchfield's offices were raided by Ernest Mayer and his colleagues. Mayer had earlier driven straight to Crutchfield's from the Waffle House, figuring he'd shoot a few surveillance pictures before formally searching the shop. But Crutchfield discovered Mayer snooping, hopped in his truck, and ran Mayer off the road. "Not one of my more fond memories," said Mayer, who returned to Lake Panasoffkee that evening, with backup.

The agents signaled to Crutchfield from the door of Catfish Johnny's, where he was eating dinner. Crutchfield refused to leave until he had finished eating. Mayer was not surprised. "Tom Crutchfield was just Tom Crutchfield, kind of an arrogant blowhard," he said. "There had been enough contacts by different agents over the years to know what he was like."

The agents spent hours placing piles of paper into plastic evidence bags and pulling hard drives from computers, while Crutchfield's staff sat in terrified silence. Crutchfield, by contrast, "was real cocky and confrontational," said Randal Berry, who watched as agents took apart his .38-caliber pistol, a gift from the boss that he kept in a desk drawer. "But it also seemed like he was expecting it."

Crutchfield was more than expecting it, and in the hours between Kloe's arrest and Mayer's search, Tom and Penny Crutchfield decided to do something they had been mulling over a long time. They would "go somewhere tropical, where they speak English, sort of retire, you know, fuck the U.S.," Crutchfield said. Both Crutchfields had been quick to demand the return of their passports once their sentences on the Fijis were served. If they were ever indicted again, there would be no need for lawyers.

THE IMPLICATIONS of Kloe's arrest were lost on nobody at the expo. Copies of the *Orlando Sentinel* flew around the lobby of the Radisson Twin Towers. Kloe had been arrested in Bushnell—no one but Crutchfield lived anywhere near Bushnell. Crutchfield, who always had the best booth at the fair, stood behind his well-placed, well-advertised table, in plain sight of the world. But few dared walk up to him, so fierce and glowering was his face.

Hank Molt ventured to Orlando for the 1996 reptile expo. It was his first foray into the reptile world since his Starbucks exile, and Molt spent most of the weekend drinking Heineken and avoiding Crutchfield—who, he was sure, would beat him up on sight. Yet Molt could not help but feel a sublime redress in everything that was happening. He had failed to finish Crutchfield, but Tom Terrific would finish himself.

ADAMM SMITH disappeared from Crutchfield's the week after the raid. More Crutchfield employees quit in the weeks and months that followed, as the target letters poured in and Ernest Mayer rolled up in their driveways in a black SUV, asking questions. Mayer had lots of new information to badger them with. Wolfgang Kloe was cooperating with prosecutors in his eagerness to whittle down what threatened to be a very long prison sentence. Adamm Smith was meeting wildlife agents in hotel rooms, desperate to cut a deal. Randal Berry remained in Crutchfield's employ until the winter of 1997, when Ernest Mayer came around for a chat. Within a day of that unsettling experience, Berry and his wife loaded all their animals and possessions into U-Hauls and drove away forever. The Little Rock Zoo gave him his job back.

CRUTCHFIELD DIDN'T wait around for the indictment. He had no way to escape a conviction when everyone who had ever worked for him seemed to be cooperating with the government.

Crutchfield's new 1997 price lists in no way indicated there was anything amiss—but then, they never did. The year of the Fiji iguana trial was Crutchfield's "most successful year yet," as he told it to his customers. The new lists were timely, long, full of interesting animals and helpful veterinary tips. The only thing different about them was a notice at the bottom:

### FOR SALE

BEAUTIFUL property in Subtropical Sumter County, Florida. Property comes complete with wild herps such as Alligators, Gopher tortoises, etc. Sumter County is still one of the most unspoiled and sparsely populated areas in Florida!!

The U.S. Fish and Wildlife Service didn't get the hint. They were busy building a case against Crutchfield, a case so damning that it took thirty pages just to summarize, and failed to notice that though Crutchfield's lists kept coming in the mail, no one had actually seen Tom Crutchfield for a while.

On May 1, 1997, Crutchfield's probation officer faxed the U.S. district judge in Tampa. He had checked in to find only Penny at home, and she'd been nervous and evasive about her husband's whereabouts. Later that night, the officer wrote,

> Tom Crutchfield called me at my home and explained that the call was primarily a courtesy call. In the course of our conversation, he said that he had left the United States and did not intend to return. He said he had researched places to go that did not extradite him back to the United States for violation of his release or any new charges that he anticipates occurring. He would not say which country he was in. He said he anticipated new criminal charges and felt that he would not receive justice in the American court system as the government has all the advantages and would ultimately win.

HANK MOLT, who had little better to do that summer but sell coffee and savor Crutchfield's misfortunes, typed up a brief "herp news bulletin" announcing Crutchfield's arrest warrant, and circulated it to what remained of his mailing list. Then he drafted a letter to Penny:

> *Mrs. Crutchfield:*
> *Just a reminder that you still owe me $5,000 that you both cheated me out of back in 1991. I realize that I will probably never see that money but at least it gives me succor to finally see your decaying empire slowly grinding to an ignominious and agonizing death.*

*With the issuance of the Federal Arrest Warrant for Tom on May 8, 1997, the final chapters of the Crutchfield saga officially began. When you next talk to FUGITIVE TOM, ask him if he remembers back in '91 when he called the Dietleins in Canada and told them that "THEY CAN RUN BUT THEY CANNOT HIDE." Tom got a big laugh out of that. I wonder who is laughing now? Who else but Tom Terrific could make the pain last this long and cost him and his family so much? Do you have anyone you can solicit perjury from this time to try to save your butts? Why not hire the great Fred Ohlinger to save you from the Feds once again. He certainly was the best lawyer I ever came across.*

*As your and Tom's peregrination of pain plays out just remember that you two people have contrived your own ruin with a finality that not even your worst enemy could have achieved by unremitting malice. You and Tom have proven that there are no half-measures in treachery. No decisions can be made without a price, but if the wrong decision is made the future will take its inevitable revenge . . .*

*With a special appreciation of a delicate moment,*
*I remain faithfully yours,*
*Hank Molt*
***INCARCERATION THRU STUPIDITY!!!***

The letter never reached Penny Crutchfield. By then she had packed her family's possessions into shipping containers, gathered her daughters and her aging, infirm mother, sold the crocodiles, sold the farm, and joined her husband in Belize.

# 16

## Belize

Tom Crutchfield didn't know exactly what to do with himself in Belize, but he had enough money to start some sort of business, and when his wife and three of his daughters arrived, in the summer of 1997, it was agreed that the business would be rental cars. The girls made runs to Texas, buying Isuzu Troopers that they drove down the east coast of Mexico and into Belize. Crutchfield leased office space in the Biltmore Plaza Hotel in Belize City. When the family had enough Troopers, they opened shop as Iguana Car Rentals.

At first everything about Belize seemed to confirm Crutchfield's good judgment in moving there. He had an excuse to walk around with a machete a lot. He had spent much of his life dreaming about jungles, and here he was, so close that he could sometimes hear the throaty calls of jaguars at night. The girls loved wildlife as much as their father did, and were nearly as tough. On weekends they marched off into the forest with their dad and their binoculars and a Catholic priest who taught science at a local college and whom Crutchfield liked to interrogate about exorcisms.

The girls attended private schools, just as they had in Florida. It was important to Crutchfield that his daughters have certain advantages, because he had grown up poor. The family moved into a six-bedroom house. At night, the Crutchfields read books and ate fresh avocados and cracked each other up with conversations in Creole. Even Penny's mother, who was very sick with Alzheimer's, took well to her new surroundings, as "she didn't know what the hell was going on," said Crutchfield.

But then there were the inevitable third-world moments when it became painfully clear how far they were from home. A motorcycle crashed in front of the house, and the badly injured victim fell into a canal, forcing Crutchfield's fourteen-year-old daughter to jump in and save him, with no ambulance arriving for an hour. Everyone had to be bribed all the time. Crutchfield had to bribe officials with each new Trooper he registered, or else he would have paid 80 percent of its value in taxes. He did not, however, seek to bribe his way to quick Belizean citizenship—a move that would have guaranteed his freedom—because the going rate was $50,000, "which seemed a little stiff to me," he said, especially after buying all the cars. Instead, he decided to go about becoming Belizean the normal, non-fugitive way, by applying for temporary residency, the first step toward permanent residency and citizenship.

The U.S. Fish and Wildlife Service and the Justice Department figured out where Crutchfield was soon enough. They mailed him certified letters, which Crutchfield ignored, concentrating instead on designing ecotours he would run in addition to the car business. Already he'd taken a few car-rental clients into the jungles and to Mayan ruins, and he found himself to be good at it. He changed his business materials to read "Iguana Car Rentals and Eco Tours."

It had not occurred to Crutchfield that the U.S. government might want him—or any other reptile smuggler—badly enough to come get him. Ernest Mayer was tasked with extricating Crutchfield from his jungle paradise, "a pain in the ass," said Mayer. An extradition could take years, and Belize was not inclined to extradite, which was why Crutchfield had chosen it. "We needed to figure out how to get him arrested and held," Mayer said, but that was going to require some creativity.

In early 1998, Crutchfield began to wonder if he was under some sort of surveillance. His daughters claimed they'd been followed on their way home from school. One weekend, he was visiting the southern part of the country, hunting snakes with a friend, when he spied from his hotel window two white guys outside on the patio. They had that law-enforcement look, a look Crutchfield had come to recognize. Crutchfield dispersed them by storming onto the patio with a pissed-off expression and a machete in his hand. Suddenly, he wished he had fled to Thailand instead.

The next sign of something amiss was when a Belize City police officer was spotted parked outside the Biltmore Plaza, showing people a picture of Crutchfield before giving up and leaving. Crutchfield wondered if the cop would have arrested him or just questioned him. He received word from his friends that the cops were under pressure to arrest him from the U.S. government, which had, months before and totally unbeknownst to Crutchfield, flown two Belizean officers up to Miami for some Christmas shopping. This was Ernest Mayer's idea. "Belize was just so corrupt," Crutchfield said, which was fine when it came to avoiding duties on cars, but not when his freedom was at stake.

In late February 1998, nearly a year after his arrival in Belize, Crutchfield was arrested and taken to the Racoon Street jail in Belize City. Crutchfield found the Racoon Street jail to be about the most disgusting place he'd ever set foot in, until after three days he was transferred to the Hattieville prison, which was worse, and farther from his family's home. The United States had not made a formal extradition request, but merely asked Belize to expel Crutchfield. This Belize had every right to do, but no particular reason to do it, except as a favor to the Americans. Expulsion was like a backdoor extradition—and a contingency that Crutchfield had never envisioned.

The Belizeans did not disguise the fact that they'd put Crutchfield in jail just to placate the United States. Penny Crutchfield protested to the local newspapers that her husband posed no threat to public safety, and the Crutchfields hired a respected solicitor to plead his case. None of it did any good.

BELIZE HAD given Crutchfield the option to be deported at any time, but he chose to stick it out until his residency expired. He spent six months in an open-air cell, unprotected from biting insects and the occasional venomous snake or ocelot, defecating in a five-gallon bucket. He dodged a cholera epidemic that swept the prison.

Having deemed this ordeal a personal crucible, there was no turning back. "All my life I've been telling people I'm a tough guy, been telling myself that I'm a tough guy, and I thought if you're such a tough guy, make yourself put up with it," he said.

Crutchfield's whole family got to share in his test of will, making twice-weekly trips to Hattieville, where they could spend thirty minutes standing in an open field divided from the prisoners by two wire fences. If it started to rain, the guards made them go home.

A representative from the U.S. embassy came now and then to drop off magazines and toiletries for Crutchfield, and also to review with him the charges against him. Each time Crutchfield would thank her politely, express his lack of interest in the case, and distribute the toiletries to the other prisoners.

In August, Belize deported Crutchfield to Miami, where he was arrested on the tarmac and held at a federal detention center in the Everglades.

Penny and the girls abandoned the Isuzu Troopers in Belize. They packed up what they could and returned to north Florida, where they would have to live with Penny's sister until they figured out something better.

Crutchfield was transferred to a jail near Orlando, and having no recourse to bail, sat there for a year, working out a plea deal. There would be no dramatic cross-examinations, no pissing matches with prosecutors, no chameleon cages on the courthouse steps. It was inevitable now that he would spend considerable time in the federal penitentiary system.

It was all right, though, being back in Florida. Crutchfield had always preferred it to anywhere else in the world.

## Part III

# Dr. Wong

**Anson Wong** wore a stylish watch and a T-shirt that read "The Legend Continues." Thick gray streaks ran through his long hair. He was fifty now, but he looked fit and youthful, sort of Californian, and though he'd seen California mostly from the inside of a prison cell, he said, he'd harbored a desire to live there ever since. Wong was no longer allowed to set foot in the United States, even in transit.

Penang was no California. It was mostly Muslim, for one, with all the accompanying rules and anxieties, and the crimes there were Gothic. During my first visit, in 2006, masked thieves broke into a computer-parts factory and chloroformed all the employees, making away with millions of dollars' worth of parts. Wong refused to see me then. Two years and a few e-mails later, I visited Penang a second time, and while I was there a man was burned alive in his car dealership while thieves drove away twelve of his Mercedes-Benzes.

Wong was relaxed and garrulous. We sat in the courtyard of an empty hotel on the beach, a hotel Wong had chosen for me, and paid for. Wong was always interrupting himself to answer his cell phone, switching languages from Malaysian to Thai to Indonesian, depending on who called.

In the e-mails we had been exchanging before my visit, Wong would say teasing things about plowshare tortoises: "Would you be interested in who actually buys the 'crown jewels of tortoises'?" Wong had written. "How they get them out?" It had been twelve years since the big theft from Madagascar, and by now so many plowshare tortoises were showing up in Southeast Asia that the Bangkok airport displayed posters of baby plowshares, warning people not to smuggle them. A suitcase containing radiated and plowshare tortoises had been intercepted recently en route to Penang, but the case was never investigated. The local newspapers tried to implicate Wong.

It was known all around that Wong had been making frequent trips to Madagascar. The U.S. Fish and Wildlife Service believed he'd established some sort of business in the north, near Mahajanga.

Wong launched into a story about running into a Chinese restaurant owner in Mahajanga who kept plowshares. Wong said he told the Chinese, in his halting Mandarin: "I want these."

I interrupted Wong to ask when this was—"Just a couple weeks ago," he said.

Then the story ended abruptly. Wong had something to do. When he returned the next day, he revised it. The restaurant incident had happened a year ago, he said; he didn't go to Madagascar anymore. He didn't enjoy the "weird food, broken-down taxis." Instead, he said, he sent his staff members, but they were only collecting fossils. One of his staff members, on a recent fossil-collecting trip, had happened upon a huge cache of plowshare tortoises in Mahajanga.

Wong opened his laptop and scrolled through a series of photos that his staff member, he said, had taken. The photos showed plowshare tortoises, large and small, on sawdust, in a duffel bag, being held at waist height by a Malagasy man, then by a woman. Wong said the tortoises in the photos cost a thousand dollars apiece. They were being sold for food, he said.

That price, and the circumstances in which they were being kept—on clean sawdust, in what looked to be a clean apartment—did not suggest to me that they were headed to the food trade. It suggested to me that they were headed for Anson Wong, or someone a lot like him. The really odd thing was why he was showing me these photos at all.

Later, when a reporter for a Malaysian newspaper interviewed Wong, he opened his laptop for her and showed her the same photos. He said he had taken them himself, while on vacation in Zanzibar.

# 17

## Anson and Friends

Anson Wong had always loved rare animals, and the "goodies," as he called the illicit species he dealt in now and then, had less to do with making him money than with assuaging his boredom. Most of his business was in giant, legal bulk shipments, millions of wild geckos and frogs that ended up in crowded aquariums at Petland, if they made it that far. Volume was how Wong made his money, but volume was dull. Less dull were the shipments of something special—say, wild star tortoises from India—laundered through a third country as captive bred, a favor Wong sometimes did for Strictly Reptiles, his biggest customer in the 1990s.

It took an animal very rare indeed to get Wong's mind racing. Even the Fiji banded iguanas that had caused the whole Crutchfield fracas hadn't had that effect. A Swiss man had arrived in Penang one day with more than one hundred of them—"Two suitcases worth," Wong said, and Wong guessed that they weren't that hard to come by in Fiji if he'd gotten so many out. Wong had bought ten and sent four to Crutchfield, later getting bored with his own six and reselling them. "They were just iguanas," Wong said; over his fifteen years in business he'd had red pandas from Burma, hyenas, a Spix's macaw. But there were still animals that did it for him, and in November 1996, when a man in New Zealand called Wong about tuataras, he had that feeling again. "I had seen them at one of the zoos once—geez, where was it? You know how you see that dress and you want it? So the next payday you have to go buy it? That's how it was," Wong said. The caller was Freddie Angell, a dedicated wildlife smuggler who had been imprisoned twice already for stealing tuataras, some of which he'd swiped from a museum menagerie. Angell was presently incarcerated again, phoning Wong from jail.

New Zealand's tuatara is arguably the strangest living reptile—strange foremost in that it lives at all, since it is the sole surviving member of an order from 200 million years ago, unrelated to any modern reptile. It looks something like a brown iguana—except it has no ear holes, and the males lack hemipenes, transferring sperm to the female through a birdlike vent instead. Amazingly, it can live a century or more. A handful of American zoos kept the more common tuatara species, *Sphenodon punctatus,* though the San Diego Zoo, never to be outdone, managed through the efforts of Thomas Schultz to acquire eight of the much rarer *Sphenodon guntheri,* which are confined to one small island in the Cook Strait and number less than a thousand. Both species are CITES I, and strictly protected by New Zealand.

Wong already had a buyer for the tuataras, someone he had never met face-to-face and had only been dealing with for a year or so, George Ross of PacRim Enterprises in California. The fact that Wong had an outstanding arrest warrant in the United States, dating back to Crutchfield's Fiji iguana trial, did not deter him from dealing in illegal animals with Americans he hardly knew. "I knew I was a wanted person," he said, but he was safe in Malaysia. For six months now, Wong had been sending Ross mislabeled shipments of Gray's monitors, Timor pythons, Indian star tortoises. "It took me away from the monotony of the usual frog and gecko shipments," Wong said.

In retrospect, Wong felt, there had been something odd about George Ross and PacRim. "When I started dealing with them, it was all so easy—anything that is too good to be true usually is. My terms are always the same: 50 percent before shipping, 50 percent after, and they said, 'No, it's not necessary, we'll just pay in advance.'"

GEORGE ROSS was George Morrison, the U.S. Fish and Wildlife agent who had introduced PacRim Enterprises by way of a classified ad in *Reptiles* magazine. The *Reptiles* ad was intended to help Morrison dispose of any legal reptiles he imported, nothing more. "The guys I care about catching are the Anson Wongs, not the lesser guys," he said. Morrison had already made contact with Wong before placing the ad, and Wong turned out to be far easier to deal with than Morrison imagined. "How did you find me?" Wong asked when Morrison phoned, and Morrison replied that everyone knew who Wong was. The answer seemed to satisfy Wong, so PacRim and Sungei Rusa Wildlife—Anson Wong had finally retired the horribly dated-sounding "Exotic Skins and Alives"—exchanged price lists.

Then the *Reptiles* ad ran, and Morrison started fielding calls from the two-bit snake nuts he expected to hear from. "In '94 and '95 you had a huge increase in people wanting to get into the business," Morrison said. One of the first calls came from an eighteen-year-old in Buckeye, Arizona, who ran his reptile business from his parents' house—such was the caliber of dealer this ad attracted. But then, six months later, the same Arizona teenager called Morrison again, to offer him Gray's monitors from the Philippines "without papers." Anson Wong was the only reptile dealer who routinely trafficked in this species. Improbable as it was, the kid had a connection to Wong.

The kid's name was Beau Lee Lewis, and youth had treated him poorly. He was freakishly tall, and suffered from muscular dystrophy, for which he had undergone three separate surgeries. He had also been treated for asthma, allergies, temper tantrums, pneumonia, suicidal thoughts, and depression, and was so socially isolated by these ailments that he had finally dropped out of high school and retreated to his bedroom, reading snake books and composing various communications for his Southwest Reptile Exchange, a business that comprised, essentially, a fax machine. Lewis had the screwy habit of corresponding in capital letters, and his grammar and spelling were appalling. Yet Lewis was not to be taken lightly if he was in touch with Anson Wong, and Morrison was quick to cultivate him.

Lewis had yet to actually smuggle any animals when he offered Morrison the Gray's monitors. All he'd ever done was sell common, cheap reptiles to local pet stores, and managed somehow to get Anson Wong to take him seriously. Wong invited Lewis to fly to Penang and take Freddie Angell's tuataras back to the United States. Wong routinely used kids Lewis's age as couriers; some frightening percentage of Penang's university students had run missions for Wong to Australia. "You have to get young people with a lot of *cojones,*" Wong explained. But Lewis refused. It was too risky, and he had bigger ambitions than to be someone's mule.

Lewis confided all this to George Morrison. Morrison and Lewis were starting to brainstorm business deals, all of which involved Anson Wong in some way or another. Lewis wanted Wong to send him animals by DHL, but wasn't sure how to make it work. Morrison was talking about cutting Lewis in on some of the big commercial shipments from Wong, letting him sell off what he could in Arizona. Lewis sent Morrison and Wong a list of his code words for Komodo dragons, false gavials, star tortoises, radiated tortoises, tuataras. Wong didn't bother to use it; as far as Wong was concerned, that stuff was for kids.

In September 1996, Lewis turned nineteen. He changed his business name to Beau Lewis Rare Reptiles Import-Export/Herpetological Brokers. Morrison helped him type his first list. Few of the tremendously pricey animals on that list were actually in his possession; most weren't even in the country. He still lived at home.

That November, Wong, Lewis, and Morrison talked almost daily about tuataras. Morrison had agreed to buy them—he'd already wired Wong a payment—but Lewis was still not inclined to pick them up. "Some of us go in for that," Morrison told Lewis, but he'd have to decide for himself. Wong used the advance from PacRim to front Freddie Angell's wife a few thousand dollars, something to tide her over until her husband was released. Angell did snare four tuataras after leaving prison, just as he promised. But police soon discovered him with nets, poles, and Mesozoic reptiles in his car.

Wong called Ross the next month with an even better offer: young plowshare tortoises, two for $13,000. Ross talked him down to $11,000.

GEORGE MORRISON regarded live-animal smugglers as congenitally different from other wildlife crooks. "When I worked ivory cases, no one was a collector of tusks," he said, and he felt both Beau Lewis and Anson Wong to be possessed of "that sickness—the same sickness you see in people who are into butterflies, insects, shells." Lewis had been chasing snakes since kindergarten, and Wong accumulated books, art, artifacts, even samples of beach and river sand.

Wong, Morrison said, "would build the animal up and talk about how beautiful it was, but there was no real love for it." Most animal dealers, however, would recognize Wong's attitude as ennui. Anyone who handles thousands of specimens gets inured to them eventually. Unless the specimen is breathtakingly rare—then the old love comes surging right back.

The wildlife agents had expected some of the famous stolen plowshare tortoises to arrive in the United States, and Morrison wasn't wholly shocked by Wong's offer. Some of Morrison's colleagues believed Wong might have masterminded the theft. "If anyone could have done it, it would be Anson," he said. Wong was offering two plowshares, but claimed he had access to dozens more. Wong told Morrison he had already sent four to Japan, using couriers who'd tied them up in pantyhose and stuffed them into backpacks.

The timing of Wong's offer was curious. It had been seven months since the theft of the plowshares, and no one had heard a thing about them until two weeks before, when Dutch authorities called U.S. Fish and Wildlife to say that thirty-five of them—just less than half the number stolen—had turned up in a small city in the Netherlands. For now, they were being held in secret while an investigation proceeded. The media had not been informed, nor had the government of Madagascar.

Wong was adamant that his plowshare tortoises were not among those stolen from the breeding program, but Morrison found that hard to believe. Morrison tortured himself trying to get Wong to say something about the tortoises' origins, let slip some hint of the chain of custody from Madagascar to Malaysia. But Wong gave him nothing. Wong, he suspected, fed him disinformation—sparingly, the only effective way. "I got the feeling that I was dealing with a very cunning and intelligent person," Morrison said.

Morrison paid in advance for the plowshares. Wong would conceal them in a shipment of other species.

Plowshare tortoises represented a sensational turn in the Wong case. But for this case to actually see a court of law, Wong would have to enter the United States, which he had no plans of ever doing. Morrison tried from time to time to interest Wong in Hawaii. "No place on earth like it," he'd say, but Wong never sounded too enthused.

AFTER THE plowshare tortoise theft of 1996, the *New York Times* began paying unusual attention to reptile crimes, placing on the cover of its Sunday magazine a photo of a radiated tortoise with the words: "I was caught in Madagascar. Peddled for 30 cents. Smuggled to Orlando. Sold for $10,000. I'm a rare, coveted tortoise—coldblooded contraband."

Radiated tortoises, which were CITES I and coveted but not all that rare, were some of the animals Wolfgang Kloe had taken delivery of that fateful morning at the Waffle House. They did not sell for $10,000, but closer to $1,000.

The *Times Magazine* story, which relied heavily on agency sources, estimated the global illegal wildlife trade as worth between $10 billion and $20 billion annually—"roughly equal to the trade in smuggled weapons," a Fish and Wildlife spokeswoman added. This was an unprecedented hyperbole. Traffic, the group established by CITES to monitor the wildlife trade, offered no estimates for the illegal trade, saying reliable ones were impossible to come by. Traffic's values for the entire *legal* trade in live animals—all the aquarium fish, birds, reptiles, and mammals exported worldwide—hovered at around $500 million a year, and the illegal trade was thought to be a fraction of that. Yet somehow, $10 billion to $20 billion were the numbers that made the *Times Magazine*. "There are a lot of mythical numbers in the wildlife trade," said Bruce Weissgold, a Fish and Wildlife agent who had formerly worked for Traffic. "I was there for the genesis of many of those numbers."

The *Times Magazine* story mentioned Kloe's pursuit and arrest, the unsolved plowshare tortoise theft, and the efforts of U.S. Fish and Wildlife to combat the global trade in illegal reptiles. It took particular care to explain why those efforts were warranted: "According to Fish and Wildlife authorities and a chorus of independent biologists and ecologists . . . if the decimation of animal populations and their habitats continues, the tapestry of life across whole blotches of the map may start to unravel. Though few scientists agree on the timing or severity of this scenario, they have given it a name: ecosystem collapse."

Privately, the Fish and Wildlife agents didn't delude themselves that their reptile campaign was winning battles for the planet. "The major impact to any wildlife resource is degradation of the environment," said Ernest Mayer. "No one can argue otherwise." Reptile smuggling was an environmental pinprick next to the carnage wrought daily by mining, logging, and conversion of wilderness to farmland. Still, smuggling was something the agents could at least attempt to control. Already they had expended tremendous energies on the Kloe case, on Crutchfield, and on a sprawling new case against Strictly Reptiles and its suppliers in Indonesia and South America. These investigations, which were supposed to have lasted a year, had gone on for two, with no end in sight. Inside the agency, the team took heat for all the time and money spent protecting animals that weren't even American, much less ducks.

In short, said Bruce Weissgold, "when Special Ops decided to mess around with Johnson's flying snakes from East Walla Walla, people said, 'What the fuck?'"

But then "ecosystem collapse" sounded pretty bad, too.

Two days after the *Times Magazine* article appeared, Anson Wong's plowshare tortoises arrived, safe and sound, at PacRim.

SMUGGLING REPTILES via one of the international parcel companies, DHL, UPS, or Federal Express, became popular in the 1990s, an upgrade of the old postal schemes. The parcel companies were fast, but you still had to label the contents as something besides animals, and this meant no one looked out for their safety. If you were an expert packer, the animals could last a week or more confined in their boxes, but if you weren't, they would die, and you could expect to be caught. Few smells are more distinctive or disgusting than that of dead snakes.

Beau Lewis pondered ways to improve on the practice, until in May 1997, he had it. After much deliberation and planning, a friend of his was hired as a FedEx driver. The friend would ensure that Lewis's parcels were pulled off the line immediately, then signed for by their fictional addressees.

The first of Lewis's FedEx shipments from Wong, labeled as medical books and addressed to "Dr. Harry Glassman," contained a Boelen's python and a false gavial. The false gavial arrived dead and the python badly injured. Lewis remained optimistic.

LEWIS MADE an impressive debut at the Orlando reptile expo that summer, renting himself one of the penthouse suites at the Radisson Twin Towers, across the hall from Wayne Hill's. Even Hank Molt was taken with the nineteen-year-old's swagger.

Molt had finally been fired by Starbucks for erratic behavior, which made him very happy, and now, with his probation period from the Crutchfield affair over, he inched his way back into the reptile business, armed only with the cash from the painful sale of his entire natural history library. He crashed in Hill's penthouse and rented a table for the expo, though all he had to offer was a pile of photocopied flyers with a blown-up drawing of a mata-mata, a bizarre fish-eating turtle from the Amazon whose head looks like a leaf. Underneath it, he reintroduced himself to the world. "I HAVE BEEN IN THE REPTILE BUSINESS SINCE 1965— I AM A QUALITY FANATIC—LET'S DO SOME GOOD DEALS: CONTACT—HANK MOLT REPTILES."

Molt had always been attracted to crazy young men. Not only did they keep him young and hopeful, they were readily persuaded to put snakes in their bags. Lewis knew of Molt by reputation. Most of the younger kids entering the business had a hard time imagining a world where if you wanted an animal, you actually had to go out and get it; their elders joked that they thought snakes came from deli cups. But Lewis was better schooled. In his penthouse, Lewis produced for Molt his photos of rare snakes, a ritual courtship gesture among reptile people. "He was clearly wanting to impress," said Molt, and Molt, never wasting an opportunity of his own to impress, regaled Lewis with his fireside chats, the forever-mutating stories of climbing trees for Fiji iguanas and setting bounties on Boelen's pythons.

After the expo Molt remembered his young friend and wrote him again. "The herp world needs more guys like you," he said.

PACRIM HAD by now purchased more than two hundred illegal animals from Anson Wong. The agents in San Francisco were stuck feeding lettuce to plowshare tortoises, and Morrison had just ordered from Wong his second Komodo dragon. It was time to shut the operation down, and yet Wong had made it clear from the start that he would not travel to the United States. It wasn't that he didn't want to meet Morrison. "I was always inviting the PacRim guys over, but they never had time," Wong said. Wong was even more amenable to a meeting now, because Morrison had announced that he was closing PacRim and starting a new, bigger business with Beau Lewis. He hoped the three of them could meet up and make plans. Wong insisted they meet somewhere in Asia.

Morrison would have to lure Wong to a country that would extradite him to the United States for animal smuggling, a crime seldom considered extradition-worthy. Morrison almost pulled it off when Wong said he'd meet Morrison in Vancouver. Canada had agreed to arrest Wong, and it had extradited a far less egregious reptile smuggler the previous year, an Ontario man connected to Frank Lehmeyer, so the prospects for an extradition were good. The Royal Canadian Mounted Police were on board to apprehend Wong when he landed. But in August 1998, just before Wong was to leave, Beau Lewis, who scanned the U.S. Fish and Wildlife Service's Web site regularly for useful tidbits, remembered something. He searched for and found an agency press release about the extradition of Lehmeyer's friend. Lewis forwarded the release to Penang, and Wong canceled his trip. "It was very stressful and a huge blow when Anson said he wouldn't come to Canada," Morrison said. The agents brainstormed. Wong loved tropical places and he loved women—maybe they could charter a boat with beautiful women and steer it into international waters? "We thought of all kinds of crazy stuff," said Ernest Mayer. In the end Morrison settled on Mexico, which had beautiful women, beautiful wildlife, and an extradition treaty.

BEAU LEWIS'S FedEx scheme grew to involve three drivers and a designated receiver, who was paid $200 for every package he signed for. Wong made a special trip to the Philippines to secure Gray's monitors for Lewis. He talked to Lewis like a colleague now, not some college kid with a backpack to rent.

Beau Lewis had by now received multiple indications that the U.S. Fish and Wildlife Service was onto him, all of which he chose to ignore. Lewis's FedEx driver had voiced suspicions that a package from Wong had been opened and resealed, and later told Lewis he'd seen Fish and Wildlife agents in the FedEx shipping office in Phoenix, inspecting parcels. In the summer of 1998, the Gray's monitors from Anson Wong—animals Lewis had been awaiting nearly three years—simply never arrived. They had been intercepted and confiscated, at George Morrison's direction, and sent to the Los Angeles Zoo.

That August, a large package from Indonesia was returned to the main

FedEx office in Phoenix, radiating a foul stench. Some brave soul at FedEx cut open the parcel to find nine dead snakes, partially liquefied from the heat. An agent from U.S. Fish and Wildlife's Phoenix office was called in to deal with the mess.

Lewis was quick to find out, and by now he was worried. It seemed inevitable that something would happen, and the first thing to happen was usually a search. But Lewis had himself covered. He'd already sent the one friend he could trust a box full of his most incriminating documents—waybills, receipts, faxes, check stubs, bank account numbers, wire transfer receipts, and every last fax to and from Anson Wong.

When he received the box, Morrison got a warrant and searched it.

GEORGE MORRISON paid for half of Anson Wong's ticket to Mexico City and bought Beau Lewis a ticket, too, though that one was dated a full day later. Morrison never intended for Lewis to make it.

Wong had some business first in Japan, so he flew from Kuala Lumpur to Osaka, then to Tokyo, and then, circumventing the United States, to Vancouver, which he deemed safe enough as a transit point. In Tokyo, a Japan Airlines representative took his passport and ticket, and then scrawled something into a notebook, which alarmed him. "I asked, 'Is this procedure normal? Is this what JAL does all the time?' And she said this is a precaution because of a Swissair crash, and for some reason that made sense to me," Wong said.

In Vancouver, Wong found a pay phone and called his wife, who was half asleep. He wandered into a shop and bought sweatshirts that said "Canada," in different sizes. He stopped at a kiosk for some sushi. "I was eating it and then happened to turn and I caught this guy following me. He had been tailing me since the phones. Could I have turned back at that moment? I think yes."

But Wong boarded the flight to Mexico City. He would recognize George, he'd been told, by his Orlando reptile expo T-shirt.

ON SEPTEMBER 14, 1998, Mexican agents grabbed Anson Wong out of an immigration line at the airport, where he was standing next to Morrison, and pushed him into a line of his own. "Anson was looking around wondering what was going on. He seemed very confused," Morrison said. The Mexicans stamped his passport, then arrested him.

The same day, Beau Lewis was arrested in Buckeye, Arizona.

THE REPTILE sting was wrapping up nicely. By the day of Wong's capture, German officials had arrested Frank Lehmeyer, albeit only for tax evasion. Belize was then on the verge of expelling Tom Crutchfield. Wolfgang Kloe had been sentenced to forty-six months in federal prison, a sentence that would have been a lot shorter had he not gone running across the East-West Expressway. Mike Van Nostrand of Strictly Reptiles had been caught laundering frilled dragons through Jakarta to Holland and then reexporting them to the United States, among other offenses. He was sentenced to eight months in prison and forced to pay $250,000 to the World Wildlife Fund. Dwayne Cunningham was convicted following years of smallish entanglements with Strictly Reptiles, Crutchfield, and Frank Lehmeyer.

The government had made good use of Adamm Smith, Crutchfield's former manager, as an informant. After serving up Crutchfield, which he didn't feel all that bad about, Smith provided wildlife agents with just what they needed to begin investigating Thomas Schultz of the San Diego Zoo, someone they'd been eyeing for years. "I really regret that—I can't express to you how much I regret it," Smith said about Schultz. "That was the one thing that pained me the most. I was complicit in costing him his career. I don't think Tom did anything the zoo didn't know about, but publicly he took the fall."

Zoos had always presented a problem for the Fish and Wildlife agents, who weren't stupid—they knew that zoos continued to acquire and dispose of animals in dubious ways—but their will to police them was limited. Zoos provided a reliable outlet for their seized animals. Ernest Mayer had investigated six zoos in his career, but never made a significant case against any of them. Wildlife laws were complex and fungible, and "when it comes to surplus animals zoos are kind of stuck," Mayer said. "It's just one of those things."

In the course of his zoo career, Tom Schultz had provided countless surplus reptiles to Tom Crutchfield. This was in keeping with the San Diego Zoo's fairly liberal protocols for disposing of surplus animals. The zoo, throughout the 1990s, was found to have sold or donated a full third of its unwanted stock to private businesses, which in itself was no crime. But using zoo permits to import snakes, then selling them to Tom Crutchfield for cash, then not reporting the sale to the zoo, was fraud.

For Fish and Wildlife to go after the largest and perhaps best zoo in North America, a zoo that prided itself on breeding seventy-two endangered species, took some audacity, but the agents had been hearing whispers about Schultz since Crutchfield's Fiji iguana trial. In August 1999, Schultz pleaded guilty to two charges of fraud.

The San Diego Zoo defended Schultz, paid his legal bills, and encouraged other employees to pen commendatory letters to the judge, on zoo stationery. No one at the zoo believed Schultz had traded animals for cash and pocketed the money, as the Feds were insinuating. All you had to do was stroll through the reptile house to see what the money had bought. Wrote the zoo's director of collections:

Collecting trips have been part of the history of this institution, and they are not confined solely to the reptile department. Often times these travels take us to remote parts of the world, such as Papua New Guinea, where literacy is at a very low rate and life is primitive. I can assure you from my own experience, your Honor, that it is not always possible to provide receipts from those with whom one has a financial obligation, i.e., indigenous people collecting in the bush . . .

Curators at other zoos, who cringed at the thought of Schultz's fate befalling them, wrote their own letters to the judge, all arguing the same point—that any truly good collection requires some thinking outside the box. Absent, not surprisingly, were letters from the more progressive factions of the zoological community—John Behler in the Bronx, or anyone at the American Zoo and Aquarium Association.

Schultz was sentenced to three years' probation, forced to retire, and ordered to pay $75,000 in fines. He never kept a reptile again.

ANSON WONG, naked but for his shoes and boxer shorts, spent his first night in prison awake on the floor of a cell without beds. The cell's twenty-odd prisoners, who had been curled up on the floor like millipedes when Wong was brought in, were then kicked into the corridor. The cell now held only Wong and a giant man covered by a blanket, and though Wong was very cold, he refused his cellmate's offer to come share it. At dawn, when Wong looked out the window, he saw that a queue of visitors had formed by the gate. They were families of the prisoners, who had come to celebrate Mexico's Independence Day, waiting, carrying whole hams and baskets of food. He was hungry and tired, and what he was experiencing "wasn't fun," he said, "but it was new." Then, later that morning, "I heard banging on metal doors like angry bulls," Wong said. "We heard shots fired and we quickly went back to the cells," where the prisoners put milk on their faces to protect them from pepper spray. "The visitors started the riot because they were trying to control the main gate and they thought they were being shut out," Wong said.

Wong spoke seven languages, but Spanish was not among them. When he couldn't respond to the word *"nombre,"* a guard kicked him in the shin. "Shit," Wong said, and the guard punched him in the stomach. He was transferred to a cell with a brain-damaged prisoner who'd decorated it with "feces all over, some of it dried, some of it fresh," said Wong. He was grateful for his shoes. When the food cart came around, Wong split a plastic Coke bottle in two. He now had a bowl and a cup, which he stuck through the bars.

Wong's extradition to the United States was by no means guaranteed. The Americans wanted Wong to volunteer to leave Mexico. Wong refused them—he would stay. His wife managed his animal business in Penang. He began to learn Spanish from an American drug smuggler named Fred, who also translated his legal documents. One afternoon, "Fred and I were having a tortilla when someone came up and stabbed another guy like four feet away, and Fred looked at his tortilla and there was blood on it!" Wong said. It did not occur to him that prison in the United States federal system might be a cleaner and safer experience. "I figured they were all the same," he said. After two years, with the encouragement of his American lawyer, he gave up the fight. When the U.S. marshals came to put him on a plane, he demanded time for good-byes with his Mexican friends. His Spanish was very good by then, though it had a noticeably rough edge to it.

ALL THE delays in getting Wong to the United States caused Beau Lewis's trial to be pushed back by two years. Part of Wong's plea agreement was that he would testify against Lewis, the boy who'd been recruited to bait him. It was the second time in twenty years that the agency had recruited a teenager to ensnare reptile smugglers, then prosecuted the recruit aggressively. Lewis pleaded not guilty; Morrison, he said, had entrapped him. Physicians and psychologists testified to Lewis's immaturity and suggestibility and copious illnesses. Lewis was found guilty and sentenced to three years in prison. But an appeals court ruled that all the government's delays in waiting for Wong violated Lewis's right to a speedy trial, and reversed his convictions. Lewis was retried and convicted, and his case was dismissed again, on rulings. A decade later, Lewis was still waiting to see if the government would indict a third time. He had suffered two heart attacks in the meantime, or so he told people.

ANSON WONG pleaded guilty to pretty much everything, and signed his plea agreement like a movie star might, sideways, with a swirling loop around the letters. Days later, one of Wong's Komodo dragons, by then a permanent resident of the Los Angeles Zoo, bit off a chunk of Sharon Stone's husband's foot during a private tour of its enclosure. "Phil screamed and we heard this crunching sound," the actress told *Time* magazine. "The deal is, they pull you off your feet and apparently then try to eat you."

Fish and Wildlife issued a triumphant press release about Wong. The World Wildlife Fund issued another.

> WWF believes that the world's endangered species are one small step safer with the recent sentencing of Keng Liang "Anson" Wong to 71 months in federal prison, sending a signal that illegal wildlife trade will not be tolerated. Wong, a notorious dealer of threatened and endangered wildlife, was sentenced last Thursday in federal court in San Francisco and ordered to pay a US $60,000 fine . . .

Actually, the judge had given Wong credit for time served, so Wong would spend only two more years at the low-security federal correctional facility in Dublin, California, where the amenities were top-notch. "Gosh, it was nice," Wong said. "The guards were courteous. They called you 'inmate,' 'sir,' not 'asshole.'" All Wong lacked were animals. He volunteered for leaf-raking duty so he could look for lizards. On New Year's Eve 2003, Wong was freed. He had not seen his family in five years and four months. Wong knew he was not reformed—no reptile smuggler ever was. But it had been an ordeal, for sure, "and it kind of gives me a perspective on things when I want to do something bad," he said.

Wong's lawyer bought him Kenneth Cole shirts and shoes and new jeans, then put him on a plane for Taipei, where he would board another for Penang. Wong upgraded himself to business class. He was given the choice of lobster or duck. He asked if he could have both, and the stewardess said, "Of course," which made him start crying. Eventually he pulled himself together and asked for ice cream.

# 18

## Whatever Happened to the Plowshare Tortoises?

The story of the plowshare tortoises neither began nor ended with Anson Wong, but remained entwined in a long and fragmented chain of events that started minutes past midnight on March 19, 1993, when four Germans emerged onto a road from a forest trail in Ampijoroa, Madagascar, and were shot.

The Germans had been collecting reptiles. When they walked out of the forest, they were apprehended by Malagasy gendarmes, who then opened fire. Three of the Germans were wounded; two died of their wounds en route to the hospital, and one, a well-known museum herpetologist named Fritz Jürgen Obst, lost an eye. The fourth man, unharmed in the shooting, escaped into the forest and reemerged after daybreak, shivering, soaked, and disoriented. Such are most of the agreed-upon facts about the incident. On other points, the accounts are so divergent as to be irreconcilable.

The way Obst recalled it, at eight p.m. on March 18, he and his three companions, amateur reptile hobbyists, were dropped off by their driver at the entrance to a forest path at Ampijoroa. They wore headlamps and carried batteries and reptile-collecting supplies and managed to bag two species of chameleon and three species of gecko, one of which they suspected to be new to science. At midnight, they emerged on the path to meet their driver, who was normally punctual, and were surprised not to find him waiting. Moments later, they saw the lights of a car approaching, but it was not their Mercedes; this one was a car marked with the emblem of the Jersey Wildlife Preservation Trust, a British zoo whose many conservation projects included a tortoise-breeding center in Ampijoroa. The Germans flashed their head-lamps to signal the car. It stopped. To their surprise, uniformed Malagasy gendarmes emerged from the backseat, carrying automatic weapons.

The armed men seemed agitated, and shouted for passports. One of Obst's companions, who spoke French, answered that the passports were in the Mercedes, which was nowhere to be found. The gendarmes pointed weapons at the Germans, who had switched off their headlamps and, with the car's headlights pointed at them, had a hard time seeing what was happen-ing. None of the Germans was armed, but all four were ordered to put their hands in the air, then to lie on their stomachs and spread their limbs. Obst felt safer once he was prone on the road, thinking the gendarmes would relax when they realized the group was harmless. But then one of the Ger-mans recalled that his passport was in his pocket, and jumped up from the ground. There was a flash, and suddenly Obst realized that he had been shot.

Obst was bleeding from his head and throat. One of his companions had been shot so badly in the legs that they seemed to be coming off his body; another, the youngest, had lost part of an arm, most of a leg, and enough of his chest that lungs were exposed. He now begged the gen-darmes to kill him. The fourth man, who had jumped up, was unharmed. He started running. Obst yelled at him to stop, but he disappeared.

Obst begged for help, though he could not discern, through the darkness and his bleeding eye, if anyone was still present. Obst noticed that one of the Malagasy gendarmes was lying on the ground with them. The gendarme, he saw, was dead. The bullet meant for the fourth German had killed him instead.

The rest of the gendarmes had fled.

The escaped German, a gecko collector named Robert Seipp, had not run far. He hid in a bush close enough to the scene to see a white man return in a Land Cruiser, and with the help of a Malagasy friend load the two worst wounded into the truck bed. Obst was able to sit up, in the back. The dead gendarme was left on the road.

After the Land Cruiser had driven off, Seipp heard more cars coming—for him, he felt sure—and he ran deeper into the forest reserve. In the moonlight he saw a lake, and he waded in. Seipp stayed underwater for hours, breathing through a reed. The next morning, Seipp was discovered soaked and despairing on the roadside by more gendarmes, who pointed weapons at him. Again Seipp feared for his life. Then a car pulled up. The driver was the same white man from the night before, who had carried off Obst and the others.

The white man identified himself as Don Reid, the station manager for the Jersey Wildlife Preservation Trust at Ampijoroa. Reid ran a program breeding plowshare tortoises, one of Madagascar's most endangered reptiles.

It was Don Reid who had first noticed the Germans' Mercedes, with a driver inside, parked on the edge of the forest reserve the night before. Reid demanded that the driver let him inspect the car, whose trunk contained boxes suitable for carrying reptiles, a live chameleon, one dead snake in preserving fluid, and several dead lizards. The driver explained that he was waiting for a group of Germans to emerge from the forest. Reid sent the driver away, and traveled to a gendarme station in a neighboring city, as only gendarmes could make a poaching arrest. Reid ferried them back to Ampijoroa in the Jersey Wildlife Preservation Trust's car. There they all waited by the forest until the Germans emerged. The gendarmes had come heavily armed. But Reid had hardly expected they would shoot.

Reid informed Seipp that two from his group were dead but that Fritz Jürgen Obst had survived. The previous night, as Reid was driving the three wounded, the roads had been terribly bumpy and Obst's two badly injured companions, bleeding continuously without compresses or first aid, shouted in pain and begged for water in the back of the vehicle; one, delusional, began addressing a nonexistent "Monsieur le docteur." Obst led them in praying the Our Father, over and over. Half an hour before they reached the hospital, both were dead. Reid left Obst with the Malagasy doctors and drove with the bodies to the morgue.

In the morning, the German embassy sent a Cessna from the capital to remove Obst. A team of German aid workers was dispatched to Ampijoroa to collect Seipp, who was being held on the roadside by Reid and, now, more gendarmes. The aid workers took Seipp back to Mahajanga, where he was reunited with Obst and flown out of the country. Don Reid waited a few days before telling his bosses in Jersey about the affair.

Save for a brief and sketchy report in a British newspaper, the international news media paid no attention to the Ampijoroa killings. The whole affair would likely been forgotten, except by the families of the dead, had the Jersey Wildlife Preservation Trust not written triumphantly about it in its newsletter, three months later, in an article titled "Reptile Rustlers Meet Tragic End." The rustlers, the article said, had come awfully close to the trust's colony of plowshare tortoises, the rarest tortoises in the world.

THE REASON the plowshare tortoises needed a breeding colony was that they were presumed to be all but extinct. In fact the plowshare had always been presumed to be all but extinct, though there was never much consensus as to why.

The beautiful golden tortoises, called *angonoka* by locals and *Geochelone yniphora* officially, spelled "plowshares" by the Americans and "ploughshares" by the British, are the largest of Madagascar's four tortoise species, and the only ones possessing an elongated lower shell that protrudes like a plowshare, restricting free movement of the tortoises' heads and necks. The males need the protrusions to batter and flip over one another during the mating season, but they look so acutely uncomfortable that Malagasy families keeping plowshares— usually tethered up in their chicken yards out of a belief that they keep poultry from getting sick—were known to saw them off out of pity.

The first evidence of the species had been a carapace toted into Paris's Muséum nationale d'Histoire naturelle in 1885 by a man who'd purchased it from sailors. In the early twentieth century, living plowshares were first observed in a patch of bamboo forests in northwestern Madagascar, near the coastal town of Soalala. They remained little studied after that, but were believed to be terrifically rare. A 1950 report predicted that the species would be completely extinct within a few years, and until 1971, when the geologist James Juvik of the University of Hawaii set out to rediscover the tortoises, that sad prognosis had been the last word on plowshares.

Juvik found plowshare tortoises in the bamboo thickets around Soalala, but only a handful, and he wondered whether they might be the last of their kind. Juvik could see no reason for populations to be so low. The tortoises were not eaten or exported for food, the way radiated tortoises, a related and more common species, often were. Wild pigs roamed the area, and though Juvik was sure the pigs ate young plowshares and eggs, "this factor alone is probably insufficient in explaining the species' near extinction," he wrote in an article describing his trip. "Man's indirect effect, such as the alteration of the native forest, appears modest in the region, where human densities are low." Juvik thought the species might simply be dying out, unaided by humans, "undergoing extinction as a natural and inevitable process common to all species," he wrote. But, in spite of his concerns that populations were dangerously low, Juvik removed six adults of breeding age from Madagascar to the Honolulu Zoo, confident that Hawaii's tropical climate, combined with the zoo's record of success breeding other tortoise species, made it the ideal place to conserve them for posterity.

In the early 1970s, after Juvik's trip proved that plowshares still existed, the Texan animal dealer Leon Leopard traveled to Madagascar and took home a pair, which eventually ended up in Honolulu, too. A Connecticut dentist imported one from France, where a former colonial administrator had kept it as a pet. The dentist loaned that plowshare to the Bronx Zoo, where his good friend John Behler shared his interest in Madagascan tortoises. But Behler's keepers saw fit to put the tortoise on sand, which it swallowed too much of and died.

After the passage of CITES and the Endangered Species Act, there was no longer any legal way to obtain plowshare tortoises from Madagascar. And by then the Honolulu Zoo, the one sizable repository of plowshares outside Madagascar, was not only failing to breed them, it was starting to kill them off. After the zoo's attempt to electro-ejaculate the males, one died of an infection on its penis. A female had to be sterilized because of an ovarian infection, and another plowshare died of unknown causes. After a decade's efforts, only one baby plowshare was ever hatched in Honolulu.

Honolulu gave up on its breeding program. It kept the sterile female and the baby, then sent two to the dentist in Connecticut, one of which died the day after its arrival, and the last three to the Bronx Zoo.

The dentist, Bill Zovickian, was a tortoise hobbyist well regarded in the zoo community, and he remained very close with John Behler, even after the Bronx Zoo had killed his first plowshare. Zovickian forgave that accident and loaned his new pair to Behler, too, believing that the animals would be likelier to breed if kept in a group. Behler did not put the five plowshares on display in New York, but rather housed them at the zoo's Wildlife Survival Center, its breeding sanctuary for endangered species, on St. Catherines Island, Georgia. In the winter of 1985, the heating system at St. Catherines failed, and one of Zovickian's plowshares, the female, froze to death. In the early 1990s, three more died, of unknown causes, and Zovickian demanded his surviving male back.

Honolulu's baby plowshare died of a calcium deficiency.

By 1993, Zovickian's old male and Honolulu's sterile female were the only known plowshares in captivity.

IN MADAGASCAR, meanwhile, the Jersey Wildlife Preservation Trust was having a surprising degree of success breeding plowshares in semiwild conditions.

The Jersey Wildlife Preservation Trust was not an ordinary zoo, nor was its founder, the legendary author and television personality Gerald Durrell, an ordinary zoo director. Durrell, like many zoo men of his generation, had gotten his start as a freelance animal collector, traveling to Cameroon on a small inheritance and returning with a hundred crates full of antelopes and crocodiles and warthogs for English zoos.

In the late 1950s, Durrell built a zoo of his own on the Channel Island of Jersey, between England and France. His Jersey Zoo developed into a noble and serious affair, with keen attention paid to breeding endangered species. Durrell was an early adopter of the "ark" philosophy, and also one of the first zoo directors to acknowledge its limitations, realizing by the mid-1970s—a full decade before the rest of the zoo world—that breeding rare animals was far better done, for reasons both political and biological, in their countries of origin.

So Durrell's Jersey Zoo formed a trust to fund overseas conservation projects, and in the 1970s began the hard work that saved the kestrels and pink pigeons of the island of Mauritius, and the fruit bats of its neighboring Rodrigues. In the 1980s, after Durrell had married Lee McGeorge, an animal behaviorist who specialized in Madagascar, the trust started exploring the possibility of conservation work in that country, too. The World Wildlife Fund and CITES were especially interested in plowshare tortoises—new studies had estimated the remaining population to be as low as a hundred animals. The WWF would provide the money, and Jersey would handle the rest.

But while Mauritius was a pleasant place to do conservation work, with the languid feel of a Caribbean island, nearby Madagascar was a mess. A postcolonial Marxist government had expelled the French, driven out foreign investment, redistributed land, and plunged the country into political isolation and seemingly unstoppable economic decline. Madagascar's environment suffered along with its people, who in their impoverishment began to eat many of the island's famous endemic species, and reembraced with nationalist zeal the burning of land for grazing, a traditional practice that the French had discouraged. By the 1980s, Madagascar was burned over and bankrupt.

Still, the Durrells were committed, and so was Don Reid, the man they'd chosen to manage the project. Reid had worked as a bait-and-tackle salesman, and earlier as a reptile keeper at a small English zoo. Reid was the one human being the Durrells could find willing to put up with the discomforts of Madagascar, where in 1987, the year of Reid's arrival, it was hard for a foreigner to locate toothpaste.

Reid established camp in Ampijoroa, a village eight to twelve hours north of the capital, depending on road conditions, near one of Madagascar's largest forest reserves. The Madagascar government had rounded up a group of adult plowshares from chicken yards, and these served as Reid's breeders.

To Reid's surprise, he liked living in a brick-and-raffia hut without running water or a toilet, with only a motorcycle to get around on. He learned French. "I was the only honky for a long way around," Reid said, and that pleased him.

Reid's plowshares mated right away—it was something about the climate, or the forest plants Reid harvested to feed them, or the bamboo and shade palms he put in their pens—whatever it was, they felt at home enough to have sex. In April 1987, a female laid three eggs. "We had absolutely no idea when they would hatch," Reid said. "We put wire over them to protect them from civets and we waited, waited, waited. And one day in November we went out to have a look and the center of the nest had fallen. I dug the nest up with a spoon and there was just one baby."

The next year there were seven nests. By 1990, when Gerald and Lee Durrell first visited the site, more than thirty babies had hatched. The Durrells were thrilled and touched.

"No matter how comprehensive the reports of man on the ground are, there is nothing like seeing and holding the fruit of your labors," wrote Gerald in *The Aye-Aye and I,* his book about the Madagascar trip. "Cupped in our hands, these funny little pie-crust babies represented the future of their race."

John Behler of the Bronx Zoo also visited Reid at Ampijoroa in 1990, after which he formally recommended, as a member the IUCN–World Conservation Union's Madagascar committee, that Jersey send the Bronx Zoo one of its adult male plowshares. Behler wanted a second male for his group on St. Catherines Island, which at the time was still limping along.

It was a neat trick of Behler's to recommend, as the chair of a supposedly neutral conservation committee, the donation of a tortoise to his own zoo. But this was easier said than done. The Durrells had been careful to establish that any animals they collected in Madagascar, and their offspring, remained the sovereign property of Madagascar, and that it was the Madagascar government, not Jersey, that determined their fate. Such an agreement was hardly standard practice among zoos, but the Durrells felt that they had done the right thing. "We invented this stipulation as a safeguard because many countries felt that outsiders were only interested in grabbing the fauna and running, as it were," wrote Gerald in *The Aye-Aye and I.* The trust saw no reason to export any plowshare tortoises, even to its own zoo in Jersey, when they were doing so well in Madagascar.

In the early 1990s, Jersey took over complete control of the plowshare project, including its fund-raising, and turned "the world's rarest tortoise," which happened to be a very pretty tortoise, into its flagship conservation cause. The plowshare was not, strictly speaking, the world's rarest tortoise.

There were at least ten turtle and tortoise species, most of them in Asia, of which only a handful of individuals survived. And as Madagascar opened up to Western researchers, the discovery of other, isolated populations of plowshares raised estimates to a few hundred animals, or even as many as a thousand. The plowshare was getting less rare by the minute, but donations poured in, affording Don Reid a proper vehicle, a house not made of raffia, and a toilet. The Jersey Wildlife Preservation Trust, having secured the good-will of Madagascar, started new programs for lemurs, jumping rats, aye-ayes, and native fish. The plowshares produced more golden babies every year.

Then the Germans were killed.

AT FIRST, the Jersey Wildlife Preservation Trust had written rather glibly about the Germans' deaths in its newsletter, referring to Fritz Jürgen Obst, curator-in-charge of the Dresden Zoological Museum and author of several well-regarded books on reptiles, as a "reptile rustler." The trust also made note of the Germans' proximity to the plowshare tortoise colony at the time of the shooting, complaining, in what seemed to be a fund-raising plea, that the altercation would drive up the costs of protecting the tortoises. When the surviving Germans responded with outrage—they had never tried to nor intended to steal any of the trust's plowshare tortoises, they wrote, and they weren't "reptile rustlers"—the trust, in a subsequent newsletter, apologized. But it stood by its original accusation, which was probably true, that Obst and the others had been removing reptiles from a national park illegally.

A phone number Don Reid had discovered in one of the dead men's pockets seemed to confirm that. The number belonged to Olaf Pronk, a Dutch expatriate animal dealer well known to Jersey. Pronk had shown up in Madagascar in late 1988, only a year after Jersey set up its plowshare program, and while the trust aimed to ensure that Madagascar's endemic reptiles stayed in the country, Pronk found clever ways to assure that they wound up in European terrariums.

What Obst's team was doing, collecting without scientific permits, was hardly unheard-of. To export specimens from Madagascar it was far easier for scientists to get an invoice from a licensed animal dealer like Pronk and export them as products of a commercial, not scientific, venture. This was the only way to obtain a good number of specimens. Otherwise, you had to buy computers for the university, house Malagasy exchange students, and perform all kinds of expensive, time-consuming favors, just to get permits for two chameleons. Olaf Pronk had provided Obst's team with a driver who had a commercial collecting license of his own, an arrangement that went a long way toward solving their problem.

Some of the most respected herpetologists in the world counted Olaf Pronk among their friends. Curators from the University of Michigan and the American Museum of Natural History stopped by on their frequent visits to Madagascar, and Pronk, about as sophisticated a naturalist as an animal dealer ever was, gave them specimens he recognized as extraordinary. But the conservation groups working in Madagascar—particularly the World Wildlife Fund and Jersey—did not appreciate Pronk's generosity or sophistication. What they saw were Pronk's wholesale exports of native fauna. Pronk had almost single-handedly started a chameleon craze in Europe; more recently he had discovered legal loopholes that allowed him to export hundreds of Madagascar *Pyxis,* little woodland tortoises of a genus considered seriously threatened.

By Jersey's reasoning, anyone associated with Olaf Pronk was a reptile rustler.

THE TRIBUNAL set up to investigate the Ampijoroa killings—whose results the two surviving Germans eagerly awaited—ended almost as soon as it began. Don Reid was questioned by two or three Malagasy judges, and no one was censured. "The whole thing just sort of blew over," Reid said.

In the couple of years that followed, Reid's plowshare project continued to produce exceptional results, with the females digging as many as seven nests a year. The juveniles were getting stronger—strong enough, almost, to be invulnerable to bush pigs, which meant they could soon be released.

But Reid felt himself souring on Ampijoroa. He was haunted for a while by the recollection of one of the dying German's lungs exposed and inflating outside his body. The assignment he'd originally signed on to for one year, back in 1987, had become eight. His assistant had "gotten into drugs," Reid said, and had to be replaced. In January 1995, Gerald Durrell died, at age seventy, of liver cancer. Durrell's loss, to Reid and to the zoo world in general, was hard felt.

Reid contracted malaria repeatedly and missed cricket, his favorite sport. He thought he might be getting a little weird, "going bush," he said.

In February 1996, Reid, with the backing of Gerald Durrell's widow, Lee, who was now in charge of the organization, wrote to Madagascar's Ministère des Eaux et Forêts to propose a completely new strategy for the plowshares. Splitting the colony was an idea that John Behler of the Bronx Zoo had first floated on a visit two years earlier. Half the tortoises would remain in Madagascar, according to this plan, and the other half would be placed in the control of a zoo or conservation group abroad. In his letter to the government, Reid cited four threats that necessitated such a radical change of course:

1. Disease
2. Falling trees and storms
3. Theft
4. Vandalism

Reid advocated exporting half the tortoises to Mauritius, where Jersey had a permanent conservation station. He also mentioned the idea of moving half the plowshares to the Jersey Zoo, though he conceded the climate would not be ideal for them, or to "other zoos," which he did not name.

Madagascar denied Reid's request. Two months later, half the tortoises were stolen.

ON MAY 6, 1996, a thief or thieves cut two holes in the wire fence surrounding the tortoise pens at Ampijoroa, and made away with two adult
and seventy-two juvenile plowshares. Or two adults and seventy-three juveniles—the number was never certain. Such a huge haul was perplexing
for a number of reasons—it seemed too big and audacious a feat to have
been performed without being caught, at a site where people had died for
much less. It also defied the conventional reptile-smuggling wisdom to
take only as many animals as could conceivably be sold.

The *New York Times* called the theft "one of the heists of the century."
Turtle people all over the world received e-mail alerts from John Behler,
urging them to report any word of the stolen plowshares. The U.S. Fish
and Wildlife Service offered to help Jersey recover the tortoises, since no
one expected Madagascar to launch a serious investigation. Agent Bruce
Weissgold requested the guest ledger from Ampijoroa, only to receive no
response, "which I thought was weird," Weissgold said.

Jersey never cooperated with the Americans, but instead allowed a
Dutch national named Wil Luiijf to pursue his own investigation. Luiijf
later claimed that Lee Durrell tapped him for the job; Durrell insisted that
Luiijf volunteered.

Luiijf had in the early 1990s worked as an inspector for Holland's
Algemene Inspectiedienst, an agricultural agency that also made cases
against wildlife smugglers. By the time of the plowshare theft, Luiijf had
quit or been fired from the agency and worked from home as a freelance
investigator, sometimes picking up assignments for the World Wildlife
Fund and Traffic, sometimes taking it upon himself to investigate wildlife
smugglers for nothing more than his own satisfaction. Weissgold and other
Fish and Wildlife agents who knew Luiijf were wary of him, particularly
since he no longer had any governmental authority, and because he was
a tortoise collector himself. It did not take long for Luiijf to produce a
suspect.

LUIIJF HAD known and despised Olaf Pronk long before Pronk had even moved to Madagascar, when Pronk ran a shop in the Hague that specialized in high-end collectible fauna. In the 1980s, Dutch law made it illegal to keep European tortoises as pets, but Pronk had special permission to export them to foreign customers. Pronk also had an extraordinary permit that allowed him to possess any CITES-listed animals, as long as he declared them within three months of importation.

Pronk claimed that his problems with Luiijf began when Luiijf tried to buy a tortoise that could not be sold in Holland. Then, Pronk said, there was another dispute over another tortoise that died after Luiijf had strapped it to his back and driven it home on a moped in the middle of winter.

Luiijf always said he opposed Pronk on principle—that Pronk was a criminal, albeit a shrewd one who had yet to be caught. In 1988, Luiijf persuaded Dutch tax authorities to pursue an investigation of Pronk. Luiijf accompanied them on the raid, and confiscated a number of *Pyxis* tortoises and two Fiji banded iguanas from Pronk's apartment, along with piles of documents. The Fijis were sent to the Rotterdam Zoo, and Pronk's special permit was not renewed.

Luiijf also found among Pronk's effects a fax to Japan in which Pronk seemed to be offering a plowshare tortoise for sale. Luiijf attempted to make a legal case based on the fax, but there was much legal wrangling about its authenticity, and a court ruled in Pronk's favor.

That year Pronk decided he was through with Holland, and set up shop in Antananarivo, Madagascar. Three years later, Pronk was arrested there after the Madagascar government received a letter from Luiijf, signed also by Traffic, Jersey, and World Wildlife Fund officials, claiming that Pronk had fled Holland to avoid a tax fine. The Dutch embassy came to Pronk's aid, and he was released after four days.

In 1993, the year that the Germans were killed, Luiijf flew to New York and gave a presentation to conservationists on the horrors of the international wild-tortoise trade. He showed slides he'd taken in his inspector days, of tortoises crushed and maimed in their shipping crates. There Luiijf met John Behler, and they talked about Madagascar. Both already knew Don Reid and his plowshare project; now they discussed Olaf Pronk, who since his arrest had married a well-connected Malagasy woman and was enjoying much warmer relations with the Madagascar government.

Behler's relationships with animal traders had always been tense, and he was particularly irked by Madagascar's. The Bronx Zoo's parent organization, the Wildlife Conservation Society, was becoming very active in Madagascar in the 1990s, developing its own conservation projects on a scale similar to Jersey's. "What seems so incredulous here is the disparity between how scientific pursuits are scrutinized by Eaux et Forêts and the way dealers operate with impunity," Behler wrote colleagues after a 1994 visit. "A dealer can somehow send out 10,000 reptiles and amphibians on his collecting permit and we have to have an *accord*—perhaps two of them—to collect 1/10 cc of reptile blood and pick up a tortoise shell." Behler singled Pronk out in that same letter as "a Dutch resident, with a highly placed Malagasy wife, who has repeatedly been implicated in the illicit trade of Madagascan herpetofauna by Dutch and Traffic European authorities." Those authorities together comprised Wil Luiijf.

JOHN BEHLER, Wil Luiijf, and Don Reid were all quoted in the *New York Times* article about the plowshare theft, all seemingly eager to direct suspicion toward Olaf Pronk. Luiijf described a "a very nasty Dutch reptile salesman in Madagascar who in the past has been known to sell wild plowshares to Japanese fellows." Reid told the paper that some Germans had stopped by Ampijoroa and informed him that a Dutch reptile dealer had offered them plowshares a month before the theft. "The Madagascar Government is completely involved," Behler told the *Times*.

When Olaf Pronk read this, at his hillside home in Antananarivo, "I knew I was in trouble. I started sweating," he said. Only one day after the article was published, the tortoises made their first appearance, not at the Orlando reptile expo, as everyone predicted, but in the small Dutch city of Eindhoven. "When I heard they were in Holland," Pronk said, "it was even worse."

IN THE fall of 1996, the national police in Eindhoven got a call, late at night, from someone whom they never identified. The caller had a friend, he said, who possessed thirty-five of the young plowshare tortoises, and was thinking of killing and burying them all. Unless something could be worked out first.

It was Wil Luiijf, the freelance investigator, who hand-delivered the first two tortoises to the police. Days later, the remaining thirty-three were placed in a Styrofoam cooler and left near the Eindhoven train station, where police picked them up. No suspects were charged, or questioned: the deal, whatever it consisted of, had been accepted.

Henny Smits, the officer who'd brokered the deal, claimed that it was done for the good of the tortoises. U.S. Fish and Wildlife agents, when they found out what Smits had done, were flabbergasted, but had no choice but to let it go.

The thirty-five recovered plowshares were confiscated by the Dutch government and moved to Reptile Zoo Iguana, a small, private animal exhibit on the North Sea. Iguana was an odd choice for so large a quantity of high-profile animals—the Rotterdam or Amsterdam zoos, with their ample space and top-notch vets, would have seemed to make more sense. But the Iguana Zoo and Wil Luiijf had a long-standing relationship, and Iguana was obscure enough that the tortoises could be kept there indefinitely without attracting notice.

In December, Don Reid traveled to Reptile Zoo Iguana and identified the plowshares as the stolen ones. Unfortunately, Reid wrote in a statement to Dutch authorities, the tortoises "cannot be returned to Madagascar, since they could be carrying a disease that could wipe out the world population of the species."

Reid did not say where they would or should go instead.

A DUTCH name began to emerge in connection with the theft, and, curiously, it wasn't Olaf Pronk's.

Don Reid had told the *New York Times* that two Germans had stopped by Ampijoroa shortly after the theft, and informed him that a Dutch dealer had offered them plowshares. The Germans were Tom Crutchfield's friends Frank Lehmeyer and Wolfgang Kloe. Reid was on good terms with both of them despite their reptile-snatching tendencies; he'd by then resigned himself to the larcenous habits of German and Dutch enthusiasts.

The Dutch reptile dealer who'd offered Lehmeyer plowshares was a man by the name of Wim Janssens, a detested rival of Olaf Pronk's and an old informant of Wil Luiijf's from Luiijf's time as an airport inspector. Like most reptile smugglers of any real ambition, Janssens was also friendly with Anson Wong.

Janssens was scoping for potential buyers for baby plowshares in the month before the theft, and Lehmeyer agreed to make a few phone calls for him. The first call was to Tom Crutchfield's Reptile Enterprises, where no one was interested. "There is some honesty among thieves," Crutchfield said.

IN FEBRUARY 1997, two plowshare tortoises the size of grapefruits arrived at PacRim enterprises, the U.S. Fish and Wildlife Service's California front company. Anson Wong had concealed them in a shipment of other reptiles. It was the first evidence of the stolen plowshares having made it to the United States, and a chance for American wildlife officials to rescue the case from the abortive stewardship of the Dutch.

But Wong did not make things easy for them. He told George Morrison, PacRim's undercover agent, that the plowshares came not from Ampijoroa but from somewhere in Asia, though this seemed hardly likely, considering their size.

Wong stuck to his story that the tortoises had come from Asia. He knew nothing more about them, he insisted.

The two Wong plowshares went to the Los Angeles Zoo while the investigation into Wong progressed. One died within a few months; the other took a little longer.

OLAF PRONK decided to launch his own investigation of the plowshare theft. "I was worried from the beginning that people would think I'm behind it," he said. "That was my first and main concern. And then it became very important to prove that I was not involved and to try and get the original thieves."

Pronk heard from his sources in Madagascar that a Dutch diving instructor, who taught for long stretches at a resort on the northwest coast, had been paid to remove the tortoises from the site. The Dutch diver "was kind of a general criminal, a little of this, a little of that," Pronk said, and knew the wife of Wim Janssens, who traveled to Madagascar for her husband and often stayed at that resort.

In the course of these investigations, Pronk made frequent contact with the CITES and World Wildlife Fund authorities in Madagascar, popping into their Antananarivo offices to update them on his findings. After one such visit, Lee Durrell phoned Pronk. Their conversation was stiff, Pronk said, as "I didn't trust her and of course she didn't trust me." But Durrell, Pronk recalled, didn't seem to be harboring any suspicion that he was involved.

Pronk had by then learned that the tortoises had been confiscated in Holland. But Durrell professed to know nothing. "I have been unable to verify this," Durrell wrote Pronk in an e-mail. "There have been so many rumors. Bangladesh, Japan, Czech Republic, France. And the police have been very tight-lipped on the subject." Except Durrell knew exactly where the tortoises were, since her own employee, Don Reid, had traveled to the Netherlands and identified them. Wil Luiijf knew where they were, as did the U.S. Fish and Wildlife Service. It was also likely, given his contacts with Luiijf, Reid, and Durrell, that John Behler knew by then, too. Only Madagascar, the tortoises' legal owner, was kept in the dark about their whereabouts.

The secrecy was mystifying. The animals were not needed as evidence, since there had been no investigation—why should the Dutch continue to hold them?

Pronk got the sense that another sort of deal was being made.

MORE THAN a year after the theft, Lee Durrell continued to insist, publicly, that the tortoises had not been recovered. At Olaf Pronk's urging, Madagascar wrote CITES officials in Geneva, asking for information on the tortoises; it never received a response. Jersey's rationale for leaving the tortoises tucked away at Reptile Zoo Iguana had been the threat of disease, but after more than a year there, the tortoises had not been tested for disease and appeared healthy.

Some suspected that Jersey had lost its enthusiasm for the plowshare program, and that the theft was providing an excuse to abandon it. "There's such a thing as donor fatigue," Fish and Wildlife's Bruce Weissgold said. "Ten years is a long time for them to be running a conservation program. The objective is always to turn it over to the native people; even if that's not humanly possible, that is always the stated objective."

In late 1997, Don Reid left Madagascar for England, and the trust did not replace him at Ampijoroa.

ONCE OLAF Pronk knew for sure where the thirty-five tortoises were, he found a lawyer who would represent Madagascar and demand their repatriation. The animals would not be returned to Ampijoroa, since Jersey now didn't want them, but rather to Pronk's own hillside compound outside Antananarivo. Pronk and the government of Madagascar had arrived at a plan, a signed agreement declaring that the plowshares and their future offspring remained the property of the state of Madagascar. Pronk would care for the tortoises and pay the bills.

On one level, Pronk acknowledged, this was a sort of revenge. But there were few other places for the plowshares to go. "Jersey said they couldn't come back to Ampijoroa because they were ill. Madagascar wanted the animals back. There were not many options—the zoo here is really not an option," Pronk said.

In December 1998, a Dutch attorney representing Madagascar filed a request for an emergency hearing in the district court nearest the Iguana Zoo. He filed on a Monday, stating his intent to demand the return of thirty-five tortoises to Madagascar. The hearing was scheduled for that Friday.

In the middle of the week, thirty-three of the plowshares were flown, under special emergency permits, to the Bronx Zoo. The two remaining tortoises were never accounted for again.

THE OSTENSIBLE "emergency" necessitating that thirty-three plowshare tortoises be flown to New York in the dead of winter was a medical one, John Behler explained in a memo to colleagues.

As chair of the turtle and tortoise specialist group for the IUCN, Behler wrote, "I was asked for advice on placement of seized tortoises and health assessment issues. Most suggestions (program sites and Europe or Mauritius, collaborators there, diagnostics) were not acceptable for political or economic reasons. I finally offered our medical facilities at WCS."

Behler had once again recommended, as head of an ostensibly impartial conservation committee, that tortoises be transferred to himself. This time, the trick worked.

Lee Durrell, in a half-hour phone interview more than a decade later, said she was "a little hazy" as to the decision-making process that had led to the tortoises being flown to the Bronx Zoo days after Madagascar filed its intention to demand them. It was "purely and simply a health thing,"

Durrell said at first. But then, Durrell acknowledged what seemed patently obvious—that it was the prospect of their being sent to Olaf Pronk that compelled the evacuation to New York. "We were all very concerned that the animals were going to go back," Durrell said. "We did not want them to go back to our facility and we would not have accepted them back there, and we felt it was foolish to get them repatriated, especially to Pronk."

Someone had influenced Dutch CITES officials to approve an emergency export permit for the animals, possibly Wil Luiijf. The Bronx Zoo would insist that the plowshares' New York sojourn was not meant to be permanent—"They couldn't be properly cared for in Holland, so we agreed to hold them temporarily," said zoo spokesman Stephen Sautner. But Behler did not see the arrangement as temporary, since no sooner had the tortoises arrived than he offered five to his dentist friend Bill Zovickian.

Zovickian drove to the Bronx from Connecticut in the winter of 1999 to view Behler's new charges. The tortoises "were under strict quarantine," Zovickian recalled. "You had to put on a sterile suit to even look at them—they were getting the best of care." Behler, Zovickian said, told him to pick out five. "I picked out the five biggest," he said. Once the quarantine was over, Behler promised, Zovickian could take his tortoises home.

ONE PARTY to the importation of the tortoises came to regret it soon afterward: the U.S. Fish and Wildlife Service. Someone in the agency had approved Behler's emergency CITES import permit believing that the tortoises were sick, and when it became clear that not only were they not sick, but that Madagascar was about to make an international incident of it, the agency had a serious problem.

"A number of us were aghast when the tortoises came to Behler," said Ernest Mayer. "Under CITES, the country of origin has the rights to any animals seized—when we learned Behler wanted the animals, we said bullshit. I don't know how the permit got issued. It was a huge mistake—a huge faux pas."

Olaf Pronk was spurring Madagascar on in its outrage, of course. Without his help and the help of his Dutch attorney friend, Pronk acknowledged, the plowshare case "would never have seen the light of day." But it didn't matter, for it was the sovereign state of Madagascar, not Olaf Pronk, taking the matter to court again, and this time, it was a national court in the Hague. The Dutch government was the defendant, and the question before the court was whether the Dutch had acted improperly in allowing the tortoises to be flown to New York.

The U.S. Fish and Wildlife Service tried to placate Madagascar with a formal apology, and sent Behler stiff instructions that the tortoises not be loaned or moved until after the Dutch court's decision. John Behler had enjoyed two decades of close relations with the agency, helping it to investigate wildlife smugglers. Now the agency was treating him like one.

Behler apologized to Madagascar on behalf of the zoo. "We deeply regret any misunderstanding that our well-intentioned import of these confiscated tortoises caused," he wrote, then blamed his underlings for the whole fiasco: "I acknowledge that my staff became overly concerned about the health status of the tortoises." He agreed to honor the Dutch court's ruling.

"We weren't fighting to keep the animals, so we have no comment on the international flap," said the Bronx Zoo's Stephen Sautner, years later. But in March 1999, the Dutch government argued a case that sounded very much as though it was acting as proxy for the zoo. The tortoises were adjusting well in New York and had gained weight, the Dutch told the judge; the Bronx's facility was among the best in the world, and preparations for the tortoises' stay were already in the advanced stage. Then, incredibly, the Dutch also argued that though the tortoises were shown not to be carrying harmful viruses or bacteria upon arrival at the Bronx Zoo, five of them had since tested positive for *Salmonella*. If they weren't sick when they got to the Bronx, according to this logic, they were now, and they shouldn't go back.

The court ruled that the tortoises be returned to Madagascar within six weeks.

"When the order came down, John flipped out—he did," said Bill Zovickian. "They had spent a lot of money."

A FEW days after the Dutch court's ruling, Behler circulated his version of events in an e-mail to colleagues labeled "HIGHLY CONFIDENTIAL," which assured, of course, that it went far and wide.

> *The basics are that the Netherlands recovered 33 (or maybe 35) G. yniphora in late 1996 and held them at the Iguana Zoo until December of 1998.*
>
> *Very few people knew that these tortoises had been recovered (including me). The investigation was (still is) ongoing and Dutch authorities didn't want anyone to know. That included Madagascar for apparently good reason . . .*
>
> *Madagascar went ballistic when it found out that they had been moved from NL and demanded that the tortoises be returned within two weeks, "or else." They threatened full diplomatic legal action against WCS. They threatened to close our office in Tana and close our multimillion dollar USAID project on the Masoala peninsula.*
>
> *Fury was (and is) driven by Olaf Pronk, the Dutch expat that is wanted in his country. He (many believe that he masterminded the heist in the first place) personally wants the tortoises back in Mad and hired a lawyer friend in the NL. The solicitor took the angonoka business to small claims court. The judge ruled that the tortoises must be returned. So you may ask "what does a small claims court have to do with an international treaty?" Good question . . .*
>
> *I believe that Pronk will be fully exposed at some point and Madagascar will be so embarrassed by their relationship with him that they will quickly distance themselves from him. I am hoping that NL will try to extradite him. I am keeping my fingers crossed.*

The letter was full of lies: Behler had surely known about the confiscation of the tortoises all along; the investigation had long ago been canceled; Pronk was not wanted for a crime or in danger of extradition. The case had not been heard in a "small claims" court, but in the equivalent of a U.S. federal court. No one close to the case still believed Pronk had masterminded the theft.

But as payback, it was pretty good. And Behler wasn't finished.

WHEN BILL Zovickian heard what John Behler wanted him to do with his dental drill, he refused. "I couldn't deface those animals," Zovickian said. So Behler found his own drill and did the best he could. Into the carapace of each tortoise he carved the initials MEF—for Ministère des Eaux et Forêts.

Plowshares have famously thick shells, allowing the drill to cut deep, and the effect was stark. The freshly marked tortoises were crated up and sent first to Holland, where CITES officials deemed them healthy enough to continue on to Madagascar. Not until the tortoises arrived at the Antananarivo airport, where Pronk and his friends in the Ministère des Eaux et Forêts awaited them, were the markings discovered. The officials were not flattered, Pronk said. "Can you believe it? Imagine getting your famous painting back and the painter's name is scratched over?"

The thirty-three tortoises were sent to Pronk's compound, as promised. Five years later, John Behler died of a heart attack.

PRONK LIVED on a hilltop near the Antananarivo airport. It was election season, and he drove his Land Cruiser past angry-looking rallies on denuded mounds of red dirt. On the roadsides, children squeezed into oxcarts pulled by other children, and hapless toddlers emerged from ditches, watched by no one, legs coated in red dust. Zebus were everywhere, yoked in the roads and neck-deep in flooded fields, and hillsides had been stripped of their clay to an ugly and probably dangerous degree. In the village nearest to Pronk's home, a dozen people had recently died of bubonic plague.

"It's hard to live here and getting harder," he said. "I don't notice the misery anymore. But every time I am in Holland I find myself reluctant to leave."

Pronk was a tall man with a long, rectangular face, around fifty years old, and like so many Dutch a skilled linguist, with all his English idioms in order. Madagascar, he kept saying, was hopeless. "We have all the major conservation organizations here in Madagascar. They're driving around in Land Rovers or Land Cruisers like mine, maybe three or four in a family. These people know there is nothing they can do to stop this as long as the population explosion continues. They see the country burning every year. The wildlife of Madagascar will be gone in twenty-five years. There will be nothing left but maybe a few pathetic lemurs in a preserve. The biodiversity of Madagascar is doomed, seriously doomed," he said.

Pronk had by now largely abandoned the reptile trade and was exporting chameleons only to a handful of German customers. It was widely assumed that new reptile export quotas by Madagascar, probably long overdue, had forced Pronk into the plant business, and he had become as well-known for plants—particularly obscure ones—as he once was for reptiles. He had a good relationship with the botanists who came through, who lately had named a species of aloe after him. Unlike in the reptile world, botanists and the plant dealers get along, Pronk said, because they're glad someone is propagating the species instead of watching them get burned for charcoal.

At Pronk's house, enclosed by a fence embedded with glass shards, a silent corps of servants opened gates, brought forth plates and silverware, and watered plants. Pronk was no longer married, and lived with a girlfriend many years younger.

Pronk was surprised to hear of John Behler's death. He was pretty far out of the loop of Behler's friends.

"I'm sure many zoo curators—if you want to call them that, I'd rather call them head animal keepers because that's what they are—it's not embarrassing," he said. "If you like animals and you're able to work with them, well, it's the best there is. I would never have started trading animals if I would have had the possibility to keep a large collection living in Holland. It's all I like. And there are many Behlers. Behler is not just one person, it's a stereotype."

After lunch, Pronk dispatched one of his silent servants to the pen where he kept the plowshares—there were thirty-two now, since one had died. Every night, he said, he moved the animals from the pen and locked them up. The servant carried back in a box one high-domed golden tortoise that was now a teenager and looking very hardy. Its shell, though, was still quite defaced; after many years the deep grooves of the "MEF" had not faded at all, only widened as the shell got bigger, like a tattoo on a growing boy.

These tortoises were not yet of breeding age, but coming close. Pronk would not be able to sell their offspring, under the terms of his contract with Madagascar, so there was little point in trying to make more plowshares, he said. "Even if Madagascar were stupid enough to issue a captive-bred CITES I permit for the babies resulting from these animals, no country would ever allow the import of them," he said.

He'd thought about renting the tortoises out to foreign zoos to raise funds for Madagascar's wildlife reserves, the way China did with its pandas. But what zoo would want a tortoise with the letters MEF carved into its back?

The sharp smell of smoke floated into Pronk's garden.

"Madagascar," he said.

WIL LUIIJF drove a Land Rover around his hometown of Breda, a town only a few miles from Eindhoven, where the plowshares were recovered. He resembled his nemesis Olaf Pronk physically, with a similar rectangular face and balding pate and bright eyes, and seemed to be about the same age. In the front yard of Luiijf's modest brick house, there was an enclosure for some animal, probably a large tortoise, and in his living room, a baby redfoot tortoise ambled about in a terrarium.

Luiijf had owned any number of tortoises over the years, but denied, despite the evidence to the contrary, any personal interest in tortoises as a hobby. "If you want to work your way into tortoises, you have to talk their talk," he explained. Luiijf had recently created an organization that he called the Fast Forward Foundation, whose icon was a cartoon tortoise. Its purpose was "blaming and shaming everyone I can," Luiijf said, adding that

he'd recently bought or intended to buy the domain name wildlifecrime
.org, a site with similar intentions. Two years later, the site was still not active.

Olaf Pronk, Luiijf conceded, probably hadn't stolen the plowshares. But
as far as he was concerned, Pronk was still a criminal, even if he'd never
been convicted of a crime. "He can play the holy boy—forget it," Luiijf said.

Then Luiijf burst out with something surprising.

"I would be a wildlife smuggler," he said. "It's a lovely life! Running
around the forest, flying from this place to that—it would be so fun! If I
didn't have the conscience, this is what I'd do."

The Dutch, he said, were the best smugglers in the world, better even
than the Germans. "We know the trade routes and we're good at zoos,"
he said.

Only thirty-three of the thirty-five plowshares had been flown to
New York in December 1998. Two more had remained in Holland, never
accounted for.

Luiijf, confronted with this fact, said he was surprised to hear it and
that it couldn't possibly be true. He never responded to another e-mail or
phone call.

BEFORE THE plowshare theft, Luiijf's former informant Wim Janssens had
for many years owned a pet store in Antwerp. Afterward, Janssens was never
in one place for long. For a while he had a zoo in southern Spain, then a
farm in Brazil, then a reptile business with a German partner. Lately he was
raising crocodiles in Xai Xai, Mozambique. "I have NEVER been involved
in ANY way in this affair, nor has ever my name come up in this story, and
I prefer to keep this situation like this," he wrote in response to an e-mail
about the plowshare theft. He decried Wil Luiijf as "a poor looser [sic] and
ordinary thief," then never wrote again.

MANY WONDERED what role, if any, Anson Wong had in the theft. Wong told prosecutors after his plea agreement that he had bought eleven young plowshares shortly after the theft from a Chinese middleman, and had never asked where they came from. One died, Wong said; he kept two, sent PacRim two more, and sold the rest to customers in Asia.

But Wong could just as easily have been involved in the theft's planning. Wong knew Wim Janssens well. Not long after offering George Morrison the two plowshares, Wong claimed to have access to dozens more. Either Wong was in touch with the Dutch smugglers or he or someone he knew in Asia had received the other forty stolen plowshares. The prosecutors who deposed Wong in 2001 hoped he would shed some light on what had happened, but he couldn't, or wouldn't. "I was as forthcoming as I could be with them," Wong said, "since by then it didn't matter."

Later he told a reporter for the *Kuala Lumpur Star* the opposite—that he'd fed the American officials only what they wanted to hear. "They bought my story—hook, line and sinker," Wong told the newspaper. "I was not obliged to tell them the truth. In this business, you can't reveal your network. You'd be done in if you did."

IMMEDIATELY AFTER the plowshare theft, the Jersey Wildlife Preservation Trust—soon to be named the Durrell Wildlife Trust in its late founder's honor—secured the remaining tortoises in pens of reinforced concrete, and installed an infrared alarm system to guard them from intruders. But ten years later the trust was again flirting with the idea of splitting the colony, proposing to export fifty to American and European zoos. To export plowshares required the approval of Madagascar, which was far from certain and would take years. Plowshares, meanwhile, were turning up in Thailand and Singapore with a regularity that alarmed conservation groups. None of the tortoises appeared to be captive-bred. On Kingsnake .com, the reptile-trading Web site, no one was stupid enough to post pictures of *G. yniphora* for sale, but in a section of the site for sharing photos, anonymous users in the Philippines, Indonesia, and Thailand showed off pictures of their plowshares. Thinly disguised inquiries followed from France, Australia, Japan: "nice yniphora very round shell and orange. please email me for share idea how to keep yniphora." Though U.S. officials had always asserted that plowshares were worth $30,000 apiece on the black market, none had ever been known to sell for more than $5,500, and that was the pair Wong had sold to George Morrison in 1996 for $11,000. Now, by most accounts, they were about $1,000 each.

Olaf Pronk, with characteristic cynicism, thought this might have something to do with Durrell's renewed desire to offload the world's rarest tortoise. "Plowshare tortoises were made a flagship species for conservation organizations," he said. "That's how these organizations work. They need flagship species to raise funds, the giant panda as far as mammals go and there are other animals you can think of. And this is a rare species. It's always had a limited distribution, it's certainly not a species that could sustain a commercial trade. But just the number of them now in Southeast Asia alone proves that these animals are not as rare as people think they are, and the species no longer has its flagship status."

IN 2008 the Bronx Zoo opened a $62-million permanent exhibit called Madagascar! to house its lemurs and fossas and radiated tortoises and *Pyxis* tortoises. A reviewer for the *New York Times* was unusually critical, finding the tone of the exhibit "self-consciously virtuous and explicitly self-promotional," as its captions focused more on the zoo's good deeds in Madagascar than on the animals on display.

Absent among the species on exhibit was, of course, *Geochelone yniphora*. A more glamorous cage for the world's rarest tortoise could hardly be imagined, but this one seemed destined to remain empty at least a little while longer.

# Part IV

# Old Age and Treachery

**By August** 2001, Wayne Hill's annual reptile expo had moved from Orlando to a larger space in Daytona Beach, Florida. The reptile craze had probably already peaked by then, but it was huge compared to what it had been only five years earlier. Every weekend of the year saw as many as twenty reptile shows across the country, some nearly as large. Germany now had a show that was bigger than Hill's, and it took place every few months.

It was my first time back since 1996, the summer the plowshare tortoises were stolen and Wolfgang Kloe ran across the East-West Expressway. Tom Crutchfield was there, too, also for the first time since 1996. His hair had turned white, and he was walking around in a T-shirt stenciled with a Fiji banded iguana.

Hank Molt looked just as he had five years before, except his turgid eyes were a little darker underneath, and vertical wrinkles slashed the surface of his forehead.

Every so often in recent years, Molt had circulated an erratic, elaborately designed price list. He made his animals sound so good that even people who hated snakes might be tempted to buy one of his Sifnos Island vipers from the Aegean Sea, with "tiny cinnamon flecks over entire body"; or a Yangtze mamushi "with bold chevrons of red, orange, brown & white, the most INCREDIBLY BEAUTIFUL small montane Asian pit viper." No one believed that Molt actually had any of these animals, but people liked the lists, not least because they never saw price lists anymore; the reptile business had migrated to the Internet. Web sites like Kingsnake.com threatened to make even the magazines, like *Reptiles,* obsolete.

On the convention floor, Molt sat alone at a table, wearing a name tag, with nothing to sell. He complained that he was bored. The whole snake world had gotten too sanitized, too industrial, for his taste. If I was interested in something different, he said, a small but much better show was coming up in Hamburg, Pennsylvania. In Hamburg, "a sixteen-year-old can buy a black mamba and take it back to Manhattan!" Molt said, laughing.

I took Molt's business card, which bore a skull and crossbones.

That October, I flew to Pittsburgh, and Molt met me at the airport wearing hunter's camouflage. We waited for his zookeeper friend Randal Berry to fly in from Arkansas, and then the three of us drove north toward Hamburg, where Molt and Berry planned to meet up with Molt's old compatriot Eddie Celebucki. They had pooled funds to rent a table at the show.

Berry and Molt had been friends since the 1996 reptile expo, when Tom Crutchfield's enterprise entered its death throes. Crutchfield had warned Berry to stay away from Molt, but the advice never took, and Molt and Berry bonded over a fear of Crutchfield so deep that after the expo, as Molt was giving Berry a ride back to his house near Lake Panasoffkee, they scrambled to find hiding places in a highway rest stop when they saw the Crutchfields pulling in.

In Hamburg, Molt, Berry, and I checked into a hotel and visited some reptile dealers down the hall. In a room whose corners were stacked with plastic boxes of live vipers, cobras, and rattlesnakes, a young boy reclined on a bed, watching television. The boy's father, with forefingers bent and stiff from snakebite, reached into a knotted pillowcase and emptied a Gaboon viper onto the same bed, for no obvious reason. The snake's venom glands had been removed, supposedly, but it was still a Gaboon viper, a thick, starkly patterned monster of a snake with a head like a slice of pie. The boy barely blinked as the snake slowly navigated the duvet.

The next day, Eddie Celebucki, gently spoken and wearing a shirt printed with a Chinese dragon, tried earnestly to explain why anyone kept these things. "A venomous animal gives someone a sense of power and a sense of adventure in an otherwise mundane life. Maybe they have a job that's not really fitting to who they are and what they do. But they can go home and control this deadly animal," he said. Celebucki now owned a swingers' club in Cleveland—actually his karate school, converted on weekends into a labyrinth of beds and a dance floor—and he believed it attracted a similar sort of person.

Molt and Celebucki had not stayed apart for long after their falling out in the 1990s. When they met up again, a year or two after Celebucki left federal prison, their first instinct was to hug. After that they were as inseparable as before. Celebucki blamed Molt for sending him to prison, which had cost him his second marriage among other things, but then, he reasoned, he probably would have been caught eventually anyway. Molt was never comfortable talking about what he'd done to his friend, except to defend himself in a big-picture sort of way. "Once you're a smuggler, you're an equal smuggler," he said. "We were all knowingly involved in criminal activities. Our senses of guilt and stuff were quite diminished compared to normal people. If you can say, 'I'm gonna smuggle these tortoises because they're gonna be eaten anyway,' you can put something on a fake credit card, you can do a lot of things. It's a very weak code of honor."

No one thought much of Molt's code of honor, that was clear. At the Hamburg show, people I'd never met volunteered their assessments of his character, and they were uniformly terrible.

But watching Molt's eyes brighten as he sold a child a cheap turtle, then scrambled to find a container for the turtle as though he were taken aback by the sale, then launched into a lecture on turtle husbandry, I found it hard not to like him. "You have the same obligation to a five-dollar animal as you do to a five-thousand-dollar animal," he explained.

For the remainder of the decade, Molt was a part of my life. His friends, his enemies, and the ghosts of his past were never far behind.

# 19

## The Hurricane

Hank Molt was a mystery even to the people who knew him best. They could not imagine where his money came from, whether he had a secret trust fund or some sort of disability income or help from his wife. Molt's wife they knew only from the phone, and his daughter only Eddie Celebucki had ever met, when she was nine; now she was married with a son of her own. None of them had even visited Molt's home in suburban Atlanta, while Molt made himself a constant presence in their homes.

Molt dropped in for weeks at Randal Berry's, and at the Winter Haven, Florida, home of Wayne Hill, the owner of the breeders' expo, and lately he'd been spending lots of time at Celebucki's Loving Couples Dance Club in Cleveland, which was starting to become a problem for Celebucki. Molt drank too much in the club, which was bad swinger etiquette. But Celebucki felt he couldn't say anything to Molt about it.

Molt called frequently, usually from the road. He called after waking up in his car in Birmingham, Alabama; he called while wandering on the Arizona side of the Sonoran Desert just after the rainy season, with snake tongs hidden in his pack; he called to say he couldn't make a reptile show because he'd run out of money. He could, he insisted, "make $40,000 or $50,000 in one week," but this wasn't one of those weeks. Celebucki, Molt reported, was having problems with his girlfriend, and the future of the Loving Couples Dance Club was uncertain.

THINGS BEGAN to brighten up for Molt in the spring of 2003, when Wayne Hill invited Molt on a trip to Germany and the Netherlands, where they visited zoos and reptile dealers and a Dutch friend of theirs named Eddy Postma, whom Molt spoke of in reverent tones. Postma was legendary among Holland's prolific reptile smugglers. Postma had a handsome, salt-and-pepper look that reminded people of George Clooney. Molt and Hill had gotten to know Postma in the late 1990s, when he'd been caught at the Orlando airport with baby radiated tortoises in his socks, and spent months in a halfway house. Molt and Hill had visited Postma as often as they could in Orlando, lunching with him at the Perkins restaurant, for which the halfway-house prisoners had vouchers. Postma specialized in rare geckos from Mauritius, the Seychelles, and Madagascar. He reminded Molt of his old friend Stefan Schwarz, with all his discipline and secrecy and love of a good project. In Europe, Molt and Postma made plans, big, fantastic plans involving China and Fiji that they proposed and expanded and hashed out, then rejected and proposed anew. Molt proceeded to alarm Postma by disappearing overnight in Amsterdam's red light district. A kindly prostitute was letting Molt sleep off his drunk, but Postma feared Molt had drowned in a canal.

After that trip, Molt began soliciting European customers. The Europeans' tastes in reptiles tended to align with Molt's, as they were much more partial to rare species than to rare morphs. But Molt had also burned so many bridges at home—where no sooner had he reemerged on the reptile scene than he gained a reputation for nonpayment, and even outright fraud—that he had to look abroad for business.

He gave up writing his formidable price lists, and finally bought himself a Web site, which he called globalherp.com. Molt designed the site the way he'd once designed his lists, with all manner of illustrations and graphic embellishments. But people complained that not only did Molt not have the vast majority of the animals he listed on globalherp.com, he also stole photos of other people's animals off *their* Web sites and pasted them onto his.

That summer, Wayne Hill, who had a tremendous soft spot for Molt, felt confident enough in his old friend to put him in charge of a new, separate venomous snake show to be held concurrently with the regular expo. Molt, whose last paying job, at Starbucks, had ended disgracefully in 1997, proved ill-suited for the task. During the registration period in the hotel, when vendors signed for their tables and collected their name tags, Molt was drunk. The next day he went missing for most of the show, leaving Randal Berry to run it. Molt was avoiding a German reptile dealer who'd sent him snakes but hadn't been paid, and he was dancing delicately around a Finnish collector who'd sent Molt money but received no snakes.

MOLT SEEMED relieved when the expo was finally over. He and Eddie Celebucki always stayed an extra day or two to swim in the ocean and enjoy Daytona's prolific strip clubs, and in their room in a 1950s-era cinderblock motel called the Esquire, they entertained some new friends, a Swiss and a German. The German was nearly seven feet tall, with a leonine face and a radiant mane of pale frizzy hair. Molt had nicknamed him Butterbean, a nickname he liked. In turn he called Molt Grandpa, a nickname Molt tolerated. Butterbean was a builder from a town near Münster; his teeth were black, and he had tattoos on his arms of a nun having sex with the Pope. The Swiss was younger, smaller, not tattooed, and bespectacled. He served as spokesman for Butterbean, who did not have much English. They were venomous snake dealers, new to the American scene, and the type of people Molt described admiringly as "hard-core," his euphemism for crooks. They were friendly with Eddy Postma.

The Swiss, Benjamin Bucks, was in fact an American citizen, born in Zurich of a lapsed Mormon father from Lehi, Utah. Bucks was only in his early twenties, but already well-known to wildlife officials in Somalia, Kenya, and Uganda. He had lived in East Africa, in one country or another, since the age of sixteen. He carried with him photos of his teenage girlfriends, many of them in the act of exposing their breasts, and of his snakes.

In the room at the Esquire, Molt and Bucks talked and talked. Something Bucks was saying caused Molt to smile a lot and his eyes to light up. Something about Ethiopian vipers.

SEVERAL OF the foreign reptile species most coveted by collectors—Fiji iguanas, Komodo dragons, plowshare tortoises, Boelen's pythons—remained nearly as prized in 2003 as they had been in 1973. But countless other species had arrived in the Western world to great fanfare but then faded in value and prestige as they began to be bred in quantity. *Sanzinia,* Womas, radiated tortoises, Bismarck ringed pythons: All were middlebrow by now. To find something truly novel had become difficult, which was part of the reason the trade had come to focus on new mutations rather than new species. Ball pythons with ugly patches of white along their bodies—a mutation called piebald—sold for $30,000 apiece on the expo floor that summer. But snakes like that meant nothing to Hank Molt, or to Benjamin Bucks, who was young but had old-fashioned tastes.

Molt, Celebucki, Butterbean, and Bucks left the Esquire hotel and walked over to Lollipops, a Daytona Beach strip club the size of a box store. Molt retreated with Bucks to a table in the back, where they talked intensely for hours and coldly dismissed the girls who approached their table, until the girls knew to avoid them.

The snake they were talking about was *Bitis parviocula,* the small-eyed viper or Ethiopian mountain viper, a heavy, velvety snake that is a beautiful greenish gold with geometric markings of yellow and black along its spine. *Parviocula* was first described by a German herpetologist in 1977—very late for a large and ornate snake. Most of *parviocula*'s equally pretty, equally deadly brethren in the *Bitis* genus, which include rhinoceros vipers and Gaboon vipers, had been described a hundred years earlier. Yet since 1977, three labeled specimens in a Bonn museum still represented most of what was known about *parviocula.*

*Parviocula* remained obscure because it occurs at altitudes of eight thousand feet or higher, and the only place it comes into contact with humans is in the cool, coffee-growing highlands of southwest Ethiopia. Only when the coffee fields get cleared are the snakes exposed and easily caught. In 2002, after one coffee harvest, an Ethiopian exporter had sent a couple of the snakes, mixed in with more common species, to a dealer in Florida.

This was not strictly legal. Ethiopia bans exports of its endemic species, and one of the very few things known about *parviocula* was that it occurs only in Ethiopia. To import it to the United States would have violated the Lacey Act, but few if any wildlife inspectors would recognize such a snake—indeed few herpetologists would. It was not a CITES-listed animal, thanks to its obscurity, and without the international protections afforded by CITES, it was up to Ethiopia to police exports of *parviocula,* and Ethiopia didn't bother. In short, *Bitis parviocula* was illegal enough to be interesting, and not illegal enough to send you to jail.

Molt had in his possession that weekend the sole survivor among the *parviocula* that had come in the previous year, an old scuffed-up male. He kept the snake in his hotel room during the expo. When he wasn't avoiding angry customers, he invited friends back for private viewings, and everyone marveled. Zoos didn't have *Bitis parviocula,* but Hank Molt did.

And yet a single *parviocula*—particularly an old, beat-up one—didn't quite cut it, and that was where Benjamin Bucks came in. Bucks had infuriated conservationists in Africa by exporting quantities of another protected *Bitis* species, *B. worthingtoni,* the Kenya mountain adder. Now CITES officials were considering listing *worthingtoni,* just to stop Bucks. Bucks knew Africa, and he knew his loopholes. He could get more *parviocula,* he told Molt.

Nothing brightened Molt's spirits like a project, though it would be years before anything came of this one. And when it finally did, everyone involved would wish *Bitis parviocula* had remained undiscovered, left to its own in the cool coffee-growing highlands.

MOLT SAID his good-byes to Butterbean and Bucks, and just before leaving Daytona Beach, he abandoned most of his animals, including the male *parviocula,* to the care of a twenty-year-old kid from Oklahoma whom he barely knew. Molt was always entrusting reptiles to others to save himself the trouble of caring for them. Only a few animals would accompany him back to Atlanta, including a Gila monster that he'd somehow acquired over the weekend. Minutes before he was about to leave, he took a hard fall in the concrete courtyard of the Esquire motel, twisting his ankle.

On his ten-hour drive back to Atlanta, with his injured foot on the gas, Molt reached into a bag and was bitten by the Gila monster. Gila monsters hang on and chew, grinding in their venom, and the pain was enough that Molt ran his Jeep off the road and ended up in a rural Georgia hospital, which he escaped from the next morning without paying.

MOLT DROVE to Florida frequently that fall, sometimes with a canoe atop his Jeep, and would paddle out onto the clear spring runs, or walk the soft beaches at Cape Canaveral, finding giant bleached-out turtle skeletons and mysterious bivalves. Nature calmed him, and imparted to him a gentle and thoughtful affect that contrasted with his loud, Heineken-fueled persona at the expos. He liked to rewind history in his mind, to imagine places stripped of civilization, the whole of Florida as seen by the first Spaniards landing there.

The rest of his life was in disarray. His wife had recently moved to South Carolina and he was expected to follow, but had yet to. His daughter was angry with him about something, and it looked as though he would spend Thanksgiving alone, "eating pepperoni," he said. He drank an awful lot. He was constantly generating plans, most of which were not to be realized. He talked about collecting Costa Rican tree frogs for the Atlanta Botanical Garden; about starting a reptile expo in Japan; about constructing a breeding facility in South Carolina. Molt's future was always brighter than his present, which tended to consist of contingencies: friends turned adversaries, missing funds, dead snakes, undelivered merchandise. He left his phone turned off for weeks at a time. His new European customers took to the reptile Web sites to broadcast their discontent:

> *Greetings, fellow herpers and anyone this may relate to.*
> *First of all, let me begin by introducing myself; I am a venomous snake hobbyist from Finland with primary interest in arboreal vipers. Before I begin, I politely ask you to take a while to read through this letter. It will only take a moment of your time, and in doing so, may save you from big trouble. The point is, as you will find out, to prevent anyone from suffering grave losses, such as mine, by dealing with one of the biggest con-men in the reptile hobby . . .*

Molt never responded to his accusers. "It's the reptile business," he said.

THINGS CONTINUED to get worse. Not just for Molt.

In the spring of 2004, Molt's German friend Butterbean was bitten by a mamba and had to be helicoptered to a hospital in Hamburg and shot up with antivenin. When he finally pulled through, his wife threatened to leave and take the kids.

Then Eddie Celebucki's Loving Couples Dance Club was raided by police. Celebucki had never applied for an occupancy permit for the club, which he ran in the same industrial loft where he also lived, taught karate, and kept his snake collection. Molt happened to be visiting Celebucki the weekend of the raid. The police had arrived before the club's guests, fortunately, so no one was naked, but it was a slow news day in Cleveland, and the local television stations played what seemed to Celebucki an endless loop of "Karate School by Day—Sex Club by Night. Do YOUR Kids Go There?" Celebucki's children were mortified. The police locked the entire building, so Celebucki was now bereft of his regular business, his lucrative club, his snakes, and an apartment. Later that weekend, when things had calmed down, Molt and Celebucki broke into the building to retrieve the snakes and other valuable items, such as a giant fiberglass dinosaur and a sit-on motorized vibrator. Cleveland's karate community was quick to shun the formerly popular "Grand Master Celebucki," whose only material assets after the raid were snakes—thousands of dollars' worth of Angola, Woma, and Boelen's pythons. Molt offered to sell them on Celebucki's behalf, and Celebucki let him. "All Hank gave me was what I paid for them," Celebucki said. "He profited significantly."

Even that year's expo proved a disaster of rare proportions. In the days before it started, Hurricane Charley, the first of four hurricanes to hit Florida that year, flirted ominously with the Gulf Coast, approaching land and then skirting back seaward, as though rearing itself to charge. Forecasts had it effectively ripping the state in half. But Wayne Hill didn't cancel the reptile expo.

Molt and Hill acted tense around each other now, and Molt was unnerved to the point of mania by the appearance of his old girlfriend Colette, who had emerged in recent years a remarried, elegant, and eminently respectable reptile curator. She had come to the expo to raise funds for her award-winning crocodile conservation program, which Molt had seeded in the 1970s with smuggled Philippine crocodiles. She seemed equally on edge to have Molt around.

Benjamin Bucks was busy with a new daughter in Africa, but Butterbean made it over from Germany, fully recovered from the physical effects of his mamba bite, though there had been other repercussions. His wife had had enough of his snakes, and he'd spent a few weeks in jail after putting a man in the hospital for calling him a "hippie." The first night of the expo, Butterbean had to exile himself for hours on a bench facing the ocean, trying to resist an urge to beat up an American reptile dealer who owed him $900 and was flagrantly blowing him off. Molt egged on Butterbean to fight, but Butterbean held fast to the bench, battling the urge. "I am a man of honor," he repeated to himself, again and again. Butterbean shared a room at the Thunderbird, a motel roughly identical to the Esquire, with a German mortician whose cell phone was filled with pictures of corpses. Molt, Celebucki, and Celebucki's girlfriend shared a room down the hall. Tom Crutchfield was staying at the Thunderbird, too, but on the far side of the building. Any fears Molt had of Crutchfield physically attacking him had dissipated long ago, but the two had not spoken for a decade, and did not much enjoy crossing paths.

On Saturday evening, Hurricane Charley made landfall on the west coast of Florida, snapping light poles in half, and tore through to Daytona Beach in a little over an hour. The reptiles in the convention center were unharmed, but flying objects and pebbles broke the windows of cars in the lots. Street signs came unbolted and flew bladelike through the air.

Molt, Celebucki and his girlfriend, and the Germans all convened in one room, listening to the glass breaking outside. Electricity was sporadic. The Germans wore only their underpants. Molt and Celebucki, high on the chaos and beer, told them the story of the swingers' club raid as the lights flickered.

The next day the expo opened for business, though smashed signs littered the roads and food was hard to find. A young man got himself bitten by a rattlesnake, right on the floor of the expo, and had to go to the hospital. That evening the strip clubs bravely reopened.

IN THE weeks after the expo, Molt found himself at the center of a hurricane of his own making. The Oklahoma kid he'd entrusted his reptiles to the previous year had cheated him, he decided, and stolen the animals Molt had deposited with him for safekeeping, including many of dubious legality. The kid begged to differ. Several of the animals had died, he claimed, and Molt had been out of contact for months.

Molt drove all the way to Oklahoma to demand the return of whatever snakes were left by that point, showing up on the kid's doorstep and terrorizing him. Molt called the police on the kid, and the police sent state game officers to confiscate the venomous snakes, which were then sent to the Oklahoma City Zoo. The kid called the U.S. Fish and Wildlife Service, reporting that Molt possessed Gila monsters and other questionable reptiles.

Molt and the kid lashed out at each other on the reptile Web sites, Molt calling the kid a thief and the kid calling Molt "a washed up drunk old time smuggler." Somehow Randal Berry got dragged into the whole mess, causing Molt to lash out at him, too. Berry secured a trespass warning from the police, in case Molt ever showed up on his doorstep the way he'd shown up on the kid's. Now that friendship was over.

But at least Molt managed to get back his one scratched-up *Bitis parviocula.*

MOLT DROVE the *parviocula* to Arlington, Virginia, where he entrusted it to another young associate. Amazingly, he never seemed to run out of these. This young man was far more valuable to Molt than the kid in Oklahoma, or Randal Berry, or any of them, because he had money, quite a lot of it, and was particularly guileless.

Peter Nguyen was a self-employed businessman in his mid-thirties, but he looked to be in his early twenties. Nguyen owned a fantastic assortment of rare venomous snakes. Nguyen also had Asperger syndrome, which affected his willingness to socialize. He flew to the reptile expo almost annually but never ventured down to the raucous hotel bar. "I'm just this dork who likes to be left alone to play with my snakes," Nguyen said.

As a young boy, Nguyen had bested his elders, including many zoo curators, during the old reptile symposium's annual slide show competition, where contestants identified species from close-up photos of just a few scales. He had known Molt since that time, but only lately had they become close.

In the fall of 2004, Molt placed in Nguyen's care his sickly *Bitis parviocula,* a rarity among rarities, which pleased Nguyen to no end. "I'd had this snake in mind since it was discovered," said Nguyen, who was eight years old in 1977. If you can keep it alive, Molt had told him, it's yours.

Nguyen got to work researching what scarce information existed about *parviocula*'s natural history. He knew it would need to be kept cold, since it lived at high altitudes, and that it liked having something to grasp with its tail, if it had been collected, as was rumored, in the tangled roots of coffee trees. There would be no point in giving a *parviocula* standing water, since a snake like that would lick the rain off its own scales.

The *parviocula* thrived.

Like everyone else who ever encountered *parviocula,* Nguyen couldn't help wanting more. He had a male—now what he needed was a female. "I would have donated a kidney for that snake," he said.

IN LATE October 2004, Molt holed himself up in New Smyrna Beach, Florida, where he'd rented a hotel room on the hurricane-chewed beach. He wouldn't say what he was doing there. It was late at night; Molt was sober, and seemed depressed. He sat outside at a table in the wavering blue light of the pool.

Eddy Postma, Molt's Dutch friend, had disappeared in the Galapagos Islands, and now Postma was presumed dead, at age forty-four. A taxi driver was the last person to see Postma alive. Postma's body was yet to be found.

The official story was that Postma was in the Galapagos to take photos, but Molt knew that Postma was planning to smuggle the pink-tinged land iguanas of Isabela Island, whose females dig their nests in the soft, warm ash atop the precipitous crater of an active volcano, a mile above sea level. Galapagos land iguanas are normally yellowish; the pink subspecies was one evolutionary novelty missed by Charles Darwin, indeed missed by science altogether until 1986, which was understandable, given the species's habits.

Molt was sad for Postma, but mourned even more the projects that died with him, the reptiles they would never smuggle, the places they would never go: China, Costa Rica, Fiji, all into a crater.

Molt had been homeless for eight weeks. His wife had moved to South Carolina, and he would have to figure something out. For now, all he had was his Jeep and his fury. Eight weeks he'd spent on the road, harassing and intimidating the Oklahoma kid and Randal Berry and whomever else. He'd done it before, he said—slept in his car, eaten only crackers, spent hundreds of dollars on gas—all to avenge himself on his enemies.

He quoted a favorite proverb: "Old age and treachery will always overcome youth and skill." It was becoming his mantra, he said.

"The thing you have to understand about the reptile business is, we're not good people, not me, not Ed—none of us. We're users," Molt said.

He feared he might be facing federal charges again, over the Gila monsters and snakes in Oklahoma. He had a plan if he ever wound up in court: He would rent a catheter and a walker and stand before the judge and act infirm. He'd already scoped out a place to rent them.

"I live from obsession to obsession," he said, and when there was no project to obsess over, his enemies filled the void. "I'm an old man, what else am I gonna do? I have no property, no money, just the clothes on my back," and even those were getting frayed.

The reptile business "is a disease," he said, and you can't retire from a disease.

# 20

## Curse of the *Bitis parviocula*

It was mostly thanks to Benjamin Bucks, the Swiss American snake wunderkind, that Hank Molt was able to wrest himself from his cycle of futile retaliations and regroup in the service of a project.

The project remained the elusive *Bitis parviocula*. Molt had let *parviocula* slide for about a year until his friend and financial backer Peter Nguyen noticed, in the summer of 2005, a classified ad on Kingsnake: A German dealer was taking deposits for a shipment of *parviocula* from Ethiopia. Molt would soon lose his bragging rights to the species, and if he wanted any for himself and Nguyen, would have to pay the German's price: $7,500 apiece. Molt told Nguyen that he knew who could fix this situation at once: Benjamin Bucks. Nguyen had never heard of Benjamin Bucks. "He was presented to me as 'our man in Havana,'" Nguyen said. "Hank made sure I didn't know too much about him."

Molt and Bucks began e-mailing each other again after a long, unexplained silence from Molt, who had moved, finally, to South Carolina. The German dealer was advertising *parviocula,* but he didn't have the snakes yet. This meant that someone in Ethiopia had a stock of *parviocula,* ready to ship. There was only one snake dealer in Ethiopia. Bucks had worked with him years before, and the two didn't get along.

Molt e-mailed the German posing as an interested customer, just to get a sense of how many snakes were involved, and how long he and Bucks would have to scuttle the deal. There were thirteen snakes, and they had two weeks. Bucks also e-mailed the German, posing as an Ethiopian customs officer, informing him that he would be prosecuted if he attempted to import this protected endemic snake. The German's ads disappeared.

Nguyen, at Molt's urging, wired some money to Benjamin Bucks, and Bucks flew to Addis Ababa to try to patch things up with the dealer there. Bucks arrived with an offer: sell us all your *Bitis parviocula* for $20,000 cash, and we'll get you a tourist visa to the United States. The Ethiopian accepted, not least because he'd met a woman online who lived in Seattle, and he was very eager to meet her in person.

The visa was Molt's idea, and something of a long shot, but Molt began writing the State Department. The $20,000 belonged to Nguyen, who knew very little about the deal save that he would get a female *parviocula* to match up with his own male, and hopefully recoup his investment from Molt's sales of the rest. It wasn't hard to envision, since the Ethiopian sold the snakes for $1,300 apiece, and collectors would pay $7,500.

The summer seemed interminable to Nguyen, who wanted that female snake badly. Nguyen attended the Daytona expo that year, but seldom left his room. On the trading floor, Molt and Wayne Hill set up a little shrine for their disappeared Dutch friend Eddy Postma, complete with wooden clogs.

Meanwhile, in Addis Ababa, Bucks imposed himself awkwardly on the Ethiopian, making sure the *parviocula* were healthy and ready to ship. Molt had full confidence in his abilities.

BENJAMIN BUCKS'S father was a biochemist, and it seemed natural enough that Bucks, a precocious youth, would also endeavor to become a man of science. But Bucks had barely penned his first and only scientific article, "Further Contributions to the Knowledge of *Bradypodion uthmoelleri* (Müller 1938) from Tanzania," for the German herpetology journal *Salamandra* when he was seized by the urge to run away to Africa. Bucks bought a ticket and took off for Uganda, his parents unable or unwilling to stop him. It was 1994. Bucks was sixteen.

At sixteen, Bucks was somewhat familiar with Africa already. He'd gone on safari almost annually with one parent or another, and had once smuggled a chameleon—the same *Bradypodion uthmoelleri* he would write a paper about—back to Zurich in his sock. His father had taught him the sock technique, which the senior Bucks used to smuggle king snakes from his native Utah to Switzerland.

The Buckses were more adventurous than the usual upper-middle-class Swiss family, but Benjamin outdid all of them with his departure for Uganda. He arrived at the Entebbe airport with no plans except some vague idea to export reptiles. Bucks helped a woman with her heavy baggage, and she offered him a ride into town, but they would have to stop at cargo first, she said. She was transporting the casket of her brother, who had died in New York. "I thought, 'This is brilliant, what a cool start,'" Bucks said.

At his hostel outside Kampala, Bucks chatted with a former Tutsi rebel, fresh from the war in Rwanda. Suddenly Bucks had the urge to visit Rwanda. He bought a bus ticket. "Welcome, traveler," the Tutsi soldiers said at the border, and Bucks thought he would be fine until he saw the shot-up walls and burned, abandoned houses of Kigali. "I suddenly realized what I had done," he said, and Bucks, who had nowhere to sleep, got a lift halfway back to the Ugandan border, and walked the rest of the way, and ended up, soon afterward, in Mombasa, Kenya.

Two years later, American reptile dealers started receiving mysterious, crude price lists hand-scribbled on stationery from Kenyan hotels. They didn't know Bucks was a teenager; they didn't know anything about him save that he was selling such rare snakes as *Atheris ceratophora,* a horned viper from a small range in Tanzania. His boxes of snakes made it out thanks to an arrangement with certain bureaucrats in the Kenyan agricultural ministry. That ministry didn't have the authority to approve wildlife exports, but American and European customs inspectors didn't know that. Well after he'd learned to bribe, bluff, and intimidate—all the skills needed to run a business in Africa—Bucks got around to losing his virginity, to a Kenyan woman ten years his senior. He emerged from the experience so terrified of AIDS that he shunned women for a whole year. He slept in an apartment behind a Mombasa nightclub where in the wee hours the bouncers tied petty thieves to chairs and beat them for stealing empty beer bottles.

By the time he showed up at the Daytona reptile expo in 2003, Bucks had already built and lost three reptile-exporting businesses. He'd gotten over his sexual reservations to the point where he was keeping a computer log of his ladies, complete with details such as "habitat," for where they lived, and "payment," for what they took in exchange for sex—beer, in most cases, or, in one, two tomatoes and an egg.

Just as his computer sex diary was getting epic, Kenya decided it had had enough of Bucks. The government put Bucks on a plane for Switzerland, but Bucks flew straight back to Africa, circumventing Kenya for Addis Ababa, and worked six months hunting snakes with the Ethiopian reptile dealer who now had a cache of *parviocula*. Bucks and the Ethiopian came to be more adversaries than friends, and parted ways. Bucks moved to Uganda, occasionally returning to Kenya, where he once again attracted notice for exporting rare vipers. He met the giant Butterbean at a reptile show in Germany, and enlisted him as the European broker for his snakes. When they'd saturated Europe with their product, they took what was left to the United States, and met Molt.

MOLT AND BUCKS harbored two simultaneous plans for *Bitis parviocula*.

Plan A was the official, five-way plan already under way, involving Bucks, Molt, Butterbean, Peter Nguyen, and the Ethiopian. Nguyen would buy the thirteen snakes at the Ethiopian's price. The snakes would be sent to Butterbean in Germany, mislabeled as puff adders or some other common species. The snakes would arrive for the Terrastika Hamm reptile show in September, a huge, practically lawless affair dwarfing any reptile show in the United States, even the Daytona expo. Molt, Butterbean, and Nguyen would all meet up in Hamm, Germany, sell some of the *parviocula,* take the rest back to the United States, and divide the proceeds, although "we never really figured out how exactly they would be divided," Molt said.

In September 2005, it seemed as though Plan A had worked. The mislabeled snakes arrived safely in Frankfurt. Molt arrived next. Nguyen was supposed to fly with Molt to Germany, but decided at the last minute to stay home, entrusting Molt to deal with everything.

At the show, Molt and Butterbean sold a pair of *parviocula* off the bat, for $7,500 apiece—a $6,200 profit per snake. All the unsold snakes Molt took back to Butterbean's house and left there. Butterbean was a government-licensed snake keeper with a well-organized setup in his basement, and Molt decided that Butterbean's house would be a fine place for the *parviocula* to rest and fatten up after their hard journey. Butterbean was in good form that weekend, cooking sausages and sauerkraut for his guests; his wife had forgiven him, finally, for being bitten by the mamba the year before.

Nguyen was flabbergasted when Molt failed to return with any *parviocula,* but then, Nguyen had no knowledge of Plan B.

PLAN B hinged on the unlikely prospect of the United States granting the Ethiopian a visa.

Molt had filled out the paperwork for once, and if it came through, Molt and Bucks were fairly sure the Ethiopian would hop on a plane that day, since he couldn't stop talking about the woman in Seattle. With the Ethiopian safely abroad, Bucks could travel to the village where *parviocula* is found and grab a fresh, low-cost batch for himself and Molt. The Ethiopian paid the villagers sixty dollars apiece for the snakes. Bucks would offer $120, which was fairer to them, and far less painful to Bucks and Molt than the $1,300 per snake they'd paid the Ethiopian. Getting the snakes out of Ethiopia was not going to be easy, but Bucks knew of a border crossing to Kenya where a guard might be bribed. Then the snakes could be sent to Europe or the United States, depending—that part they would work out later. Nguyen "was to be cut out of the deal completely," said Molt, except to be encouraged to entertain the Ethiopian during his visit.

In October 2005, the Ethiopian's visa came through, and, just as Molt and Bucks expected, he needed little encouragement to travel. He would head first to Seattle and see how that went, then fly to Florida to visit some reptile dealers who owed him money. Nguyen offered to meet the Ethiopian in Florida and drive with him to Washington, D.C., where he could spend a few days touring the Mall and the Smithsonian. And then it was back to Addis Ababa.

Bucks was on standby alert in Kenya when Molt phoned. The Ethiopian was safely in the country, Molt reported, but something had not gone well in Seattle, and he had already left for Florida. Bucks now had only a matter of days to collect the *parviocula* and get them out.

Bucks flew to Addis Ababa, and that evening made it to the village of Bedele, where he met with one of the Ethiopian's collectors. The collector informed Bucks that within a day or so he could get him five *parviocula*. Bucks took a cab back to the capital to await the delivery: the collector would hop a beer truck from Bedele and bring the snakes to his hotel. But then Bucks had second thoughts. The Ethiopian would probably find out, sooner rather than later, that the blond, rather hard-to-miss Benjamin Bucks had shown up in Bedele. The Ethiopian knew what hotels Bucks liked; he even knew the cab driver Bucks always used.

Bucks thought about leaving the hotel, but the collector was on his way there with a box of snakes. Bucks called his taxi driver to come collect him, the snake collector, and the box of snakes and get them all somewhere safer. Just then, the phone rang at the front desk. It was the Ethiopian, demanding to know if a blond man had checked in. Bucks mimed to the receptionist—he wasn't there.

"That was when Hank called," said Bucks.

Molt called Bucks's cell phone to inform him that the Ethiopian had not only gotten wind of Bucks's incursions, he was now so mad that he'd canceled his travel plans and was making an emergency flight home from Miami. Peter Nguyen had been driving down I-95 to pick up the Ethiopian for their scheduled tour of D.C. when the Ethiopian called him and canceled. Nguyen phoned Molt to tell him what had happened.

By the time Molt reached Bucks, Bucks was standing in a hotel lobby with a snake collector holding a box of five *parviocula,* "freaking out," Molt said. Someone had informed on Bucks—maybe the collector, maybe the taxi driver—"and then just that minute, I see the taxi driver pull up to the hotel with some guys I didn't know," Bucks said. He figured them to be wildlife agents.

He abandoned the snakes and the collector, ran to his room, grabbed his passport and bag, and escaped through the basement kitchen of the hotel.

Bucks expected that there would be an alert for him at the airport, where he arrived hours later. He already had a ticket to Nairobi, but they would be looking for him in the international wing. So he purchased a second, local plane ticket, and hid in domestic departures until the last moment, when he crossed terminals—African airport security could be helpfully relaxed—and boarded.

Bucks had managed to save his skin, but not his snakes.

PETER NGUYEN wasn't sure what to make of Bucks's adventures in Ethiopia. Molt insisted to Nguyen that whatever Bucks was doing was between Bucks and the Ethiopian, some old private score-settling with no bearing on Nguyen.

Nguyen didn't care, as long as he got his snakes. By now it was December, time for the next Terrastika Hamm show in Germany. Molt had promised to fly over and return with the snakes, and though Nguyen wanted to believe Molt, he wasn't counting on him. Nguyen knew Molt well enough by now to expect delays, absences, and preposterous excuses. Nguyen had visited Molt's apartment once, to find it barely habitable, just a bare cell, but for Molt's books and papers "and literally no furniture but a card table and folding plastic chair," said Nguyen, who was saddened by the sight.

So Nguyen asked some American reptile dealers, who were also headed to the German show, to bring the snakes back for him. "It just seemed like I was unburdening Hank of a task he couldn't complete," he said.

AT THE Hamm reptile show, Molt and Butterbean sold a second pair of *parviocula* to the same German collector who'd bought the first pair two months before. That night the collector called Butterbean, upset. One of the new *parviocula,* he reported, had flopped on its back and died.

"We were stumped," Molt said. "He provided the dead snake, which he hadn't paid for yet. He was a private collector, a very honest, nerdy, studious reptile guy, so we believed him. We said we could replace it." But before the weekend was over, the replacement snake died, too.

Something was sorely wrong—the snakes had been exposed to a virus or a bacterium, probably. But Butterbean had taken pains with the *parviocula,* isolating them from his other snakes and disinfecting every surface and using only fresh containers. It didn't make sense.

Nguyen's friends confronted Molt and Butterbean, demanding they hand over the remaining *parviocula* to bring back to the United States. Molt refused them.

When his friends returned empty-handed, Nguyen wondered whether Molt had meant to defraud him all along. He chose to believe otherwise. "My guess is they were trying to sell the snakes in Germany, then use [Bucks] to get enough of them cheap to fulfill the order to me," he said.

The way Molt saw it, it was Nguyen's fault for trusting him. Nguyen "did not take charge of the situation," Molt said. "He lost $20,000, got no snakes, nothing."

It was the reptile business, it went without saying.

THE FALLOUT from the *parviocula* was immediate and nasty. On New Year's Eve, Benjamin Bucks was arrested and thrown into a Kenyan jail. Kenya now had a long list of grievances against Bucks, as did wildlife officials in neighboring countries, particularly Ethiopia.

When Bucks got out of jail, Kenya began rescinding his various business licenses. Bucks was thinking about giving up Africa for good when, that March, he visited his brother in Zurich. When he tried to return, Kenya blocked his reentry. CITES officials made note of this triumph at their annual conference:

> Surveillance on a notorious reptile smuggler has been going on and was being conducted by intelligence personnel from Kenya, Ethiopia and Uganda. The smuggler was arrested at Ukunda on 31st December, 2005. KWS made an application for the smuggler to be declared a prohibited immigrant. The request was granted in March, 2006.

Hank Molt resumed his schedule of reprisals as effortlessly as if the *Bitis parviocula* affair had merely pressed the pause button on them, and added Nguyen to his roster of enemies, sending him vague, threatening letters with no return address.

MOLT FLEW to Germany again. Butterbean's recent silence seemed ominous, and the Terrastika Hamm show was approaching. Molt rented a car in Frankfurt and drove it to Butterbean's in Münster. Butterbean's yard, Molt saw, was full of empty terrariums half buried in the March snow.

Inside, the house was cold, the family had moved out, and there was Butterbean, his gaunt giant's body outstretched on a couch.

The *parviocula* were all dead, labeled in bags in the freezer. Butterbean's veterinarian had performed necropsies on the snakes and determined the culprit to be ophidian paramyxovirus, a pathogen that had wiped out whole snake collections in zoos.

"He was almost suicidally depressed," Molt said of Butterbean. "He refused to go to Hamm because he was too embarrassed. Lying on the couch all day without the heat on, listening to Gothic music."

In Butterbean's cold living room, Molt noticed an escaped rattlesnake, coiled up on a bookshelf. Eventually, Butterbean had to be hospitalized.

PETER NGUYEN would never speak a civil word to Molt again. He blamed his Asperger's for making him unable to detect Molt's deceptions, but probably he should have blamed his all-consuming snake lust, the kind of lust that had made fools out of people smarter than him.

And yet Nguyen could not bring himself to hate Molt. "He is an unrepentant smuggler," Nguyen said. "But he loved the animals. He has magnificent taste in herps—a gentleman's taste. He can in a single phrase encapsulate the essence of an animal, in a short little burst of telegraphic text until you just say, 'I can't live without this thing.'

"He is a man whom, had he been born a hundred years before, there would have been bronzes of," Nguyen continued, "and that kills him. He wants to be Alfred Russel Wallace, with a bit of Barnum thrown in. He was born a century late and it kills him, it eats him alive."

# 21

## The Partial Rehabilitation of Tom Crutchfield

Shortly after Tom Crutchfield was released from a federal correctional complex in Yazoo City, Mississippi, where he entertained very few visitors and lit his cigarettes through a hole in the wall, he left Penny, his wife of thirty years. This surprised him almost as much as it did everyone else. Even his new girlfriend, Patty, had trouble believing it. "He told me, 'I'll never leave my wife,'" Patty said. "I never thought he would."

Patty waited tables at Joanie's Blue Crab Café, a restaurant in Everglades City where Crutchfield took his Everglades Day Safari customers for lunch. Patty sometimes worked barefoot, or in a bikini. She was seventeen years younger than Crutchfield, already a widow, and had no great love for snakes. She was pretty, if tough, with chipped teeth and a smoky voice. Crutchfield thoroughly approved of lower-back tattoos and pierced nipples. Patty also tuned up Crutchfield's car and even proved amenable to arduous days at the gym, where Crutchfield would place an eighty-pound barbell on her back and make her do lunges.

Patty stood no chance with Crutchfield's daughters, at least not for many years, and she confounded Crutchfield's friends, who mistakenly called her "Penny," then caught themselves. How could he leave a woman who had fled with him to Belize? Maybe Penny had dumped *him*, they speculated.

Crutchfield and Patty showed up without fail for the reptile expo in Daytona. In the years while Crutchfield remained on probation, while he worked as a guide in the Everglades, they sold no animals but rented a small table and sold Crutchfield's book collection, along with what was left of his handmade knives and spears. Crutchfield's Mercedes was gone, replaced by a Ford Escort wagon. Sometimes he would be recognized by former customers indifferently flipping through his books. "Are you—?"

"Yep!" he would say.

"Man, I bought my first snake from you."

"A lot of people did."

Here were Crutchfield's former jerks and assholes regarding him with wonder and pity, like émigrés who'd discovered their exiled king washing dishes at Denny's. He was as obliging to them as could be. Molt, who kept an extremely polite distance from Crutchfield at the expos, thought that his old nemesis had become too mellow, too nice, that the fire had gone out of his eyes.

TWO YEARS later, when his probation period ended, Crutchfield broke up with Patty, quit the Everglades Day Safari, and moved from Fort Myers to Miami. He lived with a wealthy Miami physician, an old friend, who kept too many animals in squalid conditions in his otherwise lovely home. The doctor frequently forgot to feed them, and his wife did her best to keep them alive. Still, the rhinoceros iguanas banged their noses on wire cages all day, demanding lettuce, and from the snake room adjacent to the house came the smell of something dead. Feral green iguanas sunned themselves on the mangroves near the doctor's docked yacht, and these iguanas, left to their own devices, were doing better than any of his captives.

The doctor was wan and frail and slept all day. At night he drank white rum and smoked cigarettes until, by dawn, a ziggurat of butts arose from his ashtray. He was a former small-time smuggler himself, who in 2001 had been caught trying to sneak in boas from the Bahamas, and later pleaded guilty. He had recently been bitten by a fer-de-lance in Suriname. He claimed not to have seen the snake, but no one believed him. Not only was he drunk a lot of the time, but he had an uncontrollable urge to capture animals, all kinds of animals. The doctor videotaped the progress of the snakebite, his waxy swollen hand with its blackening index finger, narrating the progress of his symptoms. He distributed DVDs of the event to fellow snake enthusiasts; now, his left index finger was stiffened and useless.

Before Crutchfield arrived, the doctor had tried to open a reptile shop on a busy stretch in North Miami, only to lose his inventory to incompetence and neglect. Crutchfield tried his best to manage the store, but found the walk-in customers hard to bear. In the retail pet business, every day was J&A day. But Crutchfield had finally managed to save some money. He didn't know whether he'd stay in Miami and help the doctor for a while, or move to rural North Florida, where he could afford property.

Mostly what Crutchfield wanted was to import reptiles again. The doctor came in handy for this, since he had valid import permits despite his Bahamas transgression, and the Feds weren't about to reissue Crutchfield's. A crate of a thousand baby iguanas, most of them dying, sat in a back room of the shop. The doctor had ordered them on a whim, and that was a recurrent problem. Many ended up as food for the other reptiles.

AFTER A few months' separation, Crutchfield and Patty decided they couldn't live without each other after all. The pet store proved a money pit, so the doctor closed it and bought an overgrown property in Ft. Lauderdale, a compound with two houses for snake breeding and a third house for Crutchfield and Patty to live in while they managed all the snakes. This sounded good on paper, but ultimately translated into full-time servitude for Patty, who was soon at her wits' end.

"Snake shit," she said. "That's all I do, is clean snake shit." If she wasn't cleaning cages, she was cleaning house, or cooking, or on a cigarette run.

She feared Crutchfield had become dependent on the painkillers he took for his bad back, and that the drugs were making him surly. Lately she had broken a whole set of dishes in a fight.

Patty kept ducks for pleasure, one of the few pleasures she had, but Crutchfield's escaped snakes ate her ducklings. When she got a day or two alone, she would lock herself in a room with her fluffy white cat, and let the snake shit pile up.

WITHIN A year, Crutchfield's snake collection filled both back buildings of the compound and a good part of the living area. Patty thought painkillers were turning Crutchfield mean, but being around snakes again seemed to bring out some of the harder aspects of Crutchfield's personality, the impulsiveness, competitiveness, and short-temperedness for which he was notorious. His one employee, a skilled and friendly Cuban, had already quit, tired of Crutchfield's badgering. Patty had fallen in love with Crutch-field when he was flat on his back. He wasn't on his feet quite yet, but he was sitting up, and the ghost limb of his ego was regenerating.

Inevitably, Crutchfield began feeling the urge to travel again.

He was lately fixated on a snake in the Dominican Republic. He had a mission in mind to collect and take field notes on a red strain of *Epicrates striatus,* the Haitian boa. Most Haitian boas were a granite color, but a rare few were a bright, ketchupy red. The Bronx Zoo maintained a small colony of red Haitian boas, so these were not unknown to science, yet Crutchfield was unshakably convinced that the red ones were a separate, new species mistakenly lumped in with the others, a species "hidden in plain sight," he said. Back in the 1970s, Crutchfield had collected a gecko new to science, and was mildly disappointed when it was not named for him. This boa was a different story. If Crutchfield could manage to get this snake named after himself—even as a subspecies—the vanity factor would be exponentially greater.

Crutchfield's plan was to collect as many red boas as he could in the mountainous eastern part of the Dominican Republic, then pay the zoo in Santo Domingo to provide the CITES export permits to move them out, and then, after some schmoozing and chip-cashing up at the University of Florida, submit the blood samples for DNA, and get them designated a new species named, what else? *Epicrates crutchfieldii,* or *Epicrates striatus crutchfieldii,* if it wound up being a subspecies. The doctor would provide the money, as usual, and come along for the ride. The doctor spoke good Spanish, which helped, but he was always drunk and that meant Crutchfield would have to babysit him, "make sure he doesn't fall off a cliff or something," he said.

Red Haitian boas were worth about $5,000 a pair to collectors, meaning that Crutchfield's venture was not purely scientific in intent. It certainly lacked the exhaustive planning of a scientific venture. Crutchfield waited until the day before leaving to secure himself a new passport, resulting in a moody, seven-hour wait with Patty in the Miami passport office. On the morning of the trip, when he went to get cash, his bank account was overdrawn.

Crutchfield, the doctor, and the doctor's son took along a snake hook, four fancy new LED flashlights, and an awful lot of narcotic painkillers. Just to be on the safe side, as there were no truly venomous species on Hispaniola, the doctor packed medicines for anaphylactic shock. Crutchfield announced he would use the opportunity of the trip to quit smoking, but he'd nonetheless packed a carton of Marlboro lights, which he smoked without pause.

The doctor had stopped drinking following a pancreatitis episode over the winter, but fell off the wagon at the airport bar, where he ordered a Tom Collins. Crutchfield ambled over to duty free to check prices on Obsession, his favorite cologne. About half a dozen bottles of it graced his dresser at home, but he could always use more. "It costs less at Walgreens," he said, dismayed. As the flight boarded, the doctor tried to sneak a cigarette in the airport bathroom, forcing his son to intervene.

A YOUNG snake hunter named Alfred met Crutchfield in Santo Domingo. Alfred was a Dominican who had grown up in New York and had worked as an intern for John Behler at the Bronx Zoo. Alfred had been such a talented teenage herpetologist that he could find wild salamanders in Manhattan, but in his twenties he wound up serving two and a half years in state prison for drug crimes. Now Alfred was thirty, supposedly reformed, and hunting Hispaniola reptiles with every smuggler or scientist who needed his aid. He didn't discriminate.

Over beers outside a bodega, Alfred shared two inconvenient facts. The first was that a Smithsonian biologist had already done the DNA work on red Haitian boas, and determined them to be, without a doubt, the same species as the black ones: *Epicrates striatus.* The second was that Alfred himself had helped a German visitor collect more than a hundred red boas the previous year, and the German had successfully pressed the zoo for export permits. In all likelihood, the zoo gave the German a permit for four or five snakes, and he suitcased the other ninety-five, but still. If the German succeeded in breeding the boas, or at least keeping most of them alive, the market might soon be flooded with red *Epicrates striatus,* ruining Crutchfield's plans.

Crutchfield shrugged at the news that snakes were not new to science. Once the scientific pretensions of the trip were effectively disposed of, there was the German competition to worry about. But Crutchfield wasn't sweating that, either.

Crutchfield just wanted those red boas. They all did. They wanted a lot of them, and they wanted them that day. They got in Alfred's truck and started off.

"I never fail on these trips," Crutchfield said as Alfred drove. "Not like Hank."

CRUTCHFIELD SAID he expected to return from this trip with forty thousand dollars' worth of snakes, and that first night, in a patch of jungle within Santo Domingo, the group netted two normal black Haitian boas, and at least a thousand dollars' worth of a small, delicate species, the Haitian dwarf boa. Alfred drank white rum as he hunted. "Something about it opens up my senses," he said, passing around his bottle. The rum was working; Alfred was seeing snakes everywhere, even while driving, and would come to a screeching halt if a movement in a tree caught his eye. Crutchfield pronounced Alfred "the best fucking snake hunter I've ever seen." The doctor's son was also an adept hunter. Only Crutchfield seemed to have trouble seeing snakes in this environment. It had been two decades since he'd last set foot on Hispaniola, and nearly a decade since Belize. He had gained some weight, and his back and hips bothered him, making him wobbly on the alternately rock-strewn and spongy ground. "I'm getting old," he said. "Much as I hate to admit it."

In the morning, Alfred arrived at the hotel eager to hunt snakes in the town of Baní. Coincidentally, little rural Baní was famous for its beautiful women, like something out of Ovid, and was in the middle of a carnival. Baní crawled with women, in skirts, wearing cat masks, on the backs of mopeds, swishing their hips, drinking rum. But Alfred drove straight through. There were snakes to catch.

All day, they hunted muddy flats, finding nothing but shed snake skins and a toad. In the evening, when the group had migrated to a wet patch of woods that looked more promising, the frog calls were interrupted by a loud whooshing sound: the doctor's son was throwing rocks high into a tree, trying to dislodge a vine snake. The doctor and his son threw rocks at animals all the time, it turned out. Recently, to Crutchfield's lingering disgust, the doctor had thrown one at a female bobcat in the Everglades, trying to separate her from the kittens she was nursing, so he could grab one. Crutchfield threatened to let the cat shred him if he didn't stop.

The vine snake dropped to the ground. Its tail, they saw when they examined it, had been chewed by a rat.

The day's total haul was that single rat-chewed vine snake, wriggling in a bag on the dashboard of Alfred's jeep. He drove through Baní, where the carnival was winding down, and stopped on the road for a snack of pork rinds. A woman roasted them next to a tiny shack with a circle of chairs in the dirt, and on the porch of the house next door, two couples danced merengue under a bare lightbulb. Just then a young pregnant woman, in a chair near Crutchfield, suddenly fell backward and hit the dirt. "Uh, I think she's having a seizure," he said. The dancing couples stopped dancing and helped lift the limp woman into the house.

The doctor was back at the hotel—he seldom woke up before one or two p.m., and so had missed the trip—and though the doctor's son was studying to be a chiropractor, he was at a genuine loss to help the woman. His phone calls to his father's hotel room went unanswered. Screams came from within the house, and he finally entered. The woman's pulse was nearly two hundred, he reported. She needed to get to a hospital.

Her family refused. Recently a friend of hers died, they said, a young man in the village. What that was supposed to explain was unclear. Hysteria? Spirit possession? But they were adamant. "Country people," said Alfred.

The episode elicited a string of factoids from Crutchfield. "In Haiti, the *asogwe* is mounted by the *loa*," he explained on the drive back toward the capital. Alfred passed around his rum.

Then, a burst of light came from behind; it was a speeding car. Alfred hit the gas and swerved skillfully to miss it. It happened so fast that it barely registered, a flash of white headlights in the mirror. About a minute later, the speeding car, a souped-up Accord, had crashed into a Jeep and a Toyota; a small mob was pulling bodies from the smoking cars. The driver of the Accord was alive, a boy of about twenty; his companions were dead or dying, and the Toyota passengers weren't faring much better. Alfred yelled at Crutchfield to clear all the gear from the back—he would be transporting a victim. But that victim, another boy in his twenties, was seconds from being dead. His brains were falling out of his head and onto Alfred as he gripped Alfred hard and struggled to stand. A mob on the road grew and grew—young girls, old women, a fat man naked except for a towel. The crowd got increasingly nasty as young men loaded the victims into pickup trucks, while others stole their wallets and jewelry. Someone was waving a gun. "Fuck it, let's go," Alfred said. The boy he was tending to had died.

The smell of liquor permeated the truck on the way back, as though the bottle of rum had spilled. But it was the blood of the dead boy, reeking of alcohol. "I have brains on my pants," Alfred said, and all his cash was missing from his pocket. Just then, nearly an hour after the accident, a lone ambulance crossed in the opposite direction.

At the hotel, the doctor was AWOL. Neither Crutchfield nor the doctor's son had any idea where he might have gone. He had left some sort of vile mess of vomit and possibly feces in the tub before disappearing, and though his son was busy trying to clean it, Crutchfield couldn't bear to watch, and returned to the hotel lobby. "This trip is going south fast," he said, pausing for a good long while to absorb how far south it had gone. "You know who would have appreciated this day?" said Crutchfield, finally. "Hank."

He was right—it had been a Hank Molt day, a day when things go so wrong that failure itself is transfigured, with a little distance and the right telling, into a twisted sort of glory.

BY MORNING, the doctor had returned, but neither he nor his son could be roused, and so Crutchfield spent the first half of the day sitting by a cloudy stream in Santo Domingo's botanical gardens, watching Haitian slider turtles, with yellow faces, float up and dive. "You see, I actually enjoy this, just being here and seeing these turtles," Crutchfield said. The doctor, he continued, "would be out there in the water, mud all over his pants. He has an unstoppable compulsion to accumulate wildlife. He becomes possessed."

A butterfly native to Florida fluttered by, causing Crutchfield to marvel. He liked to be among the hummingbirds, the butterflies, a pond full of papyrus. Thirty years ago, he said, he was a lot like the doctor and his son—all about the snake. He might even have thrown rocks at a snake, he said. But now, that kind of behavior embarrassed him.

When Crutchfield returned to the hotel, Alfred was waiting, in clean clothes and surprisingly good spirits, though he retained a macabre bruise on his upper arm where the dying boy had grabbed him. He'd heard there were red boas in the town of San Francisco, two hours away. That got the doctor and his son out of bed. The doctor had not been hospitalized or in jail the night before, as Crutchfield had feared, but was out winning $3,000 at a casino. The doctor's fresh cash would be spread around the village of San Francisco, where eager children would scout red boas. They should write a piece for *Reptiles* magazine, Crutchfield suggested: "The Hunt for the Red Boa!" Crutchfield was smiling, excited. "We're gonna make some kids skip school!" he said. The issue of the export permits was far from resolved, but Alfred had accepted thousands of dollars of the doctor's money and assured everyone he'd take care of it later.

The next morning, as San Francisco's village square came to life, filling fast with sandwich vendors and shoe shiners and begging Haitian children, the doctor emerged from the hotel smoking a cigarette, interviewing random people in his excellent Spanish. Anyone around here hunt snakes? Red snakes? he asked a shoe shiner. Crutchfield joined the doctor, lighting a cigarette. He tried to follow the conversation, gave up, then looked the shoe shiner straight in the eye with a very intent expression.

"*Cu-le-bras ro-jas,*" he said slowly.

"Rojas," the man confirmed. Actually, yes, he did have a friend—a taxidermist—who caught red snakes. In an hour, this taxidermist friend, too, found his way to the square. He was a slender, gentle, impoverished-looking fellow, carrying a plastic grocery bag full of shoes and belts he had fashioned from Haitian boas. One of the belts was a distinct reddish orange. He extracted from his pocket a very worn photograph, protected by layers of yellowing plastic, of himself holding a live, enormous, unmistakably red Haitian boa around his neck. Alfred's tip had been right—San Francisco was red boa country! Crutchfield borrowed the man's photo and ran into the hotel to show Alfred.

The taxidermist told the doctor he wanted thirty dollars per red boa. Outrageous, countered the doctor, who offered ten. The issue of payment remained unsettled as the entire team, now including the taxidermist, squeezed into Alfred's truck. The taxidermist said he knew a cave full of red boas. That perked everyone up. Then Alfred remembered that the word for "cave" can be the same, in Spanish, as the word for "hollow of a tree." Was it a cave or a tree? A tree, said the taxidermist. "Shit," said Crutchfield. On the way they picked up another snake hunter, a friend of the taxidermist, who carried a machete and clung to the side of the jeep. The trees on the road were charred underneath from where the hunters had burned them, trying to smoke snakes out of the hollows. The sky was gray and it began to thunder.

The tree that was said to be full of red boas stood in the middle of a deteriorating old ranch. Cow pies and tangles of barbed wire were everywhere; guinea fowl and chickens ran hysterically in circles. None of the ranch hands, who were sheltering themselves from the impending rain, minded a gang of men with machetes removing snakes from the property. They were all for it.

Extracting a snake from the hollow of a tree is more art than science, and the Hank Molt adage "You can't do shit without natives" came to mind as the taxidermist climbed the tree, barefoot. His friend with the machete followed. They worked fast, chopping down branches to expose the tree's cavities. The taxidermist's long feet curled around the branches as he poked sticks into holes, looking for anything soft and alive. Crutchfield and Alfred did the same to a nearby tree, then retrieved a gas can and a narrow hose to blow gas fumes into it, fumes that would irritate a snake enough to force it out into fresh air. When that produced nothing, they started a fire, with twigs and leaves and gas, lighting it in the lowest hole of the tree, letting the smoke do the work. "This is like a needle in a haystack," said Crutchfield. "This is how snakes have survived millennia of abuse."

No one doubted there were snakes around here; the trouble was, this ranch had been pretty thoroughly hunted of them already, for shoes and belts. Most of its trees bore sooty stains from old fires. The smoking and gassing and hacking took hours, as thunder roared over the fields.

The weather was causing the cattle to cry out and the fowl to screech, but a shirtless doctor wandered alone and indifferent, looking for snakes in the ether. For a moment, it appeared as though he would be gored by a bull, which was exactly the type of thing Crutchfield expected would happen to him. "Buuuuuullll!" Crutchfield shouted in the doctor's direction. "Dad! Buuuuuuulll!" the doctor's son followed, but there was no response; the rain and wind had muted their pleas. The doctor, not one to be hurried, returned intact in his own time.

Crutchfield and Alfred had a strong fire going in one tree's core; they squatted and fanned it, looking up to see smoke emerge from its higher orifices. A sudden stench caused them to step back. "Smell that?" Alfred asked. "I sure do," said Crutchfield. Snake musk: proof positive that something was in there, ready to come out. But the taxidermist and his friend, from their vantage in the tree, had spotted something on the ground. They descended, and the taxidermist lifted with a machete the rotting carcass of a large, still visibly red Haitian boa, limp and bony as it dangled from the blade. That was what smelled. They put out Crutchfield's fire with mud.

## 22

### The Blue-Rattled Rattler

When Hank Molt failed to show up for the reptile expo in 2006, the rumor was that Peter Nguyen had put out a hit on him. Nguyen had announced on the reptile Web sites that Molt had cheated him out of twenty thousand dollars' worth of snakes, and his language was threatening in an oblique sort of way. It was a good rumor, but Nguyen was not nearly that crazy, and Molt had never let fear of creditors stop him before—his visits to the expo were marked by his cocksure defiance of people angry enough to want to kill him.

Days before the expo, Molt wrote to say that "a sudden and extremely serious medical emergency" was keeping him from getting to Florida. He alluded to a brother-in-law. Later, he acknowledged that this was not the case—he was broke and depressed, and facing some emerging debacle in South Carolina.

The cause of Molt's depression, generally speaking, was *Bitis parviocula*. It had been five months since the ignoble death of the last *parviocula* in a Münster basement. Molt, however, continued to offer the snakes under the "international inventory" section of his fabulist online price list: "Bitis parviocula. Captive born '05 the best 2 holdbacks of the litter—very rare—6000 Euros." Unless he meant frozen ones, the *parviocula* were now very rare indeed, but in Molt's experience failures were often precursors to success, and Molt could not bring himself to abandon hope that there were more *parviocula* in his future. "With the Boelen's pythons and ringed pythons we did it so many times before it worked," he said.

Molt had been quick to seek distractions after the *parviocula* debacle, and new people to spend his time with. In South Carolina, he'd met a thirty-two-year-old Mormon named Adam Stewart, who owned a pet shop in a neighboring town. Molt and Stewart drove around to reptile shows and went snake hunting in the Blue Ridge Mountains. It did not take long before their relationship bore some trappings of a business partnership. Molt consigned snakes to Stewart's pet store, and they split the earnings. Molt encouraged Stewart to obtain a live-animal shipping permit from Delta Airlines.

A couple months before the expo that he missed, Molt called Stewart with some news: Two men in Alabama, a father and a son, had asked Molt to buy out their valuable, partly illegal collection of venomous snakes and lizards. The collection included Gila monsters and rare rattlesnakes that the pair had caught in the Arizona deserts, and had flown home in their luggage. The son was getting married and his fiancée was not keen on this hard-gotten collection. The father wasn't willing to risk caring for it in his own house, since Alabama law barred the keeping of venomous snakes.

Molt was not the most loved or trusted reptile dealer in the country, but he remained a useful contact for people in a pinch.

Molt wanted the rattlesnakes and Gila monsters, but had no money with which to buy them. Adam Stewart had a credit card that allowed for cash advances. Molt agreed to take two of the rarer rattlesnakes as his finder's fee if Stewart took over the deal. Stewart negotiated a price of $5,200 for the collection, which was worth easily twice that. Molt drove with Stewart in Molt's Jeep to Guntersville, Alabama.

It would have been a cut-and-dried affair, except that on the way to Guntersville, Stewart's $5,200, a stack of notes in a bank envelope, disappeared. Stewart seemed not to have noticed until he reached the sellers' doorstep. It made for an awkward afternoon. Molt and Stewart managed to examine the collection anyway, then retraced their path and searched gas stations, fruitlessly. They returned to South Carolina with neither snakes nor money.

Stewart extracted more money—at this point he would have to buy and resell the collection merely to break even—and picked up his snakes, alone. Later Molt stopped by Stewart's pet shop for a look at the collection, which, they both agreed, was fantastic. You should see one specimen, Stewart told Molt. It was a rare twin-spotted rattlesnake, *Crotalus pricei,* but with a *blue* rattle.

"Adam was saying, 'Isn't this neat?' He thought it was a natural thing," said Molt. "I knew right away it was a field-marked specimen." Biologists routinely paint specimens with some sort of enamel, often nail polish, to identify them. This snake had a two-toned marking of turquoise and cobalt. "I told him, 'You gotta get some nail polish remover,'" Molt said. But it was too late—Stewart had already listed the animal for sale in the classifieds section of Kingsnake.com, with a color photo. Customers were already calling.

The first "customer" to arrive was Special Agent Tom Chisdock of the U.S. Fish and Wildlife Service in Asheville.

EDDIE CELEBUCKI had expected Molt to make it to the reptile expo, since Molt had, crises and calamities notwithstanding, made it to ten years' worth of expos in a row. Celebucki in no way believed that a medical emergency prevented Molt from coming to Florida, and he seemed a little lost without his friend.

Celebucki arrived the Thursday before the expo wearing a dragon shirt, unbuttoned to the belly, and a lizard earring. Celebucki owned a whole wardrobe of rayon shirts printed with oriental motifs—dragons, phoenixes, Chinese characters. He stood on the patio deck of the big hotel, dragon shirt rippling, surveying the crashing sea. He would use this weekend, he announced, as a test to see if he could break his addiction to reptiles. Celebucki, who had opened another karate school but never replaced his snake collection after his swingers' club was raided, had money in his pocket and no reptiles, always a volatile scenario, and wanted to see if he could resist the temptation to buy them. He thought maybe he had become addicted to reptiles in the first place because "I was a lonely five-year-old, and this unusual thing distinguished me." His swinging days were over, too, he added. He was single now, a state that did not agree with him.

The movie *Snakes on a Plane* opened that night, and Celebucki raised a posse of friends to go see it. They came back wild-eyed and happy, though they could not help cataloging the scientific errors. Twelve hours later, Celebucki was wandering around with a turtle he'd just bought. That evening, Celebucki was musing aloud about returning to Papua New Guinea, figuring that all the people old enough to remember him there would be dead.

In Molt's absence, his friends felt free to talk behind his back, and Celebucki, by far the most tolerant and understanding of them all, was no exception this time. Molt hadn't bothered to come around to Cleveland once since the swingers' club closed, he complained, and hadn't called much either since Celebucki refused to put up $2,000 in the doomed *parviocula* deal, a decision that, to Celebucki, was a no-brainer. "Two thousand dollars in a Hank Molt deal—no fucking way," he said. Celebucki wasn't surprised by what had happened to Peter Nguyen, and he had a feeling about what had happened to Adam Stewart. When Molt ran into a certain type of young man, Celebucki said, someone just a little too enthusiastic for his own good, he used to point him out to Celebucki and say: "I think he's ripe for our program." Nguyen had been ripe for the program. Stewart was ripe for the program. "Hank is a herpetologist's version of a pedophile," Celebucki said.

"When I was a deputy sheriff, I dealt with a lot of sociopaths," Celebucki went on. "Hank is incapable of holding a job, of committing to a routine; he's unreliable. Always blaming his illness or someone else's illness or logistical problems." Which was, of course, what Molt was doing right then.

ONLY DAYS before the expo, Special Agent Tom Chisdock showed up at Adam Stewart's pet store to get a look at the special snake with the blue rattle. Once in the door, he dropped all pretenses of being a customer.

It was an Arizona game officer who'd seen Stewart's ad first. Wildlife officers, both state and federal, made a habit of scanning the online reptile classifieds the way they once subscribed to price lists and *Reptiles* magazine. *Crotalus pricei* was highly protected, and any specimen for sale would have set off alarms, but a *pricei* with a blue rattle was asking for it.

Before contacting Chisdock, the Arizona game officer had e-mailed the ad to a biologist who'd been working with *pricei* since 1997. The biologist confirmed that he had caught and marked that snake only months before in the Chiricahua Mountains. The game officer hoped that Chisdock could open a federal case on a snake stolen from Arizona. It wasn't easy to prove poaching under normal circumstances, but a blue rattle helped.

Stewart hadn't bothered to remove the blue enamel by the time Chisdock came around. Nor did he bother to make up any stories. He surrendered the snake.

Chisdock showed up at Molt's apartment the same day, but Molt refused to let him in, even though it was raining miserably. Chisdock wedged himself as best he could into Molt's doorway, trying not to get wet. "He'd just talked to Adam for four hours," Molt said. "He was convinced that I masterminded the whole thing, put Adam up to it."

Chisdock demanded that Molt come to the local police station for an interview. Molt refused. That weekend, while Celebucki and the rest frolicked in Florida, Molt sat at his card table, crafting mocking letters to "Agent Cheese-Dick."

In the end, Molt crumpled up his provocations and wrote Chisdock a fairly subdued letter that blamed Stewart for everything. "He also gave me a litany of failed Fish and Wildlife investigations and talked about my character and lack thereof," Chisdock recalled, but the affront was modest by Molt's standards, a mere formality.

Charges were brought against Adam Stewart and the Alabama men, who settled without trial, each paying fines of $1,000. Stewart's blue-rattled rattler was sent to a South Carolina zoo, where it began to slowly starve. Eventually the zoo sent it on to wildlife officials in Arizona, where it died.

DAVE PRIVAL, the Arizona biologist who had painted the blue-rattled rat-
tler, could not resist writing an article about the incident, in a rather dramatic narrative style, published in a journal called *Sonoran Herpetologist*.
The piece was soon reprinted in any number of conservation magazines,
since it had all the elements: Hank Molt, the cunning veteran smuggler;
Adam Stewart, the dimwitted apprentice; the father and son from Guntersville with a sack of snakes on a plane. Prival made clear his annoyance
at the low fines and lax treatment of the perpetrators by Chisdock; snake
poachers might not be much of a threat on their own, he argued, but combined with other factors, such as land conversion and global warming, they
could spell the end of a species like *pricei*.

Molt responded to Prival in an e-mail complete with quotes from Vir-
gil, Kipling, Horace, Wilde, Swift, Pliny the Elder, Galileo, and Shakespeare.

> *David,*
>
> *This is my riposte to your straggling, multifarious, elegiac and most impor-*
> *tantly, supercilious essay wherein you treat of Hank Molt, Adam Stew-*
> *art, the Hammonds, a tragic little rattlesnake, geography, the history of*
> *how some villages came to be named, the family tree of Will Rogers, the*
> *height of a unique cement tower in SC, wildlife legislation, the Lacey Act,*
> *the heartbreaking lament that eager beavers no longer frolic in the Santa*
> *Cruz River near Tucson, your thralldom over the superiority of AZ to any*
> *other USA territory, global warming, human population dynamics, water*
> *use, ethics and other musings ad-nauseous, all the while arrogating unto*
> *yourself a court of judicature. I will be, with brutal probity, dissecting your*
> *many errors and mendacious obfuscation of facts . . .*

For 14,000 words, Molt continued. Though few could make it to the
end of so lavish a screed, this one did contain a few salient points. Among
them was the fact that the University of Arizona's preserved collections, to

which Prival had contributed substantially over the years, now numbered 58 twin-spotted rattlesnakes and 258 Gila monsters.

"Dead in jars," Molt added, for emphasis.

MOLT WITHDREW after that. He was mostly caring for his wife, who he said was sick. Every day he made the same tedious circuit from their apartment complex near Clemson, South Carolina, where they lived in separate, adjacent units, to the public library, the Wachovia bank, and Whole Foods or Panera, where he would settle in with a coffee for the afternoon. "I'm bored to tears," he complained. "I'm bored by my lack of crazy shit happening to me. I'm addicted to drama, but there's a couple of lines I don't want to cross. I don't want to go to prison again, I know that."

Nor did he, he said repeatedly, want to wind up like Eddy Postma. So frightened was Molt of an accident in the field that he'd begun doing exercises to strengthen his ankles, taking hikes in the uneven terrain of the Blue Ridge foothills. He was not drinking nightly anymore, but when he did drink, he had a hard time stopping.

Death was on his mind. The Crocodile Hunter, Steve Irwin, had just been killed by a stingray—Molt had known and liked Irwin since his early days with Stefan Schwarz, when they would visit Irwin's then-small zoo in Queensland, "and he was exactly the same then!" Molt said. John Behler had died that year, too, after a long battle with heart disease. For three decades, Molt had never stopped daydreaming, sometimes out loud, about being stuck in an elevator with Behler alone. And yet he e-mailed friends a sober, respectful notice about Behler's death. As much as he'd once hated Behler, he hated even more that the snake men of his generation were starting to die off.

## 23

### *Parviocula* Venom

Hank Molt moved with his wife from South Carolina to a suburb of Columbus, Ohio, where their daughter now lived. He spent hours a day on the computers at the public library, keeping tabs on the reptile world and searching for contacts. He shopped for groceries, babysat his daughter's dogs, and took his grandson skateboarding. This unremarkable pattern kept up until February 2008, when Benjamin Bucks e-mailed him with some unpleasant news.

Bucks had heard that the same Ethiopian exporter involved in their own failed attempt to smuggle *Bitis parviocula* had just sent a shipment of them directly to the United States. This was remarkable, not least because there weren't a lot of *parviocula* to begin with—anyone who knew anything about *parviocula* knew how rare this snake was—and because Ethiopian wildlife law did not allow the export of its endemic species, a shipment to America could trigger the Lacey Act. Someone calling himself "viperkeeper" was now posting videos of the snakes on YouTube, Bucks reported.

At first Molt thought that the snake he was seeing on YouTube was the same beat-up male *parviocula* he had entrusted to Nguyen before their falling out, and that Nguyen had since sold it. But then Molt realized to his amazement that there were a lot of *parviocula* in the videos, perhaps as many as twenty. New videos appeared daily, complete with dramatic titles: *"Introducing Bitis Parviocula, the Ethiopian Mountain Adder!"*

To non-snake people, the YouTube videos must have seemed incredibly boring and redundant, the same black-and-green snakes writhing about on the same blue towels. But hundreds of snake lovers followed viperkeeper's daily *parviocula* postings, always eager for the next, constantly weighing in with their flattering remarks and inquiries:

> Earthtoaster
> Hey, gratz man.
> You sound so extremely excited.
> coclhs944
> congratulations what are you going to do with all of them
> viperkeeper
> Cha-Ching!

"Viperkeeper" was a Pennsylvania man named Al Coritz, who soon informed his YouTube following that he was selling the *parviocula* for $3,000 apiece, and that several of the snakes were earmarked for major zoos. He began posting ads on Kingsnake.com:

> They like high humidity but not soaking wet. Mist daily. If you have Google Earth I can send you Lat/Long of the region they are from, think coffee plantation and you'll have the habitat.

No mention was made of the legality of all this, much less the blow dealt to the species by taking so many gravid females. Of all the Kingsnake and YouTube commenters, only Benjamin Bucks bothered to mention that the snakes were illegal and potentially endangered, and his posts were quickly removed. Coritz then changed the ads to claim the animals had been bred in captivity. Then, for a while, he stopped posting ads altogether.

MOLT RIGHTLY suspected that zoos, at least those with venomous snake collections, would be interested in the *parviocula.* He e-mailed Coritz, posing as a snake collector named Lisa, who was very interested in reserving some of the baby *parviocula* that had yet to be born. Lisa also wanted to know which zoos had purchased, or planned to purchase, *parviocula*, because, she said, "it would be neat to see a few of them in zoo collections."

Coritz replied:

> *Hi Lisa,*
> *I don't take deposits because I never know the outcome of a gravid female.*
> *Yes, some of the animals will be going to Zoo's but I cannot disclose who though. They will not be on the East Coast, mostly central & West*
> > *Your #2 on the wait list.*
> > *Al*

Lisa then inquired about the snakes' import and export documents, at which point Coritz seemed to detect Molt's ruse.

"Eat [bleep] & die asshole," Coritz replied. "I have all of the paperwork for these."

Molt readied himself for attack—no one would succeed with *Bitis parviocula* where he and his friends had failed. If any accredited zoo bought *parviocula*, he would expose it with glee for trafficking in protected wildlife.

"This isn't sour grapes," he said. "This is sour watermelons."

BENJAMIN BUCKS, who was as infuriated as Molt that someone had succeeded with *parviocula*, theorized that this Coritz, with all his videos, his ads on Kingsnake, and lately, a new Wikipedia entry that deemed *parviocula* "the world's rarest snake," wasn't the snakes' real owner.

By then the din about the snakes' legality was getting louder. A Fish and Wildlife investigation into the *parviocula* was pending. Zoo curators who had ordered *parviocula* were putting deliveries on hold, waiting to see what would happen. A month after first advertising the snakes, Coritz posted a few of the import documents on a Web site, to prove that these twenty-one wild-caught *parviocula* had, in fact, been declared to the U.S. Fish and Wildlife Service. The documents showed that the snakes were declared not as *Bitis parviocula* but under the generic label "Bitis species," which could have referred to any number of nonprotected, commonly imported snakes. The shipment had not been physically inspected.

Coritz's name was nowhere on the import papers. In the upper-left-hand corner of one waybill appeared the name of the final recipient of the Ethiopian package. The snakes had been transshipped to Washington, D.C., where they were signed for by Peter Nguyen.

NGUYEN, BY then, was very upset and harried. He had spent more than $30,000 on these snakes, which he had indeed bought straight from the same Ethiopian who'd earlier sold some to Molt and Bucks. Nguyen had arranged to sell the Dallas, San Diego, and St. Louis zoos two pairs of *parviocula* apiece. He would recoup his costs on the zoo sales, and finally get a female *parviocula* into his collection—the *parviocula* that Molt had long denied him. But Nguyen had made the mistake of sending a gravid *parviocula* to his friend Al Coritz, who went out of his way to publicize what he had—and, Nguyen suspected, sold the same zoos a few of the babies, cheap. Now the Dallas, San Diego, and St. Louis zoos weren't returning Nguyen's phone calls. Worse, a seething Hank Molt had contacted the U.S. Fish and Wildlife Service, and was now e-mailing every zoo in the country under the pseudonym "Richard Milden," concerned citizen and conservationist, proclaiming the snakes to be contraband. "There is credible evidence," Molt wrote the zoos, "that these wild caught adult Ethiopian Mountain Vipers Bitis parviocula imported into the USA in Jan and/or Feb of 2008 were illegally exported from Ethiopia and thus illegally entered into the USA in violation of the Lacey Act, customs regulations and possible international currency regulations."

Nguyen finally posted on a Web site the Ethiopian export documents for the *parviocula,* documents that looked very much as though they had been created on a home computer. The "export permit" listed fake phone and fax numbers, a nonworking e-mail address, and the signature of someone named "Lamy" or "Larry." Its text, declaring that "Bitis parviocula, an Ethiopian endemic, is added to the other exportable Reptiles," appeared to have been composed in multiple Microsoft Word fonts on a piece of white paper. About the only authentic-looking thing about the document was the purple stamp of Ethiopia's Agriculture Ministry, though it was its Wildlife Conservation Authority that dealt with wildlife exports. Benjamin Bucks was quick to recognize the possible ruse, as he'd relied for years on a similar one in Kenya.

THE U.S. Fish and Wildlife Service dropped its inquiry into the *parviocula* after one fruitless phone call to Addis Ababa. The irregularities, such as they were, had occurred on the Ethiopian side—a single, dubious piece of paper had effectively legalized the species. To make a Lacey Act case, you needed the cooperation of the foreign government, and with a country like Ethiopia it was hard. "Trying to communicate with management authorities in different countries is a nightmare," said Marie Palladini, the agent who'd sent Eddie Celebucki to jail. "It's really hard to prove if it's a violation for foreign law and the animal is not CITES. We're better off when we can catch somebody at the airport."

The summer of 2001, when Anson Wong signed his plea deal, seemed to have marked the end of an adventure for Fish and Wildlife. Afterward came September 11, and a radical reconfiguration of federal law-enforcement priorities. For most of the decade, the agency did not exhibit much energy for wildlife-smuggling cases, particularly complex international ones. The agency's covert unit, whose investigations had in the 1990s destroyed the wild parrot trade and put a very real dent in the illegal reptile trade, had been disbanded; ten years later, George Morrison, the agent who'd taken down Wong, was the sole agent working under the rubric of Special Operations.

Fish and Wildlife's chief of law enforcement, Benito Perez, acknowledged that the agency's priorities had changed. "We have to give the American public the most bang for their buck when it comes to conservation," he said. "Special Operations was a very elite unit that takes a lot of resources to maintain."

Yet the agency's law enforcement budget—around $60 million—and its number of special agents—around two hundred—had remained relatively stable even after 2001, so it seemed that there might have been other reasons the antismuggling efforts had died down. It wasn't for lack of smuggling; that continued apace. In 2007, a young man was caught in California with Fiji iguanas in his prosthetic leg, and every few months came similar reports. Catching smugglers at airports seemed to be all the agency had time for, and the physical work of that now fell to the Transportation Security Administration.

In Europe, where the market for reptiles continued to grow and where smugglers like Benjamin Bucks operated with impunity, there also were fewer big investigations than before. Wilgers Joost, a Dutch attorney who had defended a number of animal smugglers in the 1990s, said he thought the cases had proved disappointments for the governments that brought them. "It was believed that this was a billion-dollar market, the number-two to drugs and guns, very big money," he said. "Prosecutors now understand that it's not."

In March 2008, at the same time that Hank Molt was straining to elicit any sort of government action on Nguyen's *parviocula,* the Congressional Research Service issued a bizarre report attempting to link wildlife smuggling with terrorism. It was nearly fifty pages long, and recycled several of the implausible and debunked claims from the 1990s—that the illegal wildlife trade was worth an annual $20 billion, for one. The terrorism part amounted mainly to geographical overlap—smuggled animals come from hot places, the report noted, and so do terrorists.

MOLT, HAVING had no luck with the American wildlife authorities, turned to Ethiopia's. The Ethiopian government at first sent tepid responses to Molt's incessant e-mails, and then no responses at all, and soon it became clear that even they had no interest whatsoever in the *parviocula* affair.

So Molt resorted to sending Peter Nguyen malicious e-mails, the first of them a treatise on the subject of trituration, which meant, according to the definition Molt supplied, "the grinding of a substance into a fine powder." Nguyen forwarded this to a lawyer to see if it amounted to a legally actionable threat. Molt followed with arcane demands for snakes and money, including the return of the one male *parviocula* and reimbursement for "expenses of $823 in El Paso in out of pocket cash, plus wear and tear on my car"—a reference to a road trip Molt and Nguyen had made five years earlier. Molt promised "draconian measures" if his demands were not met. Then, totally out of ideas, Molt began phoning Nguyen repeatedly and hanging up.

"Hank has lost his marbles altogether," Nguyen said. "I'm sick of all this cloak-and-dagger bullshit. I just want to be left alone to play with my snakes."

Molt was on a tear, that much was clear, but he was probably not wrong about the *parviocula*. The export permits were irregular at best, and Nguyen's claims that he hadn't noticed anything amiss seemed rather hollow, since he prided himself on his ability to detect all manner of forgeries. During the first *parviocula* affair, when Bucks and Molt were encouraging Nguyen to put up the daunting sum of $20,000, Nguyen was so insistent on not being cheated that he seemed to see forgeries everywhere, offering minute analyses of shadows and pixelation in photos the Ethiopian had sent of the snakes, concluding, after days of deliberation, that the photos were doctored composites.

Molt's attempts to unnerve the zoos succeeded for only a few weeks. Eventually the curators went to Fish and Wildlife, seeking assurances that they would not be subject to prosecution if they did buy *parviocula,* as they clearly hankered to. Even Molt's ex-girlfriend Colette engaged herself in trying to dispel Molt's accusations. "Our local USFWS agent offered to speak to any zoo person that had a legitimate interest in the legality of the parviocula," she wrote colleagues. "This agent is a friend of mine and he told me the Gladys Porter Zoo could, with his blessings and support, receive shipment of those animals with a clear conscience."

The zoos went ahead and bought *parviocula*.

WHENEVER MOLT came to the end of the line, when his attempts to provoke outrage or mayhem failed, he always claimed that he was "wiping the slate clean," or, alternatively, "getting away from all the negativity," and moving on.

For months, Molt had been soliciting Butterbean and Benjamin Bucks for any sort of adventure, anywhere at all: "I am bored to tears and lust for some action, some roguery, some semi-desperado stuff that is still safe for us and profitable," he wrote Bucks. During his daily Web searches at the public library, Molt had located a German expatriate in Rio de Janeiro who sounded amenable to an illegal reptile deal, as he had responded warmly to Molt's suggestion that they "do something creative." This German had even made mention of a snake rarer yet than *parviocula*. This was *Xenoboa cropanii*, a tree boa with greatly enlarged scales that gave it a primitive, prehistoric appearance. *Cropanii* was first discovered in 1953 by researchers at the American Museum of Natural History, but was believed extinct until twenty or thirty years later, when two more specimens were collected. It had never been photographed in situ—the snake books used photos of the preserved specimens. Yet Molt's German contact insinuated that he'd seen *cropanii*, which lived in a highly protected area in a forest outside São Paulo, alive. Even *cropanii*, Molt now believed, was not outside the realm of possibility.

Molt was self-conscious that he hadn't made a big trip in a while. He was rusty, he complained, and kept talking about the need to get his "feet wet" with a warm-up venture to Mexico or Belize. Brazil was deeper waters. Still, he was determined to go, though he had confessed to Eddie Celebucki that he feared this trip could be his last. Molt was sixty-eight, and there was nothing wrong with him that Celebucki knew of, but he seemed more anxious than invigorated.

Eddie Celebucki had mixed feelings about Molt living in Ohio. It was nice to have his friend in the same state, but it also made Celebucki susceptible to being sucked into Molt's snake schemes, just when he was finally living like a normal human being again. For two years after his club was raided, Celebucki lived in the drafty basement of the small karate studio he rented, with no kitchen or proper bathroom. To shower, he had attached a hose to the sink tap, and stood in a plastic trough to catch the water. He had a bigger karate studio now, and a decent apartment, and Celebucki worried most of all that if Molt's wife ever expelled him, he'd have to let Molt move in. Celebucki was irritated at Molt, too, for making such a stink about the *parviocula*. He would have liked to buy some *parviocula* one day, but Molt had to ruin it. Even this Brazil trip seemed pointless to Celebucki. "Hank never allows himself to connect fully with the people around him," he said. "Which is why he's always lusting for the next adventure."

MOLT HAD just taken off for Brazil when the studiously elusive Peter Nguyen found himself on the front page of the *Washington Post*.

Nguyen's neighbors, sick of finding escaped Mexican rattlesnakes in their yards, had prompted the town council of Arlington, Virginia, to pass an ordinance banning venomous reptiles. The cries for a ban became louder after an incident that spring in which a plumber, summoned to fix Nguyen's hot tub, arrived to find twenty dead snakes in containers and called 911. Nguyen refused to let police officers into his house, and a five-hour standoff resulted. The reason dead snakes were rotting next to his hot tub, Nguyen told police from his window, was because he was skeletonizing them for research. Nguyen denied to the *Washington Post* that the escaped Mexican rattlesnakes, snakes worth more than a thousand dollars apiece, had been his. "It would be an impossibility of physics," he told the paper. "It's downright impossible for them to get out, much as a goldfish would have the potential to leave its bowl and go scampering about the community."

And yet, for all Nguyen's evasions, the *Post* reporter discerned something noble in his obsession:

> A snake is not something you get emotionally attached to, he explained. You research its history, anatomy and physiology. You observe its behavior. You don't handle it; you "encounter" it . . .
>
> Fea's vipers, "dazzling" bright blue natives of Himalayan cloud forests with red striping, usually die in captivity. Nguyen has three. A rare Ethiopian small-eyed viper with green and black patterns is considered the "Holy Grail" in snake collecting circles. "Only one person in the world has kept one alive for more than six months, and that was me," he said.

The town council, unmoved, gave Nguyen a month to get his snakes out of Arlington.

MOLT'S BRAZIL trip took a wrong turn at the start. Shortly after Molt and Butterbean landed, their German export contact was arrested. Wildlife officials had followed a package of snakes from Amazonia, a package intended for Molt and Butterbean, addressed to the German's eighty-year-old neighbor. When the German came to retrieve it, he was taken into custody. "He had to pay like a $15,000 fine," Molt said. "He couldn't even see us the whole time we were there." All Molt and Butterbean could do was drink beer and go to soccer games and zoos. They flew home empty-handed.

Benjamin Bucks, in an e-mail, described the trip as a "real fuckup." Butterbean, he said, "seemed to put much of the blame on Hank and said it seemed the Brazilians did not like his boasting ways and promises which all never would be realized."

But Molt had been to Brazil, which was all that mattered. He'd come out alive, and now all he could think about was going back.

PETER NGUYEN wound up in the *Washington Post* again that summer, this time because the housekeeping staff at the Hy-Way Motel in Fairfax, Virginia, had discovered seventeen snakes, twelve of them venomous and two of them dead, in a room Nguyen had rented.

Nguyen had placed the snakes in containers, which he then concealed in suitcases and the type of thermal bags used for delivering pizzas, and rented a room for them at the Hy-Way, where he failed to check up on them. It was the smell of the dead snakes that gave him away.

He explained to police that he'd already sent the rest of his now-illegal collection to Florida, and these were the last batch he had yet to find homes for. The *Post* did not mention whether there were any *parviocula* in the Hy-Way, but there were indeed.

MOLT FELL mysteriously out of touch. He missed the Daytona reptile expo, again, this time without excuse or explanation. Another month passed, and Celebucki and Bucks and Butterbean all started to worry, at once.

Bucks thought Molt might be in Latin America, in jail. Celebucki thought that someone had finally killed him. "There are so many times he's taken payment for animals that he didn't deliver," Celebucki said. No one had any way of contacting Molt's family. Molt made sure of that: he enforced a strict, almost paranoid, separation of his worlds. He used a P.O. box for his mail, and all the family's phones were unlisted.

Finally, in early October, Molt called, sounding a hundred years old.

He had suffered a perforated intestine, he said. At first he'd thought it was stomach flu, but it got worse and worse over days until finally he checked himself into the hospital, where he underwent emergency abdominal surgery. Molt had been recovering for six weeks, and he needed yet another surgery. He now had a colostomy bag attached to him, which disgusted him to no end.

PETER NGUYEN, now bereft of the snakes he loved, considered buying Molt a snake to aid his recovery. Nguyen believed that Molt's callousness was not some congenital disease, but a progressive hardening of the heart that began when he stopped keeping his own animals, abandoning them instead to the care of his friends. "The best thing Hank could do for himself," Nguyen wrote in an e-mail, "is to get himself a snake—something interesting, though not necessarily something costly—and just take care of it. Keep it. Not attempt to sell it, or to use it as a prop for an Internet scam, or anything of that sort. Hank has, I'm afraid, forgotten all about his love for the animals themselves; and seeing the animals as only a means to an end—a way to make money, which they are not and inherently cannot be—and thinking of herps in terms of their cash value has blunted Hank's enjoyment of the one and only pursuit about which he was ever really passionate, and has consequently made him bitter and insane."

Nguyen wrote again, recalling how back in 2005, during the first *parviocula* affair, there had been something strange about the way Molt insisted, over and over, that Nguyen travel with him to Germany and collect his snakes in person. "Except that if I'd gone," he wrote, "Hank couldn't have intercepted the parviocula and attempted to sell them there. I've always wondered if Hank was telling me, 'I'm about to do something unforgivable to you; I don't want to, but I can't stop myself; stop me.'"

It was hard for Nguyen to shake his enduring sympathies for Molt, but eventually he came to his senses and took the mildly vengeful step of buying Molt's domain name, globalherp.com, which Molt had allowed to lapse. He thought of filling the site with ads for dinosaurs and imaginary reptiles, lampooning Molt's excesses as many before him had done, but in the end he just left it blank.

OVER SEVERAL months, Molt's health improved. He had a second surgery to piece his intestines back together, and no longer suffered the indignity of a colostomy bag, though he remained terribly gaunt and struggled to gain weight. He began driving short distances and resumed his daily visits to the public library, where he researched a new area of interest for a future trip to Brazil.

This was the town of Tabatinga, bordering Colombia and Peru, a place where things a lot more dangerous than reptiles got smuggled all the time. "The Indians up there are really good at collecting animals," Molt said, sounding like himself again. "They hate the Brazilian government and aren't keen on their laws and will do anything for money." Some of the animals in the ill-fated package his German expat friend received had come through Tabatinga, Molt said. It would be much, much better to go in person, "to pick what you're getting and see it."

NO ONE had much idea what Peter Nguyen or his friend Al Coritz had done with all the *parviocula* they'd once had, or if some or most had died. At one point they'd had more than forty, including babies. Many zoos were rumored to possess them, yet only three had formally registered their *parviocula* in the zoo association database. The next news of *parviocula* came in the *Tampa Tribune* the following winter, when a Florida man claimed that one had been stolen from his house. The sheriff's office valued the stolen snake at $10,000, and published a toll-free number in the hope of its recovery. Later, the man was charged with filing a false police report. Apparently he'd stolen his own snake.

Nguyen said he'd left five *parviocula* with that same Florida man in his desperation to get the snakes out of Arlington. The Florida man had a lousy reputation, but so did everyone in the reptile world, so Nguyen paid no mind. Then Nguyen saw the theft reported in the *Tampa Tribune*. The same month, more *parviocula* turned up on Tom Crutchfield's price list.

TOM CRUTCHFIELD had done what no one thought he could ever do. He'd built another reptile business, and was having some success.

It began when the doctor's drinking and gambling finally caught up with him. The doctor's yacht was repossessed, and the Fort Lauderdale house he was renting to Crutchfield and Patty fell into foreclosure. Crutchfield had amassed enough animals and money by then to escape, and the foreclosure gave him the excuse. Crutchfield moved himself, the animals, and Patty to a friend's farm on the edge of the Everglades, where they built pools and pens for animals and started afresh.

In early 2009, Crutchfield introduced his new business to the world by e-mail, as Tom Crutchfield's Reptile Price List. Every month Crutchfield e-mailed a new list, full of big, colorful photos of his animals. He was farming albino iguanas and turtles, using the profits from those to buy what he loved most—Caribbean rarities, the boas and lizards that thirty years ago he had caught by hand in the West Indies, but now mostly imported from Europe.

Crutchfield had by then managed to acquire dozens of the red Haitian boas he'd failed to collect in the Dominican Republic. These came not from Europe but from a businessman in New Jersey, a snake hobbyist who had received his founding stock from the Bronx Zoo, many years before. He loved the red boas so much that he'd bred hundreds, and since he was rich enough that he never needed to sell them or trade them, no one knew he even had them.

The businessman owned his own plane, and Crutchfield flew to the Bahamas with him, searching for the black boas of Bimini. One of Crutchfield's daughters was deeply suspicious of the businessman, and the trip to the Bahamas unnerved her. The New Jersey man was becoming a constant presence in her father's life, she said, and "one day I'm scared that he's gonna offer Dad something so good he can't resist." She brought her misgivings to her father, who assured her not to worry; he'd long ago learned his lesson.

PETER NGUYEN wanted his *Bitis parviocula* back, and though he barely knew Tom Crutchfield, he phoned him, hoping for some answers. Crutchfield answered Nguyen truthfully—the snakes had come from the same Tampa guy who later reported one stolen. In other words, they were Nguyen's snakes. It was too late to do anything about it, Crutchfield told Nguyen: he'd already sold them.

Six weeks later, Crutchfield circulated an e-mail to friends and colleagues. Someone dear to him had just been bitten by a *parviocula,* he wrote, and now that friend was hospitalized, his life in the balance. Crutchfield wanted to know if anyone else had been bitten by a *parviocula,* and if so, what treatment was administered. He wouldn't say who'd been bitten. Within days, though, a newspaper in Wilson County, Texas, reported that Earl Turner, a salty old-time snake keeper, had been bitten by a *parviocula,* the "world's rarest snake." Turner asked his wife to shoot off his arm when it happened, but she refused, and he somehow lived to brag about it anyway.

The only snake collector in the country without any *parviocula,* by this point, seemed to be Peter Nguyen.

HANK MOLT was always lamenting that the trouble with reptiles was that it got harder and harder to find novel species, and as soon as you did find one, the romance of it died. *Parviocula* was a case in point: from the world's rarest snake to someone like Earl Turner begging his wife to shoot off his arm. "All the low-hanging fruit has been picked," he said. "It's very daunting to find anything new. And I have more years behind me than ahead of me at this point."

Brazil once again consumed all of Molt's energies, as he and Butterbean made new plans for the border town of Tabatinga. Butterbean had located a promising charter flight, one that ferried German families to vacation towns in Recife. Butterbean thought he'd avoid the usual customs scrutiny on such a flight, though he was a tattooed giant with black teeth and heavy-metal hair.

In the midst of Molt's preparations for Tabatinga, Eddie Celebucki fell ill with the same diverticulitis that Molt was still recovering from. Celebucki was already dealing with painful arthritis and nerve damage to his shoulder after decades of teaching karate, and was recovering from a recent cataract surgery, when he wound up in the emergency room suffering intestinal agonies. Molt drove over from Columbus to help, and stayed a week while doctors tried to decide whether to cut Celebucki open or not. The whole time, Celebucki said, Molt talked about Brazil.

It wasn't that Celebucki lacked for reptile fantasies himself. He followed the reptile classifieds carefully. He still scrutinized listings for Boelen's pythons, the snakes that had so taken hold of his imagination that they'd set the course of his life. But Celebucki had a sense of his physical limitations, at least. "We're not kids anymore," he said. "I keep telling Hank that."

Their relationship had changed. "He's been my best friend and my worst friend," Celebucki said of Molt once, and that pendulum was swinging back. Now that they were getting older, Molt came around seeking nothing but Celebucki's company.

When, a few weeks after being hospitalized for diverticulitis, Celebucki finally went back in for colon surgery, Molt showed up again to neaten up the karate school and to instruct Celebucki on converting to a high-fiber diet. Molt's extensive Brazil plans had been shelved, indefinitely, and he was talking about the Philippines now, specifically an island province in the southwest called Palawan that he'd researched rather exhaustively in his long library afternoons. On Palawan, he could live for weeks or months in a cabin on the beach, and since it was cheap to hop over to Australia from the Philippines, he could visit Stefan Schwarz, whose face he hadn't seen in twenty years. A pair of any one of a half dozen illicit but rather nice species, including *Varanus mabitang,* an arboreal fruit-eating monitor discovered only in 2001, would net him enough to pay for the trip, and breaking even was at this point, with the onset of his eighth decade looming, all Molt cared about or could dream of expecting. He had nothing in the bank, but there were always ways, and *V. mabitang* was waiting in the trees.

# Epilogue

Benjamin Bucks was arrested in February 2010 in Christchurch, New Zealand, for attempting to smuggle Otago Peninsula jeweled geckos; he spent eight weeks in prison and resumed smuggling reptiles shortly thereafter. Within six months he had earned himself enough to buy an acre of beachfront in Somalia.

Four more plowshare tortoises were stolen from the Durrell facility in Madagascar. In July 2010 two Malagasy women were arrested in the Kuala Lumpur airport, carrying radiated and plowshare tortoises in their luggage. Though wildlife authorities believed Anson Wong was connected to the smuggling, only the women were charged. Two months later Wong himself was arrested at the same airport, en route to Indonesia, with ninety-seven snakes and one turtle in his luggage. Following inevitable "snakes on a plane" headlines, Wong was sentenced to five years in a Malaysian prison. Durrell reported that two of the plowshares confiscated in Malaysia had been among those stolen from its facility; Malaysia was sending them back to Durrell in Madagascar.

Tom Crutchfield, in addition to running a sizable reptile business, was working with researchers at Loma Linda University to revise the entire *Epicrates* genus.

*Varanus bitatawa,* a nearly seven-foot-long monitor lizard covered in bright yellow spots that eats fruit, was discovered in the northeast coastal forests of Luzon, the Philippines' largest island.

Hank Molt continued, between family obligations and seemingly infinite medical and dental treatments, to plan his Philippines trip.

# Acknowledgments

My first debt is to my sources, without whose candor and generosity this book could not have been written. I thank Hank Molt for being ruthless and intelligent, full of pique and history and life, one who "stood up for evil in the Garden," as Robert Frost had it. I thank the big-hearted Tom Crutchfield and his equally big-hearted family, who asked for nothing and gave everything, including real friendship. Edmund Celebucki, Randal Berry, and "Benjamin Bucks" I consider friends as much as sources. Anson Wong, Olaf Pronk, and countless others kindly set aside their skepticism when I knocked on their doors. Joe O'Kane and Bob Standish dug through their files for me. Special thanks to Bill and Kathy Love, Bonnie Berry and her portable copier, Al Weinberg, Brian Potter, Paul Bodnar, Riana Rakotondriany, Ralph Curtis, Eric Thiss, Peter and Sibille Pritchard and the Chelonian Research Institute, Allen and Anita Salzberg, and Bruce Weissgold.

I am thankful to my wise agent, Irene Skolnick, who saw this the whole way through. My editor, Sean Desmond, along with Stephanie Chan and the designers and copy editors at Crown, worked hard and patiently to shape, refine, and prettify what was once a very unruly beast indeed. Further thanks to Ivylise Simones and Oliver Munday.

I thank the always generous Michael Suh for reading three manuscript drafts with equal attention and for his valuable counsel. I am similarly indebted to Victor LaValle for multiple reads, smart calls, and heartfelt encouragement.

Thanks to Nick Trautwein, who was ready with soothing words and level-headed advice at all stages, and to Seth Robbins for repeated close reads, for creating a makeshift portrait studio in a bad hotel room, and for coughing up a title that finally passed muster.

Thanks to the *Daytona Beach News-Journal* for allowing me to play with some of these ideas in its pages. Thanks to Luke Dempsey, who bought the book originally and continued to offer moral support. Also in the moral support department, the Kotlow and Decker families, the Robbins-Einsidler clan, Derek Catron, my grandmother Marie McGrath, my uncle Kevin Smith, my cousin Calvin Godfrey, and many more friends and relatives all helped me in different and important ways.

From the day I started researching this book in earnest to its publication, it will be just over a decade. It was not always a pleasant or easy process, and through it, the emotional help mattered as much as the logistical kind. For this (and a series of interest-free loans) I have my family—my parents, Raymond and JoAnn Smith, and my sister, Lizzie Smith—along with my boyfriend, Seth Robbins, to thank the most. All of you rescued me in more ways than I can count, with more love than I know what to do with, and without you I don't know where this thing—or I—would be.

# Selected Bibliography

Asma, Stephen T. *Stuffed Animals and Pickled Heads.* New York: Oxford University Press, 2001.

Baratay, Eric, and Elisabeth Hardoin-Fugier. *Zoo: A History of Zoological Gardens in the West.* London: Reaktion Books, 2002.

Barrow, Mark V. "The Specimen Dealer: Entrepreneurial Natural History in America's Gilded Age." *Journal of the History of Biology* 33 (2000): 493–534.

Berry, Randal. "Reptile Dealers Past and Present: A Brief History." *Reptile and Amphibian* 50 (September-October 1997).

Betts, John Rickards. "P. T. Barnum and the Popularization of Natural History." *Journal of the History of Ideas,* vol. 20, no. 1 (1959): 353–68.

Black, David, ed. *Carl Linnaeus Travels.* Twickenham, U.K.: The Felix Gluck Press, 1979.

Bown, Stephen R. *The Naturalists: Scientific Travelers in the Golden Age of Natural History.* New York: Barnes & Noble Books, 2002.

Buck, Frank, and Edward Anthony. *Bring 'Em Back Alive.* New York: Simon and Schuster, 1930.

Buck, Frank, and Ferrin Fraser. *All in a Lifetime.* New York: Robert M. McBride and Co., 1941.

———. *On Jungle Trails.* New York: World Book Co., 1936.

Camerini, Jane. "Wallace in the Field." *Osiris,* vol. 2. Journal of the History of Science Society: 44–55.

Ditmars, Raymond L. *The Forest of Adventure.* New York: The MacMillan Co., 1933.

———. *Reptiles of the World* (revised ed.). New York: The MacMillan Co., 1933.

———. *Snakes of the World.* New York: The MacMillan Co., 1931.

————. *Thrills of a Naturalist's Quest.* New York: The MacMillan Co., 1932.

Durrell, Gerald. *The Aye-Aye and I.* New York: Harper Collins, 1992.

Faber, Paul Lawrence. *Finding Order in Nature: The Naturalist Tradition from Linnaeus to E. O. Wilson.* Baltimore: The Johns Hopkins University Press, 2000.

Gratzer, Walter, ed. *A Bedside Nature: Genius and Eccentricity in Science 1869–1953.* New York: W. H. Freeman and Co., 1997.

Green, Alan. *Animal Underworld: Inside America's Black Market for Rare and Exotic Species.* New York: PublicAffairs, 1999.

Juvik, James O., and Charles P. LeBlanc. "The Angonoka of Cape Sada." *Animals,* vol. 16 (1974): 148-53.

Obst, F. J. "Report on the Events During the Trip to Madagascar in March 1993." *Bulletin of the Chicago Herpetological Society,* vol. 28, no. 8: 173–76.

Pope, Clifford H. "Fatal Bite of Captive African Rear-Fanged Snake." *Copeia,* vol. 1958, no. 4: 280–82.

————. *The Reptile World.* New York: Alfred A. Knopf, 1955.

Pritchard, Peter C. H. *Tales from the Thébaïde.* Malabar, Fla.: Krieger Publishing Co., 2007.

Purcell, Rosamond Wolf, and Stephen Jay Gould. *Finders, Keepers: Treasures and Oddities of Natural History.* New York: W. W. Norton & Co., 1992.

Reid, D. "Notes on the Reports of F. J. Obst and R. Seipp Concerning Events at Ampijoroa in March 1993." *Bulletin of the Chicago Herpetological Society,* vol. 28, no. 9: 202–3.

————. "Personal View Account of the Events Near Ampijoroa Forestry Station on 18 and 19 March 1993." *Bulletin of the Chicago Herpetological Society,* vol. 28, no. 9: 201–2.

Rothfels, Nigel. *Savages and Beasts: The Birth of the Modern Zoo.* Baltimore: The Johns Hopkins University Press, 2002.

Schmidt, Karl P., and Robert Inger. *Living Reptiles of the World.* New York: Doubleday & Co., 1957.

Smith, Charles H. "The Alfred Russel Wallace Page." Western Kentucky University Web site, 2007.

Wallace, Alfred Russel. *The Malay Archipelago.* New York: The MacMillan Co., 1869.

————. *My Life.* New York: Dodd Mead, 1905.

Wilson, E. O. *The Rarest of the Rare: Stories Behind the Treasures at the Harvard Museum of Natural History.* New York: HarperCollins Publishers, 2004.

# About the Author

Jennie Erin Smith is a freelance science reporter and a frequent reviewer on animals and natural history for the *Times Literary Supplement*. She is a recipient of the Rona Jaffe Award for women writers, a fellowship at the Fine Arts Work Center in Provincetown, Massachusetts, two first-place awards from the American Association of Sunday and Feature Editors, and the Waldo Proffitt Award for Environmental Journalism. She lives in Germany.

### HERPETOFAUNA INTERNATIONAL
### 226-B Horsham Road
### Horsham, Pennsylvania 19044
### (215) 675-1796

SEPTEMBER 1983
SPECIAL BULLETIN

1 DESERT DEATH ADDER(Acanthophis pyrrhus) 18 inches: extremly rare in collections; beautiful red color with silver, black & yellow crossbands; quite different from common Death Adder........$1000.
1 DEATH ADDER(Acanthophis antarcticus) adult: 4 year captive raised proven breeder; nice rust-orange color phase..............$ 375.
3.3 DEATH ADDERS(Acanthophis antarcticus) juveniles: captive born 3/83; all have quadrupled in size; ferocious feeders on mice; all are the very bright and rich red color phase..................$ 750.pr
1 BROWN SNAKE(Pseudonaja textilis) 30 inches: flawless captive born specimen; ferocious feeder on mice; growing fast...........$ 675.
1 BROWN SNAKE(Pseudonaja textilis) juvenile: captive born 83; feeding very well on small furred mice; growing quickly...........$ 550.
1.1 A L B I N O WESTERN DIAMONDBACK RATTLESNAKES(Crotalus atrox) 3½ feet: only 2 years old; flawless beauties growing well...........$ 900.pr
1.1 MEXICAN GREEN RATTLESNAKES(Crotalus basiliscus) 5 feet: flawless captive raised breeders...............................$ 300.pr
1.1 EMERALD TREE BOAS(Corallus canina) 3½ feet: exceptional color and both are aggressive feeders on rats; flawless............$1150.pr
1.1 DUMERIL'S BOAS(Acrantophis dumerili) yearlings; rich colors..$1000.pr
1.1 NORTHERN PINE SNAKES(Pituophis m. melanoleucus) 4 - 5 feet: captive raised breeders; no longer available from the wild.........$ 225.pr
4 A L B I N O CORN SNAKES(Elaphe guttata) juveniles..........$ 45.ea
1.0 ARIZONA MOUNTAIN KINGSNAKE(Lampropeltis pyromelana) adult....$ 175.
1.1 RUSTY MONITORS(Varanus semiremex) 30 inches: 4 year captive raised specimens; outstanding coloration - SUPER EXCEPTIONAL !!!..$1500.pr
2.2 MTBE'S PYGMY WATER MONITORS(Varanus mitchelli) 12 inches; very ly colored; feeding well on small mice; ALL (4) @....$1750./4
MONITORS(Varanus gouldi) 12 to 24 inches: all have bright & patterns; feeding on mice...ALL THREE (3) ONLY...$2000./3
BLUE-TOUNGE SKINKS(Tiligua nigrolutea) flawless.....$ 750.pr
-TAILED ROCK SKINKS(Egernia depressa) adults: very brilliant with black & white dorsal markings; hardy in captivity; one world's most beautiful & interesting lizards.........$1000.pr
& RED-FACED TORTOISE(Emydura australis) 5 inches: very rare s species; has high & very round shell; orange face with red on neck; as this species matures they develop a very huge ometimes called "BOOF-HEADED TORTOISE"...........$ 750.pr
AND COOTER(Pseudemys rugosa) 8 inches..................$ 225.
CAN TENT TORTOISES(Psammobates tentorius) adults: flawless raised examples of this rare species....TRIO.@....$1000./3
TORTOISES(Homopus areolatus) adult pair and one juvenile: htly colored captive raised beauties....TRIO @....$1000./3
SPECKLED TORTOISE(Homopus signatus) adult pair: very rare ican species resembles a Pancake Tortoise.........$1000.pr

*************

## EXOTIC SKINS AND ALIVES
DIRECTOR—ANSON K. L. WONG
17, TAMAN BERJAYA,
PENANG, MALAYSIA.
TEL: 365429

IMPORTER & EXPORTER
OF SKINS AND ALIVES

16th June 1983.

The Director
Bronx Reptiles
271 West 20031 Street
Bronx
NEW YORK 10463
U.S.A.

Dear Sir

I came to know of your address through a business colleague of mine and I am taking this opportunity to enclose herewith a list of animals that I can offer you.

The reason why the quantity and prices of some of the items are not printed is because they vary according to season and age.

Hoping to be of service to you.

Yours faithfully

Anson Wong

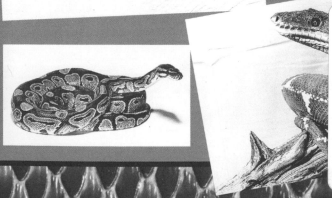